—FOR—
THE LOVE
—OF—
DONKEYS

FOR
THE LOVE
OF
DONKEYS

DR ELISABETH D. SVENDSEN MBE

Whittet Books

For Naughty Face

First published 1993

© 1993 by Dr Elisabeth D. Svendsen MBE

Whittet Books Ltd, 18 Anley Road, London W14 0BY

The right of Elisabeth D Svendsen to be identified as the author of this
work has been asserted in accordance with the Copyright, Designs and
Patents Act 1988

British Library Cataloguing-in-Publication Data.
A catalogue record for this book is available from the British Library

The Donkey Sanctuary is at Sidmouth, Devon
Tel. no. 0395 578222.
Registered charity no. 264818

Design by Paul Saunders
Layout by Richard Kelly

ISBN 1 873580 10 X

Typeset by Photoprint, Torquay, Devon
Printed and bound by Bath Press Colourbooks

THE DONKEY SANCTUARY

THE INTERNATIONAL DONKEY
PROTECTION TRUST

THE SLADE
CENTRE

THE ELISABETH SVENDSEN TRUST

Author's note: Occasionally, as this book covers the true happenings of the years since
1980, I have had to re-tell a story told in one of my previous books. I've tried to re-write
them, but as they are all true, they all come out the same, so, in fact, I have just reprinted
some. If you feel 'I've read this before somewhere', you just possibly *could* have!

I would also like to take this opportunity to thank my personal assistant, Mal, for all
her help and Sue for her assistance and the typing, and Marie for her proof-reading.

The author and publishers are grateful for the permission of the following to reproduce
pictures on the page numbers indicated:
Rita Barton, 1, 10, 37, 55, 69, 230; Birmingham Post and Mail, 240 (bottom); Rosemary
Clarke, 167 (top); Champion Marine Photography, 171 (top); Julie Courtney, 191
(bottom); Cresswell Studios, 123 (top); Daily Mail Solo, 171 (bottom); June Evers, 43, 119,
123 (bottom), 127, 137, 140 (2), 147, 149 (2), 152 (bottom), 183 (2), 185 (bottom), 195 (2), 203
(2), 215 (bottom), 240 (top), 245 (2); Exeter Express & Echo, 31 (bottom); Chinch
Gryniewicz, 152 (top); Roy Harrington, 13 (top), 49, 59 (top), 82 (top), 97 (2); Sandra
Harrington, 31 (top), 115 (top), 129, 154, 167 (bottom), 191 (top), 249 (top); Julius Mutea
Inoti, 185 (top); David Mansell/Observer, 115 (bottom); Dorothy Morris, 86 (bottom); Pan
Macmillan Children's Books, 175; Press Agency (Yorks), 233; Len Shepherd, 160;
Elisabeth Svendsen, 21 (bottom); Paul Svendsen, 2, 39 (top), 179 (3), 215 (top), 249
(bottom), 254; Nicholas Toyne, 6, 51, 59 (bottom), 63 (bottom), 71, 75, 82 (bottom), 86
(top), 95, 222 (2); University of Cambridge, 237 (bottom); University of Glasgow, 252.

CONTENTS

PREFACE

F OR THOSE of you who have not read the first part of the story of my
life and that of the Donkey Sanctuary, *Down Among the Donkeys*, the
following information may help you!

I was born in Yorkshire in 1930. I had a normal and happy childhood
and education, partly disrupted by the war, and a serious illness,
osteomyelitis, which has left my right hand 'handicapped'. My love of
donkeys must have started when I was a few years old. My grandparents
retired to St Annes, and every third weekend the family drove from
Elland to see them. My sister, Pat, and I hated the journey but for me it
was made bearable by the fact that if I worked on my father hard enough
he would add an extra three miles to the journey to pass a field with two
donkeys in! He would stop and I would clamber out and climb the bank
shouting 'donkeys' and they would always come to me.

I attended the Rachel McMillan Training College in Deptford, London,
where I obtained a first class Froebel Diploma. Having taught in a local
school for 18 months, I joined my father as secretary to the family
drainpipe works when the secretary who had helped my grandfather
found the company had a stroke. I soon learnt typing and accountancy
and then moved on to the selling side of the business – the only woman
travelling in drainpipes!

I then met and married Niels Svendsen, who was working for his
brother in the area. After a while he took a job at British Cellophane in
Bridgwater, and with our first baby, Lise, and another (Paul) on the way,
we moved there. A big problem was drying nappies, as we lived in a flat
and drying washing outside was forbidden. We designed a clothes drier,
and, with Niels representing us, we won the *News Chronicle*'s 'Get Ahead
Contest'. We developed the business, had a third child, Clive, and then
sold out to part of Thorn Industries, and were made directors. Niels
decided he would prefer to be self-employed, so we moved to Cornwall

Naughty Face, who started it all.

as business consultants, helping a boat yard, a group of garages and farm industries. Eventually we decided to purchase a hotel and bought the Salston Hotel at Ottery St Mary. I must admit the six acres of ground attracted me, as I wanted a donkey!

Naughty Face joined us in 1969 – a beautiful grey donkey with deep limpid eyes and a mournful bray that woke all the hotel guests far too early every morning! Feeling that Naughty Face might be noisy because she was lonely, I bought Angelina, and peace reigned. However, despite the hard work of the hotel and the arrival of our fourth child, Sarah, I became more and more interested in donkeys, joined the Donkey Breed Society, and after two years became Area Representative for them. In an attempt to find a suitable donkey for a local member I visited Exeter market and saw something that was to change my life – seven pathetic, sick donkeys crammed in a pen. I tried to buy the worst one to give it a good home but the dealer wanted £45 – a lot of money for such an elderly, obviously sick donkey. I asked for time to think about it, not aware that they would not be going through the auctioneer's ring, but when I returned a few moments later the last was being cruelly forced by tail twisting into a lorry. I was told they had all been sold to a beach operator. The more I thought about it, the more I became concerned, and I decided that instead of breeding donkeys I would try to save them.

By 1972 I had registered as a charity in order to provide for the 38 I had in care; the profits from the hotel were literally being swallowed up!

I had taken some desperate donkeys in from a Miss Philpin in Reading, who ran a Sanctuary, but I was totally unprepared for the phone call late on June 20th, 1973.

Mr Holman from Barclays Trust asked, 'Are you Mrs Svendsen – Mrs Elisabeth Svendsen?'

'Yes,' I replied.

'Are you sitting down, Mrs Svendsen, because you've been left a legacy.'

'A legacy?' I replied, 'I've never had a legacy before.'

'Well, it's 204 donkeys, Mrs Svendsen!'

Poor Miss Philpin had died, leaving all her donkeys to me plus court cases for unpaid livery charges and a large bank overdraft. With the help of the Charity Commissioners the two charities were merged and I took all the donkeys. Our lives changed completely. We had to sell our house in the grounds of the hotel, and bought Slade House Farm where we could keep our fast-growing family.

With my teacher training I was keen to help children, and so started a charity, the Slade Centre, to bring handicapped children and donkeys

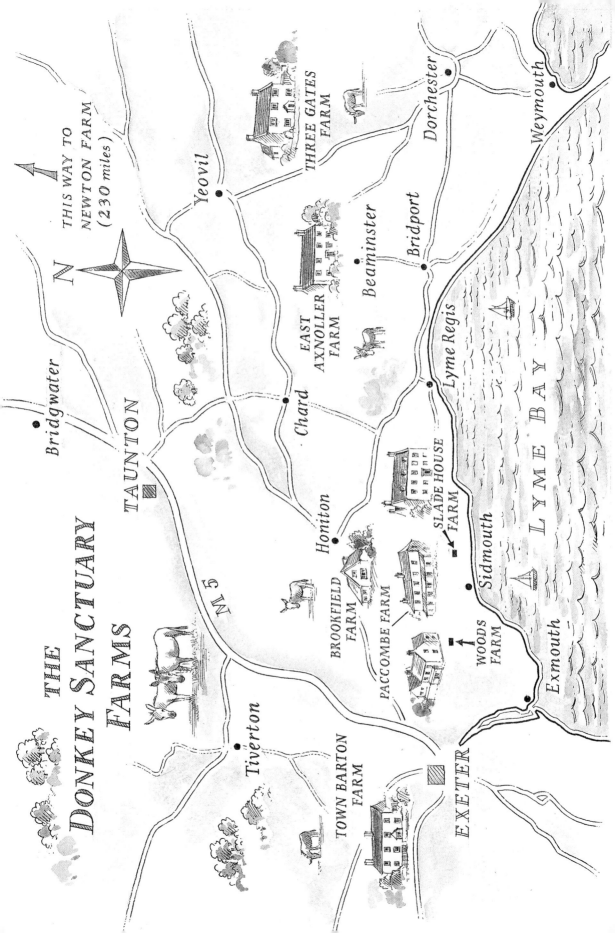

together. I was also well aware of the terrible conditions under which donkeys worked abroad, and was equally determined to help them. As each charity could only apply funds to its own aims and objects, The International Donkey Protection Trust was started for the overseas work.

Looking back I feel perhaps that Naughty Face should be blamed for the majority of the events that have affected my life since I first met her in 1969. She was such a beautiful, gentle, innocent little donkey that I fell for her the moment I saw her, and she gazed at me with her beautiful limpid eyes. I wonder if she could have had any idea of the impact she was to make on my life and my future.

I sit in my office writing this book today in the knowledge that, since Naughty Face, the Sanctuary has taken nearly 6,000 donkeys into care, has a full-time staff of 160 and owns 9 farms. The events leading up to the current total of donkeys have not been without their tragedies, their humour and their sad moments, and in this book I hope to give a small insight into what has happened during the last twelve years.

Dr Elisabeth D. Svendsen MBE

Chapter · 1

CRASH LANDING AT SALSTON
1980

B Y THE spring of 1980 we had taken 800 donkeys into care, and had three farms – Slade, Paccombe and Brookfield. Many had come from extremely poor homes and were in desperate need of love and attention; some were the results of direct cruelty, and others had just simply outgrown their owners. One of the donkey's biggest problems is, of course, its longevity. People buying a donkey rarely stop to consider that the average life expectancy in this country is 37 years old, and many can actually live as long as 50 years. This means that the owner buying a donkey for his daughter on, perhaps, her fifth birthday, is quite possibly taking on a commitment for many more years than he imagines. It is so easy, as the daughter outgrows the donkey and decides she would like a pony, to keep the donkey as a companion, and there the donkey stays, quietly and peacefully, in the orchard or the paddock, apparently needing little attention and little spent on him. As the child progresses, and a horse replaces the pony, the donkey still stays, and eventually when the child leaves home, the family has got too fond of him to turn him away. Many donkeys come in from owners who are heartbroken at having to part with their old friend, but either for financial reasons, loss of land, or even just that they are too old or ill to look after him properly, in he comes to the Sanctuary. The greatest care is particularly taken with these lifetime pets; they can pine terribly for their previous owners, and we ensure that we know exactly what titbits they have been fed, and the food they have received, so that we can try to make the adjustment as easy as possible for the donkey, and to change his lifestyle, certainly from the food point of view, as little as possible. Many of these elderly owners get tremendous pleasure from coming to see their donkeys, and it is amazing to note that, although they may be in a group of over a hundred donkeys peacefully grazing in a field, a call from the owner of 'Sammy' or 'Eeyore' is enough for that particular donkey to recognize the voice, a pair of ears prick up, and a walk or trot to the fence to meet its still-remembered past owners.

In 1980, one of our big problems was that of the beach donkeys. Many beach donkeys at this time were quite grossly overworked, and conditions were far from ideal, not only during the summer months when they were actually to be seen working on the beaches, but also in the winter when facilities provided by some beach operators were much less than satisfactory. One of my biggest problems was with the Weston-super-Mare donkeys, which a local family had been running for many years. It was brought to my attention that these donkeys were left, winter and summer, when not working on the beach, in a large field at Winterstoke Road, which backed onto the council's rubbish dump.

One would think that having worked all through the summer giving rides and pleasure to countless children, they would be entitled to regular nourishing food and comfortable shelter in the winter, but from our visits to this area it was quite apparent that the 119 donkeys and horses at Winterstoke Road were not receiving the care and attention that they required. Having spent their day on the land regained from the rubbish dump, they then waited patiently by the gate leading to the local council refuse tip. We found by watching this gate carefully that it was opened every evening and the patient donkeys waiting by the gate went straight onto the tip, where they would rummage for food all the evening. In the early morning they were herded back onto the waste land again, but, during their time on the tip, many had collected wounds from tin cans and glass, and others had drunk peculiar liquids which caused colic and, to our certain knowledge, the death of at least one donkey. We made many approaches to the Environmental Health Department of the Council, and for a long time our efforts appeared futile, although a small section of new fence was erected which prevented the donkeys going onto the dump. Roy Harrington, Superintendent of our Welfare Department, spent many hours with his team sitting by the dump monitoring the situation, and I visited the beach operator on various occasions to remonstrate with him and to suggest that he provided better facilities. On one occasion he told me he was sick of my interference, and if I didn't have such lovely blue eyes he'd 'belt me one'! Following a report in our newsletter, many people wrote to Woodspring District Council and some people sent back the reply they received which disturbed us greatly, as it intimated that the Sanctuary was spreading ill founded rumours. However, the letters and our complaints had the desired effect and eventually the donkeys were moved off the tip and the fencing was made more efficient.

(ABOVE) *Donkeys waiting at Weston-super-Mare.*

(BELOW) *Rescued donkeys Una and Twyny.*

One of the characterful donkeys who came into our care at this time was George. We first heard about him in July 1980. He had been rescued by a vicar living near Windsor, who, to put it mildly, had been sadly misled over the needs of the donkey. When he bought the donkey, to save it from slaughter, he was told that he only needed the feet done twice a year, to give it two scoops of pony nuts a day, and no mention was made of the amount of land needed to keep a donkey, worming or the need for shelter, adequate fencing, nor the fact that single donkeys tend to get very lonely and the advisability of keeping two. Despite great care from the vicar and his family, George became difficult and a call for help was made to the Sanctuary. Our Field Inspector, when she visited, realized that George was very lonely, which was why the owners were experiencing problems with him. There was insufficient acreage for George to have a friend to live with him, so our field inspector had no option but to recommend that he came into the Sanctuary. The family were very concerned as they felt they had failed George in some way, and they were genuinely sad and unhappy to see him go. However, the fact that he was coming to the Sanctuary where he could be trained to work with the disabled children at the Slade Centre was some consolation.

George arrived with the usual characteristics of donkeys who have been on their own – he was aggressive, objected vigorously to being handled or even petted, and brayed frequently; however in a short time he had settled down. We had been advised that he was about 11 years old but having inspected his teeth we established his correct age at almost 22. This made him too old to be suitable for training at the Slade Centre and for two years he joined the group of donkeys known as 'Boys Group' at Brookfield Farm. He had settled in very well at Brookfield; a good strong donkey, but he obviously liked individual attention and was always following the manager around. Because of this and his excellent condition, as well as the fact that he had made no particular friend and seemed to prefer humans, it was decided that he should be considered for rehabilitation when a very good home was offered at Chiselborough in Somerset. There were already two horses, called Breeze and Rockey, and in view of the fact that before George had been rescued by the vicar he had been in with a group of five horses, we decided he could possibly be tried in this new home. Mrs Cade, who offered the home, had been in contact with us for some time and was obviously a very knowledgeable person and had supported the Donkey Sanctuary for several years. Having received a most enthusiastic report on the prospective home from our inspector, Charles Judge, we sent George to Chiselborough, where he brought about great changes for everybody.

By October 1982 Mrs Cade decided that George should be trained to pull a small cart. The many walks she had taken him on the roads had provided good background training and a beautiful little float with side seats and a door at the back with a step up was purchased. By May of the following year basic training was over and they were both able to set off with a reasonable chance of a relaxing drive. To help the Slade Centre, an impressive open day, named Fiesta, is held. Over 6,000 people attend and generally at least £3,000 net profit is made. Large colourful posters are printed and Mrs Cade pinned one of these on the back of the cart and made a practice of going out on the B3165 every Saturday morning. As she said, this gave George practice with heavy traffic and, as they had to stay behind for some time, drivers had plenty of opportunity to read the poster. Mrs Cade wrote regularly to us with many amusing incidents with regard to our dear George and we were most amused to hear that one day, proceeding sedately along the B3165, they rounded a corner to find a combine harvester advancing towards them. The driver sensibly stopped and turned off his engine; George apparently also stopped and turned off his engine and totally refused to move either forwards or back, which caused an immediate traffic jam. Mrs Cade, realizing an impasse had been reached, gave George a flick with the whip on his shoulder, and – whether from outrage or astonishment – George moved forward immediately. Mrs Cade admitted there wasn't much room to pass but didn't think George really needed to attempt to scale the bank. Eventually, however, everything was straightened out again and as they passed the cavalcade behind the combine, one man put his head out of the window and said, 'That was well worth waiting for.' Apparently George and owner drove on with heads held high.

This road seemed to be their bête noire as, on a subsequent occasion, just when Mrs Cade thought she had met all road hazards possible, she found she had overlooked pneumatic drills. Rounding a corner, they came across a team of men repairing the road with a pneumatic drill going full blast. George came to a sudden halt and the operator very kindly stopped too. However, just after the cart had passed, the drill started again and, according to Mrs Cade, 'George shot forward like a kangaroo and this activity continued most of the way up Norton High Street.' Frequent letters from Mrs Cade, all amusing, go to show us how many people are helping the donkeys.

Many donkeys, like George, thoroughly enjoy a new life in a private home. Not only do they have everything they need but their future is guaranteed should they ever find themselves in difficulty, as they always have the chance of returning to the Sanctuary.

Visits from children to the Sanctuary demonstrated to me how much they really cared for the donkeys, and we felt it might be an idea if we could contact schools and send an actual school lesson which could be taught, and also send a book on donkeys which could be either read to the smaller children or read by the older ones in the school. With the help of Pat, my sister, who is also a teacher, a comprehensive and interesting lesson was drawn up, including a question-and-answer section, which the teachers could use with their pupils. These were sent out to over 20,000 schools and the result was so encouraging that we knew our work had been worthwhile. Many schools decided to take an interest in one of the special donkeys we had in care and we allocated Eeyore, Pancho, Ruff and Frosty, four dear little donkeys, which each school could adopt if they wished. The question of adoption of donkeys has always been difficult, and is something we have always avoided as, if somebody says they wish their money to go to a specific donkey and sends, perhaps, five pounds, they would then expect the donkey to be available for them to see whenever they called at the Sanctuary, and the administration in making this possible would more than outweigh the actual donation. The average cost of keeping a donkey is ten pounds a week and so it would be very difficult indeed for anyone to cover the whole cost for a specific donkey.

However, for the children we made an exception, and many schools loved the link they built between the Sanctuary and the school, and many school events were held, the money going towards their favourite donkeys.

At that time I was approached by Piccolo Books to write some stories about the Donkey Sanctuary; until then, the stories had always been available only from our little shop and not distributed for sale from any bookshops. All the stories were based on fact and Eve Bygrave, whom I had met earlier, did the illustrations for me. *Eeyore and the Broken Collar* and *Tansy's Rescue* proved a great success with the children. They loved the idea of Eeyore braying outside my window to tell me how ill poor old Gertrude was. It was certainly a night Niels and I remembered, as, first of all, Eeyore should not have been right under the window – he should have been safely in his stable – and we had no idea what the tremendous noise was when it gradually broke through our peaceful sleep! Eeyore had in fact broken out, having found Gertrude, one of our very elderly donkeys, who had collapsed and was in great trouble. Children also love a good rescue story and the rescue of poor Tansy, again completely true, illustrated dramatically to children the trouble that donkeys can get into;

and showed their joy and happiness at getting to the safety of the Sanctuary.

Later in the year I was delighted to hear from Scholastic Publications Limited, who supply books to schools, that they had selected *Eeyore and the Broken Collar* for a special competition they had organized. They asked the children to write a poem and name a donkey, and to their surprise they received over 5,000 replies. The winner was a little girl called Heather Hindmarch. We had offered that whoever won the competition could name the next little donkey to come into the Sanctuary and also included in the prize was an invitation to be a guest at our hotel, the Salston at Ottery St Mary, have a full day at the Donkey Sanctuary, and have a portrait made of their own donkey by Eve Bygrave.

The donkey that came in at the appropriate time had arrived on a Saturday night at about a quarter to seven. A Land Rover and trailer containing four donkeys arrived; the donkeys had been rescued by supporters from London, and they brought these donkeys down themselves. When I opened the doors of the box, two of the donkeys were extremely distressed and in very poor condition. The young colt and a filly were so nervous that I was unable to get a hand on them. With the lady's help we put them all together in a loose box with deep straw, gave them a very small warm bran mash, and left them for the night with a manger full of hay. I went in very early the next morning to look at them. The two mares were in a reasonable state, and I aged them at about three and four years respectively, but it was still very hard to get near the little colt – he was absolutely terrified. He was covered in matted hair and lice, and aged about ten months. I checked him over very, very carefully to make sure there was nothing that love, good food and care could not put right. The fourth little donkey was a filly.

When I checked her teeth I aged her at about two years old, and on continuing my examination I just could not believe my eyes; she appeared to be heavily in foal. Normally a mare is not put to a stallion until she is at least three years old, the gestation period being 11 to 13 months. I immediately rang our vet, Andrew Trawford, and all his thoughts of a well-deserved weekend off vanished as he confirmed my opinion. 'She may well abort,' he said grimly. 'The journey and the stress may cause her to deliver before term. She will have to be moved to the intensive care unit at once.' We named her Una, and put the poor little thing, not fully grown herself, into Box 3 with the little colt, whom we named Tiffin. This was the name suggested by Heather Hindmarch, and the delightful little poem she wrote about Tiffin follows:

'If I could name a donkey
Tiffin he would be
I'd like to come and visit him
And eat a big cream tea!
He might be old and sleepy
Or wobbly and young
It wouldn't really matter
Together we'd have fun.'

We spent considerable time with the two little donkeys, because Una was very young. By the following Monday we could manage to go into the box without Una shrinking, terrified, into the corner and we knew then that she had a chance. At 11.45 p.m. that night I checked her before going to bed. She was laid out, hardly breathing, with two little black legs visible. I only had a second to dash out, yelling for June Evers, my friend and a trustee, who lived in the flat above, to get Andrew quickly. Then I rushed back to Una's aid. I was lucky, as with almost her last conscious effort she strained, and with a good pull on the back legs, the foal was free. Andrew arrived in record time, and we worked together, making mare and foal comfortable. It was certainly a timely rescue for them, as there is little doubt that, had she had to cope on her own, both she and her foal could have died.

As so many schools were already in contact with us, we were delighted that Twyn Junior School at Caerphilly organized a 'hush-in' and managed to raise £160. They asked if they could name a foal Twyny after the school (the 'Twy' part to be pronounced as 'toy'), and so the dear little foal, born backwards to Una, was given this name.

With 800 donkeys in care, not only was there a great deal of physical work involved in looking after the donkeys, making sure that each was treated as an individual, but there was also the constant problem of raising sufficient funds to look after the donkeys. Sending our list of contributors our bi-annual newsletter became more and more difficult as the labels had to be addressed using a small printing machine. This was where Niels was able to come in and offer help. He was very interested in computers and went into various types available in order to select the one which would not only cope with our current needs but which would be able to expand with the charity in the future. He chose a Data General computer and, not without some trepidation, we transferred all our subscribers' names onto this system. The first mailing seemed to cause as many problems as it solved, but having seen how easily the computer could cope with our numbers, with advice and help, we began to control the system rather than the other way round. We were all very keen that not only would the computer be used for our subscriber records, but also that it could take on the recording of every donkey's entry and its medical record as it progressed through the Sanctuary. The Veterinary Department was becoming increasingly involved in recording the progress of some of the very sick donkeys we had taken into care, and to be able to bring this information before them at the touch of a button instead of having to delve through miles of records proved an invaluable asset.

The inflow of donkeys seemed never-ending, and I must admit I had many sleepless nights wondering how we would possibly cope, and we began to search actively for another farm. We had had a lot of flak locally for buying farmland in the East Devon area, and decided it might be expedient to move a little further away from Sidmouth to take the local pressure off the Sanctuary, so we started looking as far afield as Dorset. It was in fact here that we came across a beautiful farm called Three Gates. John Fry was our most experienced and trusted manager, and it was to him we turned for the management of this new farm. We went round the farm together and as we walked through the beautiful meadows and cowslip-lined banks I could see that John was as delighted as I was – it really was a perfect donkey heaven. We got more and more excited as we went, planning where we would put our new donkey shelters, and realized that with over 240 acres we should be able to place approximately 500 donkeys in this wonderful area. The house and outbuildings were in good condition, and John readily agreed to take over the management of Three Gates. Such an increase in acreage and buildings gave me a little breathing space when planning the future of the donkeys arriving, but I had yet again to find a large amount of money. Fortunately our Christmas campaign had been a marvellous success; over 30,000 letters had been received, bringing in desperately needed funds to cope, not only with the proposed purchase of Three Gates, but also with our new hospital.

We had been absolutely desperate to get better facilities for those donkeys that arrived needing urgent surgery. Our Exeter vets, under the care of Don Attenburrow, had been doing an excellent job, but it did mean transporting all the donkeys to Exeter for surgery, with the added trauma of returning them in the lorry after a stressful operation, and the thought of having our own hospital with full facilities had been uppermost in my mind for the last two years. Despite repeated planning problems we had now received permission, and the actual building was under way. During visits to almost every veterinary university through-out the country, we carefully assessed the best and worst features of their operating theatres and preparation rooms and, with these in mind, designed and planned the hospital with the help of our vet, Andrew Trawford.

My main aim was that the donkeys should have as little stress as possible, so we made a separate entrance to the operating theatre from the back of the hospital block, so that the donkey could just walk into the anaesthesia room; the floor and walls of this room were lined with blue pads. Whichever pad the donkey lay on, after the initial anaesthetic shot, could then be picked up by an overhead pulley and transported directly into the operating theatre, the doors of which were never opened until the donkey was asleep. We managed to find a company who made overhead hydraulic lifts, and on this special lift the sleeping donkey, without being handled, was transported on its pallet and manoeuvred onto the operating table. This again was hydraulically operated and, at a touch of a switch, the surgeon could either raise or lower the table. The operation having been successfully completed, the donkey, still on the same comfortable pad, was transported through the other end of the theatre into one of the two special recovery boxes, identical to that in which it had gone to sleep. Overhead heating lamps were switched on, and the donkey was allowed to come round in its own time in a completely padded area.

As you know, donkeys have very close friends, and one of the biggest advantages of this project to me was that the donkey's friend could accompany him right to the doors where he went into the anaesthesia room, so that neither donkey had any extra time to pine for the other. When the operation was over and the donkey had come round in the recovery room, both were re-united at the earliest possible moment.

On my very first day at school, when I was five years old, I had met another little girl who was equally terrified of knocking on the big wooden door which we were both facing, and since that day in 1935, June and I had been very special friends. Over the years we had always kept in contact and June had progressed to become the Superintendent of Radiography at Exeter Hospital, Wonford. So June's advice was sought, not only on the building of the X-ray room but also on what equipment to purchase. Two laboratories were planned, so that we could learn the maximum of the physiology of the donkey from the sample taken when the donkey arrived to establish its blood group, and tests taken on sick donkeys could be analysed in our own laboratory, rather than having to waste time in sending them to Exeter on every occasion.

(ABOVE) *1939 school production of 'The Tailor of Gloucester', with me cross-legged* (left) *and June* (second right).

(BELOW) *Our veterinary surgeons at work in the new hospital.*

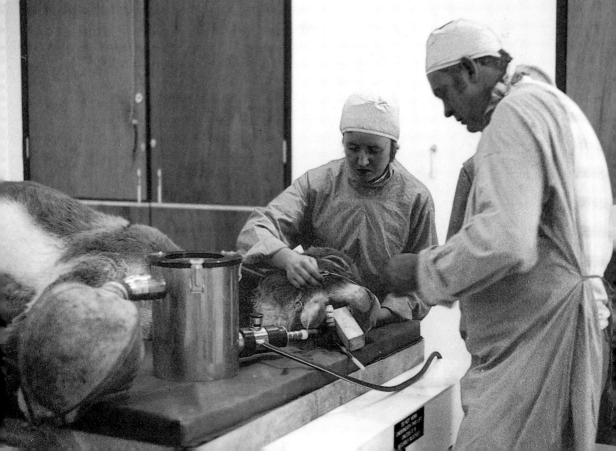

Obviously the building of the hospital was going to cost a great deal of money but, thanks to our newsletters and advertising, and to the few legacies that were now being left to the Sanctuary, we managed to keep our heads above water.

When the new hospital was nearing completion, we realized that we were going to need another vet, and Jane McNeill, recently qualified at Glasgow University, joined us. Even without the addition of the hospital, the demands of over 850 donkeys meant that more help was desperately needed, and we felt that, although it meant an extra wage, the money spent on the veterinary side was giving direct benefit to the donkeys really in need. One of the ways of raising funds and advising people of the work of the Donkey Sanctuary was to give lectures and film shows, and many hours were spent on this project, showing films and explaining to members of the Round Table at lunchtimes, and Women's Institutes and Clubs in the evening, how my life had become so involved with donkeys. June often accompanied me on these trips to work the projector, but on one particular evening she wasn't very happy. We got the projector set up after an extremely nice dinner, during which several of the audience had been imbibing rather liberally, and after the meal we all moved into another room where the film show and talk were to be given. June had spent ten minutes setting up the projector and everything was just ready to go. However, when I gave June the nod to start the film rolling, and she switched it on, somebody had jogged the table slightly and the projection failed to arrive on the screen. Before June had time to adjust it, one of the elderly gentlemen sitting in front, who I'm quite sure must have had even more wine than the average, said, 'I can do this, dear. Leave it to me.' Reaching over, he grabbed the front of the projector, completely wrenching off the lens cap and totally ruining any chance of projecting anything that night. I then had to do twenty minutes' ad-libbing to save the situation, and it certainly isn't an experience that I would like to repeat. Another lecture I was asked to give was on the Channel Islands. The Friends of Animals Group in Jersey asked me if I would come over and give a lecture to their members, as they had raised over a thousand pounds for the Sanctuary and wished to present it to me. It was a lovely evening; the Manager of Jersey Zoo was there, and they too were receiving a donation, and I was really made to feel most welcome. The following day I was picked up by the local television station for an interview with Jane Bayer. The programme was called 'Ladies First' and I met Sue Dixon, who had re-edited the wonderful Mrs Beeton's cookery book – one of the mainstays of my cooking.

My second son, Clive, had been waiting anxiously to start in the autumn at Kings College, London. We were all thrilled that he had gained a place, due not only to his academic qualifications, but also to the research work he had been doing at Woods Hole in America. He had been doing research on seaweeds there during the holiday period, and the letter sent to Kings by his professor had doubly ensured his place. I felt really sad to see him go and I knew how desperately Sarah would miss big brother. The house seemed so quiet as we lost not only Clive, but all his friends who were regular visitors to our kitchen!

It was about this time that Niels and I went to Exeter together to look at some computer equipment, and on the way back, we called in on June at her office in the Radiography Department of Exeter Hospital. Whilst there we had quite a shock; June received an emergency message that a plane had crashed at the Salston Hotel with almost 100 people on board, and all emergency services were to stand by. I can assure you, we ran out of that hospital to the car and I don't think anybody has made a quicker journey to Ottery St Mary from Exeter than we did on that particular day. As we came to the entrance to the hotel we were stopped by the police, who quickly let us through when they realized who we were. The sight that met our eyes was quite amazing; our drive was full of ambulances and police cars, and there were people reeling about in shock, having been rescued from the plane. Peter Feather, my nephew and manager of the hotel, had witnessed the accident and helped rescue many of the people.

The plane, which was on charter, had apparently been refuelled in Spain and one of the gauges had been faulty. As the pilot tried to make a landing at Exeter Airport he ran out of fuel. He missed the roof of the hotel by what people have described as 'a maximum of 20 feet' and managed to land in our field just below. By an extreme coincidence Ottery St Mary fire brigade were holding a practice in the area and the fire engine was on the scene almost before the plane had come to a complete stop. How the pilot managed to get it down we don't quite know, but he did, with little damage. Peter Feather, who had run across the field, was the first to the plane and without any thought for his own safety he climbed up onto the wing and managed to wrench the door open. He went inside and, with the shaken stewardesses, managed to get the passengers out. By this time a fleet of cars had arrived and the bewildered people were being brought up to the hotel. As I gazed round our reception area, which was covered in people lying down, crying and laughing, I could not believe my eyes, and within moments Niels and I were deeply involved in sorting out the people who needed hospital treatment and those who were just beginning to realize that they hadn't in fact landed at Exeter Airport. The pilot was amongst the last to appear and he received a resounding cheer as he walked into the hotel from those who appreciated the magnificent escape they'd had.

Dealing with the press was one of our most difficult problems, as they seemed to have no pity for many of the people who were still in severe shock, and tried to make them re-live the experience, causing them even more distress. Eventually we managed to get all the press outside the hotel and allowed them in one at a time to speak to those people we felt were able to cope, the others being allowed a time of peace and quiet until they recovered. It was about four hours before the last person climbed gratefully onto the bus to take them on to Exeter Airport, their final destination. Niels and I stood arm-in-arm in the field looking at the plane and wondering how on earth the pilot had managed to get it down, and thanking God there had been no serious injuries. I always feel that Peter did not get the recognition he deserved for his bravery; he wasn't to know whether the plane would go up in flames and his coolness in that emergency made me proud to be his aunt.

That autumn, Niels had the great delight of opening his new hotel block. He had decided earlier that he would prefer to run the hotel on his own, with my assistance when needed, he had been very keen to expand, and this beautiful new block made an extremely good addition to the hotel. Although the day of the opening was freezing cold, we were lucky: the following day the snow came.

November proved to be perhaps the happiest and most exciting month of my life. Two things happened: first of all I received a lovely letter from James Herriot telling me he would be delighted to write an introduction for *Down Among the Donkeys*, the first book I had written on the Sanctuary; and secondly I received the most surprising letter, asking me if I would accept an MBE if this was offered to me. I couldn't think why I had been selected to gain such an honour, and to this day I don't know who put my name forward, but I was very pleased to accept, as I felt it was an honour not only for me but for the donkeys and for all the staff who had helped me so very much to achieve my aims.

I got a shock in December. I had the most terrible telephone call from John Lockwood, who ran the Lockwood Home of Rest for Donkeys in Wormley. He rang late at night and said, 'I'm dying, Mrs Svendsen. Can you take 700 donkeys into your care?' John really loved all his donkeys and, although he'd had financial problems and we had helped him in the past with food for the donkeys, I certainly wasn't prepared for the phone call, and I had to urgently arrange for myself, Andrew Trawford and Roy Harrington to rush down to Wormley the following day. It was a very upsetting visit; by the time we arrived there John had been persuaded by Janet, the girl who looked after the donkeys for him and his wife, not to let us take them, and that they would be able to cope whatever happened. So it was, in the event, a wasted trip; what was particularly sad was to see John so ill and to know that another donkey lover was perhaps to be taken from the donkeys he loved.

Andrew Trawford, our vet, unfortunately decided to take a job abroad, as he had always been interested in working overseas, and his wife still missed Jamaica, where they lived for many years. It was a great disappointment when he handed in his notice, as I felt he was beginning to make headway with the general veterinary profession in the area of donkey veterinary care; he had written some important papers about our research. The one he had written on lungworm in the donkey had been extremely well received and the fact that we had a way of controlling this problem meant that people with horses could now take a donkey as a companion without risking the health of the horse. In the past it had always been thought that horses should not come into contact with donkeys – the donkey is a silent carrier of lungworm, not showing any symptoms, but able to pass it on to the horse. Only when the horse was exercised, and began coughing, did the lungworm become apparent. Although we never experimented on donkeys, standard testing of normal dung samples allowed us to treat those infected with the use of a new drug, Telmin, and we had managed to control lungworm. Andrew had been heavily involved in these trials, and I was sorry to lose his services.

On a personal note, Niels and I were both finding life becoming busier and busier. I went down to help at the hotel whenever needed, but of course nearly all my time now was being spent with the donkeys. However, we had always been an extremely close and happy family, and I desperately wanted to go and visit my son Paul, who was living in Germany, and Lise, my daughter, who was living in Denmark. Unfortunately Niels found he was unable to spare the time to get away for the long weekend and so I set off for Germany to meet up with Paul and Uschi, his wife. It was delightful to see them again and during our long conversations I suggested to Paul that perhaps if he was interested he might like to join me at the Donkey Sanctuary, as he had always had a great love for the donkeys and had really proved this by going camping at Miss Philpin's when we desperately needed someone to look after the donkeys until I was able to bring them down to Devon. We sat late into the night discussing the possibilities of his joining the Sanctuary, and both he and Uschi decided it would be really nice once he had finished his term with the RAF. So I left Germany on my way to see Lise, very happy indeed that Paul and Uschi would be joining me the following May.

Lise met me at the airport in Aarhus, along with little Mark Charlie, by then old enough to be extremely excited by Granny's visit. It didn't take long for Lise to tell me the happy news that they were expecting another baby and so once again I had a celebratory weekend with Lise and Jan happily planning their future in Denmark. Jan was employed by the hospital in Randers as a buyer, and Lise was busy teaching English at a Randers night school, eventually hoping to set up her own English language school, and it was quite amazing to me how she had picked up the Danish language. Her Danish, according to Jan's parents, was immaculate and of course this enabled her to teach her students with a thorough knowledge of both languages, and her classes were over-booked. Lise asked if it would be possible for me to come out when her baby was born, because Jan was extremely busy and she would love some help at that time, and so I promised to come out when needed.

Thanks to Julie, who had been helping me for years and had been one of my first employees, I knew I would be able to get away. Somehow in my absences she always managed to cope not only with the administration problems, but also with donkey problems. The office systems we had so painstakingly put in were under her care, and she had the wonderful gift of dealing with the often heartbroken and distressed owners when donkeys arrived. Many past owners and supporters of the Donkey Sanctuary have remained loyal partly thanks to their friendship with Julie.

Niels's back was at this time playing him up, and it was on a trip with him to his physiotherapist in Newton Abbot that we heard on the radio that I had been officially nominated to receive an MBE, and so 1980 ended on a high note.

Chapter 2

A TRIP TO THE PALACE
1981

Winter was a little kinder this year but we were still in desperate need of more comfortable winter shelter for the ever-increasing number of donkeys, which were coming in at an average rate of about five a week. It's a constant problem when these poor pathetic donkeys arrive to ensure that we continue to give them the ideal conditions that I feel are necessary. I had approached Bagwell Builders and together we had designed an extension to a small existing barn to make a large, comfortable wintering area where the very old and very sick donkeys could be close to my personal supervision.

One particular Tuesday evening Niels, who seemed to be having to work later and later at the hotel, was away, and I took the opportunity to catch up with the paperwork, which seemed to increase daily. It must have been about half-past seven in the evening when I realized there was somebody in the yard shining a large torch on the new building; wondering who it was, I left the office and went across the yard. A somewhat startled Brian Bagwell replied to my shouts and said, 'Oh, it's me, Brian Bagwell. I'm just surveying the building my brother is doing, as there seems to be some problem with the flow of the drainage.' I was very relieved to see it was somebody I knew, and I invited Brian into the office so that we could discuss the problem. He explained that, not only was the water going to the back of the barn that was being built, but also there were problems on some of my other buildings, and he said in a joking manner, 'What you need is a good surveyor to sort out all your building problems.' I replied that I needed more than a good surveyor – at the moment I could really do with somebody to help with everything, as the work was getting too much for me to cope with.

After Brian had left, I sat thinking about the visit and I thought what a marvellous person Brian would be if only I could get him to come and join our Sanctuary team. I had known him for many years and had always had a great respect for him. Being our local District Councillor and having built up his own very successful business as a house agent in Sidmouth, he was frequently in the papers and I felt his opinions coincided with my own. The more I thought about it, the more I thought how invaluable Brian would be and before I left the office that evening I phoned him at his house. I think he was extremely surprised when I asked, 'Were you serious about coming as a good surveyor?'

He laughed and said, 'Well, only half serious.'

So I said, 'How about coming and being my Deputy Administrator?'

I know this took Brian aback but he said he would think about it and I left the office that night for the first time feeling that perhaps some of the enormous weight I now had to carry, with Julie's help, was possibly going to be shared. I approached all the trustees; Niels was very much in favour, as he also liked Brian and felt he would be a marvellous addition to the Sanctuary staff, and of course Niels was fully employed with the hotel and was having less and less time to help me with Sanctuary matters.

At the same time I advertised for a part-time secretary to assist Eileen Judge who had been working hard with me as my secretary. Amongst those applying was Mal; we immediately liked each other and, although she was looking for a full-time rather than a part-time job, she said to me later that she loved the atmosphere so much, and felt she would love to work for the Donkey Sanctuary so she took the job on a part-time basis. She has proved one of my most invaluable assets.

Brian arrived on March 9th, 1981, having put his business under management so that he could devote his time to the Sanctuary, and he fitted in immediately. He had a great respect and regard for animals, enormous experience in the building trade, and, having been a Councillor for many years, had just the right attitude towards the work that we were doing. Unfortunately one of his first jobs must have taken him quite by surprise. I was awakened in the middle of the night by Niels moaning next to me, to find that once again his back had gone out, but this time extremely seriously. By the morning it was impossible for him to move. We called the doctor, who tried various types of manipulation, one of which needed two strong men to hold one of his legs down, and poor Brian got hauled up to the bedroom and, amongst the yells and shouts of an agonized Niels, joined the mêlée on the bed! Unfortunately all the ministrations of the doctor failed and within another half hour we had to call an ambulance, then I was on the way to the Nuffield with poor Niels facing up to several days of painful treatment and possible surgery. They put Niels on Valium and the change it made in him was almost unbelievable. Although it eased the pain a great deal it was a very difficult time for him.

By this time home was gradually beginning to be taken over by the Sanctuary. The cellars of the house were Tudor, probably the oldest part of the house; we opened them up and moved the Veterinary Department underneath to give them some space until the hospital building was completed. Our new vet was Trevor Duckham and he was very interested in carrying on the work with lungworm that Andrew Trawford had started.

We were also holding meetings of our managers every week at the house, providing lunch for them on the day to try and make it not only a business occasion but also a social one. This kept everybody in close contact with the main Sanctuary and made us feel we were working as a team.

That spring I received a call from an animal lover who had read our newsletter and seen the picture of terrible hooves that we had displayed on the front cover; I was horrified to hear of three donkeys with hooves that were even worse than the ones illustrated. We immediately sent our local inspector to visit, and the visit confirmed our worst fears. The donkeys were in an appalling state and needed immediate help and attention. Fortunately the owner had previously had warnings from another animal welfare society and, under pressure from our inspector, who threatened prosecution, he eventually agreed that the donkeys could be taken into the Sanctuary. They arrived during the late afternoon and I just couldn't believe the sight as they struggled off the wagon. The donkeys' feet had not only turned up, but the hooves had twisted in a spiral and on one of the donkeys was actually piercing the shin bone. We put them into a lovely warm stable with lots of straw and plenty of hay to eat, and the donkeys seemed to feel much more comfortable with the deep bedding. First thing next morning, of course, we had the farrier, and the long and painful process of trying to get those feet back to normal began. I had just received a letter from a subscriber describing horrific conditions on the Greek islands, and we were due to visit them very shortly, so we decided to name these donkeys after the islands that we wished to visit. So they became Lindos, Poros and Syros. The day after these donkeys arrived we had a donkey in that had been deliberately cruelly treated. Called Jenny A, she was bought by a man who was so appalled to see her being kicked consistently by her owner, that he bought her on the spot and took her home. Unfortunately he only had a back yard to put her in, but in this yard he gave her all the love and attention she had missed. Of course he soon realized that the donkey needed much more space and also a companion. Having met one of our supporters and being told of the Sanctuary, he rang us up and asked if she could be taken in. When Jenny arrived I was quite disturbed to see that she was heavily in foal and having been so mistreated there was a very real risk that she would abort or have a deformed foal. Luckily under our special care she recovered and eventually a small, but perfectly formed foal was born to Jenny, and Jenny at last had the chance of a happy life and future.

I had been waiting with some trepidation for the award of the MBE at Buckingham Palace and at long last, in April, the day came. They had made a special exception to their rule of only two visitors and allowed me to bring Sarah as well, as I felt it so unfair that only Niels and Clive could come and little Sarah, who would appreciate the event such a lot, would be shut out. Luckily they agreed, and we travelled up to London in a state of great excitement for the presentation. We had all bought new clothes for the occasion, and Niels and Clive hired grey top hats which looked absolutely superb. Despite the thrill of driving through the gates of Buckingham Palace, I must confess that I was extremely nervous and worried that I would do something wrong.

I needn't have worried; those about to receive honours were ushered up the staircase and put into special order. The equerry, who was there to train us, explained exactly what we had to do when our names were called. We were in a beautiful long gallery full of portraits; I could have spent hours looking at all the pictures, but it was not to be. We had to stop in front of the Queen, do a curtsy, walk forward five paces, receive our MBE, only speak when spoken to, reverse five paces and then walk out through the other exit, where we would receive the box for our medals. The equerry was wearing black tights and a special uniform; after he had explained to the gentlemen how to bow before the Queen, I was cheeky enough to ask if he would demonstrate the curtsy, as I thought he would look rather nice attempting this feat. However, he declined politely and I was disappointed. As the time for the actual presentation drew nearer and we were taken down a long hall to stand waiting outside the main chamber; we could hear the band of the Grenadier Guards playing, and suddenly the occasion became almost too much for me, and I realized quite desperately that I just had to 'spend a penny'. I went to the equerry and he looked rather disturbed. Eventually I was rushed to what appeared to be one of the marvellous glass panels down the side of the hall. This was in fact a secret door; he pushed it a

(ABOVE) *Jenny: she had been kicked consistently by her owner.*

(BELOW) *Niels, Clive, Sarah and I at Buck House (note the hats).*

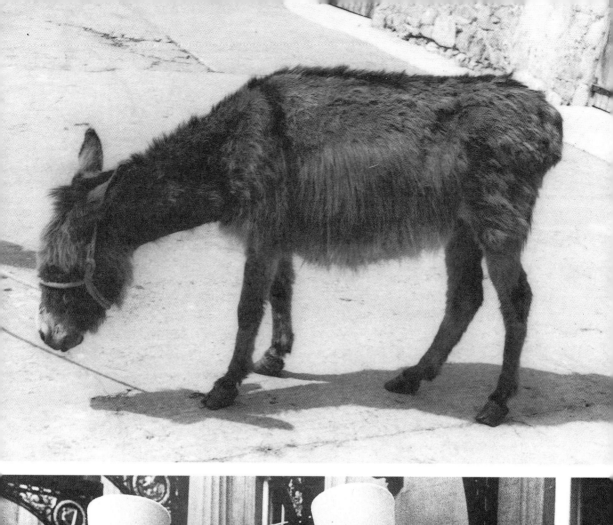

certain way, it opened, and I went into this very small room with a very elaborate washbasin and even more elaborate toilet. It was as I was sitting on this toilet that a thought came to me that I could well be sitting on the royal throne! I just managed to rejoin our line as we were led forward, and saw Lady Diana sitting at the back of the hall as we passed, obviously having been given the opportunity to watch before she married Prince Charles.

As I waited my turn I sensed the tremendous atmosphere as the Queen bestowed the honours on those in front of me. I can hardly remember doing my curtsy and my five paces and standing before the Queen, but I do remember the surprised expression she had on her face when she asked, 'And what is your work, my dear?' and I replied, 'Donkeys, Your Majesty!' A look of amazement came across her face and then I explained I also worked with donkeys and handicapped children, at which she smiled and said, 'Well done.' Having backed away and done my curtsy I left by the prescribed route. Niels, Clive and Sarah joined me when the ceremony was over, and together we stood outside in the yard of Buckingham Palace having our photographs taken, laughing and joking with those around us. I did have a special laugh when I looked at Clive and Niels because by mistake they'd picked up each other's hat, and Niels's was perched on top of his head whilst Clive's was firmly down over his eyebrows. Certainly a day that I shall never forget.

Shortly after this time I had some worrying news. Uschi rang late at night from Germany to say that Paul had been rushed to hospital with an extremely bad stomach ulcer which was bleeding profusely and they had decided to operate to remove part of his stomach. Of course I was desperately tempted to rush over to Germany to visit Paul, but Uschi explained that as it was a military hospital she thought it would be better to keep the visiting to a minimum and she would ring me as soon as the operation was over to let me know how he'd got on. You can imagine what sort of night Niels and I spent worrying about Paul; we were relieved when Uschi rang the next day to say that the operation had been a success, but Paul was going to need quite a long time to recover. This would probably mean putting off his starting date at the Sanctuary until June.

However, on June 17th Uschi and baby Dawn arrived to move into Little Slade, the house that we had recently purchased when it came on the market. Little Slade was right opposite the Donkey Sanctuary and had been owned for many years by Dr Michelmore and his wife.

Unfortunately Mrs Michelmore had died and the doctor had decided to move down to Sidmouth. It seemed too good an opportunity to miss to purchase this house, as our own house was becoming increasingly invaded by the office and Veterinary Department of the Sanctuary, and we were able to turn Little Slade into a flat overhead for Paul and Uschi and downstairs into a headquarters for our rapidly increasing Welfare Department. Roy Harrington now had two inspectors in the field full-time, and many volunteers, and really needed a headquarters rather than the half-office he was having to share with the Accounts Department. Unfortunately Paul was still delayed in hospital and didn't arrive for a further ten days. I was delighted to have the children move in opposite, and of course to know that Paul was there and was going to train as a manager was a great comfort.

Using a 'Small World' boat as a base, June and I had been round coastal areas of Turkey trying to work out how badly the donkeys were affected with parasites. I was very eager to take rather more laboratory facilities than I had done in the past, so was delighted when Niels said he would join me on a second trip carrying out the research work for me. We pulled in at a tiny port named Kas on the Turkish mainland, which overlooked an island called Kastellorizon, which is Greek. It was already late evening when we arrived but I could see two donkeys just up the hill from the boat and asked the captain if I could go off early in the morning to try and collect some dung samples, which we could then analyse. He agreed, but explained that we would be sailing at 8 a.m. I left the boat and Niels, sleeping peacefully, at about 5.15 a.m., and a local fisherman took me across the harbour and landed me at the foot of the hill. I climbed up the hill and sat down close to one donkey, waiting for it to dung, gazing out to sea, and looking at the beautiful view of the Greek island in the distance. I only became aware of the soldiers creeping towards me on their stomachs when they were just a short distance away. I sprang to my feet in horror as five or six of them suddenly rushed at me, waving guns. They wrenched the pot I was carrying to collect the dung away from me and hustled me off down the hill to the village. I was pushed roughly into what was obviously the village police station's only cell – a dank, dark room with just one small bench in it. I must have waited there nearly two hours, aware of the warning hooter from 'Small World' and I just hoped they realized I wasn't on board and hadn't made it back to the boat.

I was eventually taken into the station office for questioning and, of course, my lack of Turkish made the situation almost hilarious had it not been so frightening for me. All I could say was 'Veterinaire, veterinaire,' and they kept waving the pot at me, whilst I was trying to describe that I was waiting for a donkey to eject a dung – an almost impossible task! Eventually at 11 a.m., alerted by Niels, Iannis the captain of the boat arrived. Thank goodness back at the boat they had realized I wasn't with them. Although Iannis, being Greek, also had some language problems with the Turkish Army, he managed to persuade them that I was just an eccentric Englishwoman and was no threat to Turkey. I was only released after the local veterinary appeared, who had had to travel from Antalya, some sixty miles away. He could speak some English and was able to explain that I wasn't a spy from Greece but was in fact a genuine animal welfare worker. I can tell you they didn't let me go ashore again on my own!

Back home, the Slade Centre, under Pat's special care and management, was a pleasure to visit. I loved going across there when I got particularly tired or exhausted, just to see the children enjoying themselves so much and gaining skills that they, their teachers and parents might never have thought possible. It was a tremendous reward for me, and I was absolutely thrilled one day to be at the Slade Centre when Alfred, one of our favourite donkeys who had been with us since the very early days and absolutely loved the children, proved once and for all to me the intelligence of donkeys. On the day I visited the children were playing a special game and, accompanied by one of the headteachers from the schools, I watched as the children rode round the arena, stopping the donkey by a special rail on which were lined a number of envelopes and Christmas cards. The idea of the exercise was that the child stopped the donkey, leant across, which gave the child the opportunity to make a movement he wouldn't normally make, picked up a card and then rode the donkey right round the arena to the big posting box that stood at the other end. The child who was riding Alfred was having tremendous difficulty in picking up the card, and each time Alfred stopped and looked round patiently as his poor rider tried desperately to reach the rail, but the child was so physically handicapped that it became apparent on the third circuit that he was not going to be able to pick up the letter. To everybody's amazement, Alfred gently turned his big head and picked up the card in his mouth and, even more amazingly, he then walked round the arena and carefully stopped right by the letter box so that the card could be pushed into the hole. There were over ten startled witnesses who watched this wonderful scene; I must admit that I nearly cried to see the look on the child's face and the effect this had on all those who had watched this lovely gentle donkey helping this very handicapped child.

At Christmas we have the added joy of giving every child a present which Pat carefully selects and wraps up, and if you could only see the faces of the children when Father Christmas, in the shape of our farm manager, John Rabjohns, disguised in whiskers and long robe, rides into the arena on the sleigh pulled by a furry 'reindonk'. The Slade Centre really does bring such joy and happiness to so many children and one of the greatest pleasures is the fact that the donkeys absolutely love doing the job.

On July 27th, the long awaited and exciting telephone call came from Lise. They had a little girl, Kate. Lise asked, 'Please, Mum, can you come as soon as possible – I desperately need your help!' I decided to set off in the car, taking Sarah, who needed a treat, having had some rather painful eye treatments for her continuing problem, and to make up for her absolute hate of her current boarding school. Sarah had never taken to school at all, and when we decided that she might benefit from a boarding school, we took her down to Paignton where there was a very good school run by the Marist Convent. We decided we would just send her as a weekly boarder, as she was very much a home girl and hated being away. So every weekend Sarah had come home and she spent the whole weekend planning how she could avoid going back to school again on the Monday. Having found out that threatening sore throats, being sick and other things had very little effect on us, she had hated the car journey to school.

I had, however, promised that if she would complete the last year without complaint then I would let her leave at the end of July, so that she could attend the local school. And so it was partly as a reward for Sarah for having been good for the last year that I decided she could come to Denmark with me. Off we set to give Lise a hand. Everything was fine for the first few days and I was able to help Lise with the baby and look after Mark Charlie with Sarah's help. Unfortunately, on August 3rd, I managed to injure myself. Galloping into the bathroom with some nappies that needed washing, I tripped over the doorstep and fell against the washbasin, unfortunately cracking three ribs in the process. By the following day I could hardly move and had to go into the hospital to be X-rayed. Having seen the damage I was advised that I could not drive home, and so I had to ring Niels, who had stayed at home, to see if he could come over, pick us up and drive the car back. So Niels came over, attending the christening of Kate at the same time. We then all drove back, with me in not inconsiderable pain, and looking forward to getting back to have a little rest and recuperation. We didn't have long to rest, though, as the Slade Centre Fiesta was arranged for August 16th, and Arthur Negus was coming to perform the opening ceremony. The night before we had the pleasure of entertaining him down in our Salston Cellars, and a good time was had by all. He was a happy and jolly person, full of anecdotes and interesting stories. He had always loved the donkeys and had his own favourite donkey whom we had named Negus after him some years before, and he and his wife always insisted on going out to Brookfield so they could pat Negus and take him a special treat.

The day of Fiesta dawned beautiful and clear, and it turned out to be one of the best Fiestas we'd ever had. We made a net £4,000 and the obvious enthusiasm of Arthur Negus was a great help in the event.

On August 20th I was totally devastated when Niels left me. The family rallied round and Lise, with her babies, came over from Denmark for three weeks to comfort me, but as the weeks went on I realized it was all over and did the only thing possible for me; I devoted my life and time to my other love – that of the donkeys. One evening I sat quietly in one of the intensive care stables with just the glow of the infra-red lamp, stroking a poor little mule who had been owned by gypsies, starved almost to death and had been destined for slaughter for pet food. With his head in my lap I just prayed that, having lost the only man I had ever loved in my life and for whom I would have given my life, I would never lose the love of the donkeys.

My best friend, June Evers, who unfortunately had had to resign as a trustee as she was hoping to take up a position abroad, was living in the flat next to the house and she was the most enormous comfort to me at this time. We had been friends since we were five and I think perhaps she was the only person who knew exactly what I went through during those next few months. I felt it was particularly hard on Sarah, who, having left boarding school, was now home all the time, and I had to do my best to keep bright and happy for her. June was an immense help with this also, and we used to go out in the evenings to cheer ourselves up and to take my mind off the fact that I was now alone and had to cope for myself in the future.

All the Sanctuary staff were absolutely marvellous; Brian, who had been quietly watching everything that was being done, and picking up the aims and objects of the charity, quietly took over whilst I pulled myself together, and proved an absolute tower of strength. The work had to go on, and indeed was going on at an ever-increasing pace, and I found this the answer to my problems. I had previously been asked to attend a conference of the International Union for Conservation of Nature which was taking place in New Zealand but, of course, there had been no way I could go whilst trying to run the family home and look after Niels. I now decided this would be a good thing to do, to give myself space to think, and to occupy myself with other problems. Bill Jordan, a Trustee and a qualified Veterinary Surgeon, had asked me to accompany him to the conference and I rang him to ask if the offer was still on. So on October 24th we set off for Christchurch, and had two weeks of conference and travel which helped not only to take my mind off things but also opened a lot of new contacts that have been invaluable since. Whilst there I was approached by Professor Ramade of the Department of Zoology and Ecology at Paris University, who advised me of the terrible plight of a very endangered species of donkey called the Poitou. They had been bred in the west of France in the area known as Poitou for hundreds of years, and their main use had been to be mated with the Mulassiere mare to provide one of the biggest and strongest mules in the world. Unfortunately, due to interbreeding and mismanagement, there were now only 75 left in the world.

Returning home I found the legal documents giving the date of my decree nisi as January 22nd – the day before my birthday.

Chapter 3

A CHAPTER OF ACCIDENTS
1982

WHAT A START to 1982! The Sanctuary was completely cut off by snow for three days, during which time those of us living on the premises coped as best we could. Fortunately we'd installed a generator, so we were able to keep the infra-red lamps going on in the intensive care unit and to have the yard lights on at the height of the blizzard, when twenty-nine donkeys had to be moved from a barn which took the brunt of the gale. The Slade Centre stables provided a warm haven for the temporary evacuees. Somehow we managed – everybody got fed and donkeys were kept fit and warm. Having my family living opposite and the vets next door was a tremendous help.

Once Roy had got firmly established, my policy of getting good homes for young, fit donkeys to go out in pairs was succeeding. Roy and his team were busy in the field finding good homes and all those selected had a very full inspection indeed. Those offering homes had to prove they were doing it for the genuine good of the donkey; they must have adequate shelter, pasture and fencing, and we did get the odd complaint that it was worse taking one of our donkeys than adopting a child. I feel that our donkeys are so humble and patient they need protecting at all times. Once the inspector had accepted that the home was suitable for the donkeys, he visited every three months, and of course the donkeys always belonged to us – they were only loaned out to the owners, and if the donkeys got into real trouble and needed expensive veterinary care, we guaranteed to see that this was paid for. As Roy increased his department we were able to rehabilitate our donkeys further afield than I had been able to do in the past, with only myself, my sister and one local person, Charles Judge, to check the homes. In a newsletter I appealed to our many supporters to keep an eye open and if they possibly could make room for two donkeys, to contact us, and this came to provide many happy and satisfactory homes for our swelling number of donkeys.

(ABOVE) *'Where's our grass?'*
(BELOW) *June some years later with our five dogs.*

Following the final divorce, I decided I just had to get away for a break, and, having looked through travel books, rang up and got two last-minute seats on a plane for St Lucia in the West Indies. June was accompanying me. We had never been to St Lucia before and were entranced by the beauty and peace of the island. In the area where we stayed there was a row of little houses for sale, called 'town houses', overlooking one of the inland waterways, and we met up with the most charming people who were in charge of these. I decided to buy myself a small house there using much of the money I had received from my divorce settlement, as of course there had been the Salston Hotel and many of our joint possessions to be shared out.

We had a terrible shock one morning whilst in St Lucia, when we heard from an English person sitting near us on the beach that England had gone to war! The problems in the Falkland Islands seemed very far away until that bleak announcement, and we suddenly wished that we were back in England where we could be in touch with what was going on. We felt very cut off in another country. I returned to work much refreshed and looking forward to going over again in the winter, when the legal formalities should be completed and the St Lucian house would be mine.

I got back in time to open our new hospital. To save expense we didn't have an official opening, and almost before the whole project was finished we already had donkeys in the treatment boxes and the first operation was about to take place. Many of our loyal supporters helped to sponsor the six recovery stables and others donated large sums of money towards the construction of the hospital, and we decided to place their names on the stables or on a section of the memory wall at the hospital.

I had long been aware of the Broombank Sanctuary in Inverness, which had donkeys and other animals, and I was very disturbed when Carol Jones, who ran it, wrote to me and asked if I could possibly take her donkeys in. Well of course this was nowhere near as bad as Miss Philpin's, but even so we had 13 donkeys and Lambkins, a sheep who thought she was a donkey! These were brought down to us, and this is the letter Carol wrote to her subscribers:

Dear Adopter, It is with deep regret that I have to write to tell you that Broombank will cease to be a Sanctuary as from 10th March this year and our adoption scheme will cease as from that date. Broombank has been in desperate need of funds since November 1981. It had been hoped that by advertising more at Christmas the matter could have been righted. However, even after doing this the funds that came in were lower than for previous years. It was not possible for us to meet higher feed and medical bills for the year 1982 and onwards with less money coming in. Inflation caught us up. To prevent any harm coming to our animals we arranged for the donkeys and Lambkins to be accepted by Mrs E. Svendsen at The Donkey Sanctuary, Sidmouth, Devon.

We had just taken these donkeys in when Betty Austin of the Portland Animal Welfare Society phoned. Her husband had become allergic to donkeys and so she had to send her seven down to the Sanctuary. To crown all, yet another nine in the same week came from Cleveland, as the person who had been rescuing donkeys found that she was having to spend too much time with the donkeys and too little time with her family, and really felt she couldn't cope. As you can imagine, all these crises were stretching our resources to the limit and two more senior staff were taken on to join the Donkey Sanctuary Inspectorate – Bert Duncan to take the Midlands area and John White to cover Scotland and Ireland. Both these men had had complete and excellent training by the RSPCA and really strengthened our team.

I was very distressed to read in the papers of John Lockwood's death; I hadn't received any news from the Lockwood Sanctuary since his desperate call for help, but I just hoped that Mrs Lockwood and Janet would be able to continue looking after the donkeys in the same way John had all his life.

As I mentioned earlier, the conditions for beach donkeys had always worried me and I was very pleased that, using the expertise of my inspectors and with the help of Eric Ellis of the British Horse Society, we got together to draw up a special Code of Practice for beach donkeys and became involved in a new licensing scheme which meant that at the beginning of the season all beach operators had to attend a licensing session where their donkeys were examined by a local vet appointed by their local council, a member of the council, a member of the British Horse Society and a member of our Inspectorate. This meant that for the first time we began to have some control on the conditions for donkeys and if our inspector visited a beach and found that the recommendations were not being carried out, the operator could be reported to the council who could, by law, revoke their licence. The only problem we have had to date with licensing is that it covers only the time when the donkeys are working on the beach; bearing in mind the conditions found at Weston-super-Mare, we felt the regulations should be extended to cover the winter months.

Having such good inspectors out in the field now meant that many more donkeys were finding their way in, and our next large consignment came from Derbyshire, where a Mrs Else, who was 67, found she had to re-home her donkeys. Jack Turnell, who had been working with me for some years, stepped in to visit Mrs Else and eventually she agreed that they should come down to the Sanctuary, so yet again our numbers had a sudden increase.

Raising funds was getting more and more urgent and at the request of many people I wrote a book called *Twelve of my Favourite Donkeys*, just giving the details and life histories of twelve of the donkeys that had come into the Sanctuary. This proved immensely popular and of course was a very good fund-raiser.

Whilst in St Lucia I had been impressed by the number of donkeys I had seen working, and when I visited later in the year with June we hoped she could take some photographs for a new children's book I wanted to write, which I was going to call *Jacko – The Hurricane Donkey*. A terrible hurricane had hit St Lucia the previous year, and I had heard this delightful story from one of the young boys from the village. He had a donkey called Jacko whom he loved very dearly and looked after every day. Jacko's job during the day was to carry bananas from the plantation where he grazed until Christoff Bruno, his master, was ready to bring him home; on the day of the hurricane, Christoff Bruno heard the storm coming and saw the darkening skies, and decided he had better rush home. When Christoff Bruno got back to the village he tied Jacko up with Mary and Donko, their colt foal, and Christoff Bruno ran to his home as fast as he could to help his family secure their house. Unfortunately where the donkeys were tethered was near the sea, and as the hurricane reached its height the sea began to pour into the field and the waves began to swell up to the donkeys' knees. Christoff Bruno risked his life to rush back to the field and grab the donkeys. He climbed up into the hills, pulling the donkeys behind him, and they managed to shelter until the hurricane was over. I thought it was such a lovely story that June and I went round photographing Jacko and his owner, and also the little house where the family lived, which was now standing on only three of its legs, having been partially blown over. When the book was published I was very pleased to be able to give the family a percentage of the royalties, which certainly made a difference to their lives.

Whilst there June and I decided it would be nice to rent a boat and sail across to Martinique, the next island, and, having arranged with customs

Christoff Bruno with Jacko.

that it was all right for us to go, I was surprised to be tapped on the shoulder by an Englishman, who said, 'You two ladies can't possibly take a boat across to Martinique. You need somebody with experience.' I laughed at him and explained that I had been sailing for many years and done cross-Channel races and was quite capable of handling a small boat as far as Martinique, when he suddenly looked at me and said, 'Is your son Paul?' and to my absolute amazement it turned out to be Ted Bull, who had been my son's officer in the RAF. Paul had been on the RAF sailing team which Ted Bull had organized and been in charge of. The meeting with Ted was a great success, and he insisted on taking us back to his house from which he was running a yacht charter company and, of course, by coincidence it turned out to be three houses away from the little town house that I was attempting to purchase. Having met Ted Bull and having his promise to help me move in and keep an eye on the house whilst I was away, there was of course no more reason to doubt the purchase, and so I bought No 4 Rodney Bay and June and I came home with a new spring in our steps, and thoughts of family holidays on this beautiful island.

Niels and I had had a lovely flat in Torquay which we had used for weekends and holidays, and of course this now had to be sold as I could no longer afford, nor did I wish, to keep it. It was however quite a heartbreaking task when I had to go down to Torquay and stay over the weekend whilst arrangements were made for all the furniture to be moved. Rather than stay in the flat which had such happy memories I booked in at one of the local holiday hotels and had perhaps one of the most miserable weekends I'd had for some time. The hotel seemed full of single, elderly people, and during the time I was there, most of them sat gazing out at the view and nobody seemed to talk to anyone else. It seemed such a shame to me; I thought how these people, probably living in the north or the Midlands or some big city, saved up all the year for their annual holidays and then when they arrived in Torquay they didn't know anybody and found it difficult to make friends. In fact they probably had just as lonely a time as they did at home. I thought about this and I thought that so many of our subscribers had written to me saying how they would love to visit the Sanctuary but they lived on their own and wouldn't be able to manage the trip to Sidmouth, and I suddenly thought how nice it would be to hold a Donkey Week and invite all these people to come down to the Sanctuary. We would meet them at Exeter station and take care of all their luggage, book them into hotels in the Sidmouth area, and then arrange trips for them every single day, giving them lots of time to enjoy and love the donkeys, but also introducing them to each other and letting them make friends who had similar interests to their own. So the idea of Donkey Week was born.

When I got back to the Sanctuary on the Monday I discussed it with Brian and Julie and they both thought it was a lovely idea. We set about making arrangements for the first Donkey Week to be held the following year.

Paul was settling in very well at the Sanctuary and was busy learning donkey work right from the start. He proved popular with all the staff and had a skilful eye when assessing donkeys that was to hold him in good stead later on when he became a manager. We have always prided ourselves on the low administration overheads; at this time only 4.7 pence in every pound was being spent on administration, and this was of course due to our extremely dedicated staff. I now employed 52 full-time workers, the majority working directly with the donkeys to give them the attention they deserved, the rest of us doing every job under the sun including producing our own newsletter, printing and using our computer to keep down the ever-increasing costs of coping with the never-ending stream of letters and, thankfully, donations. The Slade Centre was managing to keep its head above water, and Fiesta this year was graced by not only Arthur Negus, who came again, but also Leslie Crowther. The children, receiving cups for bravery or just for trying, were overwhelmed by having some of their favourite figures actually cuddling them and handing them their prizes. We managed to raise £3,500.

I was also deeply involved with the International Donkey Protection Trust. I explained in the previous book that the lot of the donkey abroad is nowhere near as good as in this country and the donkey has very rightly been described as a symbol of the misery and poverty of the world, and with my own eyes I'd seen this truth when travelling. In Greece, we were giving donkeys anthelmintic paste (to control parasitic worms) and the trials were showing that the dosed donkeys should be able to live more healthy happy lives and work harder. An even larger advantage was that the donkeys should live longer; it is a disaster for the owner of a donkey in the Third World when his donkey dies, because the cost of replacing the donkey is the same pro rata as it is for us to replace a car. You can see what a great help this improvement to the donkey's longevity is, not only to the donkey but to its impoverished owner. June and I had visited Turkey and Greece, where we had dealt with many donkeys in trouble but had had a very big disappointment in Tunisia. On our last trip there, which was supposed to be a three-week project, we had been working in temperatures of over 100° Fahrenheit, and sometimes in near-blinding sandstorms, giving first aid to many of the working donkeys and mules belonging to the Arabs and the Bedouins. It had been the third year running that we had visited, mainly working in the remote areas of Touzeur, Gafsa and Nefta to assist the local 'dressers' working for SPANA, the London-based Society for the Protection of Animals in North Africa. On this particular trip we had been stopped on the tenth day by the Head of the Tunisian Government's Veterinary Service, who said we were not to continue giving treatment because we were taking work from veterinary surgeons, even though, as I pointed out, most of the locals could not possibly afford to pay for a professional service. About 95 per cent of all the donkeys we saw were in need of some first-aid treatment; they had weeping sores full of flies, rope burns and horrible wounds where the saddles had bitten deeply into their backs. It was heartbreaking to see all these animals and know that we were forbidden to treat them and it was a very sad day for us. There was one consolation, though: a carefully monitored dosing of a sample of eight donkeys and a mule over the previous year, carried out on our behalf by SPANA, confirmed our belief that by relieving the donkey or mule of its parasitic burden its general health improved overall.

Greece was a different matter to our disappointment in Tunisia. With Bill Jordan we had commenced anthelmintic trials early in 1981 and had had the opportunity to go on Greek television to try to explain the work that was being done for the donkeys there. We had an enormous amount of backing from the Agricultural Bank of Greece, who were monitoring our progress with great interest.

Just before the end of the year I was excited to get the final results on the Greek trials. For so long we had been working on this project, dosing groups of donkeys and keeping other groups as controls so that we could assess the value of the anthelmintics we were using. Each time the dung samples taken were put in refrigerated boxes and sent back to a laboratory in Athens where they were carefully analysed and the results sent to us. Suddenly all the results seemed completely meaningless to me. Donkeys who had been carefully dosed and their general welfare noted carefully began to get extremely high worm counts, whereas donkeys which had been the placebo donkeys and in fact had received nothing but plain paste with no anthelmintic in it, were being recorded as parasite-free. It suddenly dawned on me that the results were in fact upside-down, and if I looked at my sheets from the last six months and read them upside-down, these were the new results that were being reported to me by the laboratory. This meant a quick trip to Athens to try and find out what was happening and how the results were getting so mixed up. I was quite happily informed by the laboratory that, because they had to freeze the samples which had been sent, the numbers which were stuck onto each sample had come off in the freezer, but rather than disappoint us by not sending us results, they had just used the last list reversed! This of course made a complete nonsense of all our work and meant that the whole thing had to be started again.

We were also concerned about the donkeys on Santorini, where I had fallen with such disastrous consequences earlier in my life, and I was still worried about the 600 steep steps that the donkeys had to climb carrying tourists of all weights from the visiting tourist ships. Following years of effort and complaints to the government, we were delighted to hear that a telpherage (cable car) had been installed which would be able to take the heavier tourists up the cliff, thus relieving the donkeys and mules. We had many conflicting reports about its use, hearing that some tour operators were explaining to their clients that, although there was a telpherage, 'it was much more fun on a donkey', but a series of letters to the tour operators brought forth results and the terrible task of carrying overweight tourists up these torturous steps in the mid-day heat was at least reduced.

Travelling abroad always causes problems, as you can imagine, particularly in the Third World, where conditions for the animals are appalling and, for us humans, sometimes almost unbearable. Water is always a terrible problem, not only for drinking but also for washing. I remember many times as a child being delighted when, on our annual holiday on the Norfolk Broads, we had to conserve water and therefore washing became a non-priority event. However, working in countries amongst animals with the most terrible sores and diseases, and in frequent contact with humans suffering from disease, washing is very important and the lack of any sort of water a real problem. You can imagine our joy, therefore, when in one particular hostel in Turkey June and I were told that although there was no water in the room, we could use the shower in the owner's private garden. We both went out into the garden and found the shower building they had erected had only three sides. You entered from the back, which was open, and stood under the shower with privacy secured from the house by the other three walls. Being very generous I suggested June took the first shower. I happily stood there holding June's dressing gown as she was stand-ing luxuriating in the shower, thinking it would be my turn in a few moments, when I became aware of a rather strange rumbling noise. Glancing behind me, to my horror, I found that the village bus had pulled up and what we had assumed was just a high wall behind the garden was in fact the boundary to the main road. All the occupants of the bus had a full view of June's pleasantly rounded figure vigorously scrubbing away with her back to the appreciative audience! Without thinking, I called, 'June! My God, look behind you,' and she turned right around, giving a full frontal to the even more captive audience, who at this stage stood up in the bus and leaned out through the windows, shouting what we hoped were words of encouragement. I had never seen June try to get into a dressing gown so quickly in my life, and I don't think the fact that at this stage I'd started laughing helped matters.

Early one morning I received a desperate telephone call to say that three donkeys had been seen on a disused railway line where apparently they'd spent all the winter with no shelter and no food other than that which the lady who phoned had managed to give them. When the lady who had tried to feed them during the winter had complained to the owner, he had threatened to send them for slaughter, and the distressed lady on the telephone had bought them to save them from that fate, but of course she had absolutely nowhere to keep them. As she became more and more hysterical I realized that we had to act very quickly in this case as the situation was desperate. Within four hours our Sanctuary lorry was able to pick up the donkeys and bring them back to safety. We had rescued them just in the nick of time, as within two months each donkey had a delightful little foal at foot. I shudder to think what would have happened had they had to give birth to their foals in their previous living conditions. Since their arrival at the Sanctuary, the lady who sent them in has been to visit, receiving the thanks of all of us here for her commendable efforts in rescuing these poor donkeys.

We had also just taken into care Maud and Eyo, who had the most disastrously neglected feet which caused them intense pain and discomfort; also Jack, sent in by the RSPCA, whose hooves were reported to have grown to a length of one foot six inches. They were of course attended to before he was brought to the Sanctuary, but he needed a great deal of help in the hospital's intensive care unit before he was fit. Arriving at the same time was another little donkey called Lucius. Unfortunately for Lucius his owner had suffered a fatal heart attack and the field he'd been left in had been sold. When he arrived, although he was in a generally reasonable condition, his headcollar had been on for so long it was deeply embedded into his flesh and he had to

Two of the railway donkeys.

have an operation in order for the vets to remove it. Luckily we never assume that animals only get into trouble between the hours of 9 a.m. and 5 p.m.; the professional cover from our two resident vets and two resident nursing staff means that donkeys can have attention 24 hours a day. The lorry on this occasion didn't get in until late that night, and within a short time of Lucius's arrival, the headcollar had been removed from his neck.

I think I have mentioned previously that I am accident-prone, and I seemed determined to prove this at the end of August. I had just been up to visit the donkeys at the Slade Centre when, for some unknown reason, my ankle turned over and I heard the most horrible snapping noise. As I sat on the grass wondering if I dare put any weight on my extremely painful ankle, two visitors strolled up; they came and had a chat about the work of the Donkey Sanctuary and how it had all started. Somehow I managed to answer their questions and they wandered off quite happy to leave me sitting there, without querying why I was still on the ground. Fortunately John Rabjohns, our manager, was the next to walk past and he immediately realized something was wrong; I got carried back to the office and from there straight to Exeter hospital. June was very quickly on hand and I got VIP treatment as I was rushed through the X-ray Department to find that I had broken my ankle. I was duly plastered up and asked them to put a very strong plaster on, as I wanted to be able to walk around. They agreed to put what's called a 'rocker' on the foot of the plaster so that once the plaster had set firmly I would be able to move.

My biggest worry was that Ted Bull had telephoned me from St Lucia to say he was coming to spend a few days' holiday in England and would I like to go to the Boat Show in Southampton with him. Obviously I was extremely loath to miss this opportunity and so, having rung up to warn him that I'd be in a rather incapacitated state, I agreed to carry out our plans. Brian ran me up to Southampton where Ted was waiting to take over. I'd had the rocker fixed and, although it wasn't very steady, it was reasonable and I found I could stump around fairly comfortably. We thoroughly enjoyed looking at the boats on the land side of the exhibition. However, there was a gangplank down to the pontoons and both Ted and I wanted to see the boats that were afloat, so, without even thinking, I clumped down the long gangplank onto the pontoons. Alas, I had not reckoned with the gaps between each of the planks; on my first step my rocker sank out of sight and I was firmly anchored. The exhibition was quite busy and it didn't take very long, with me completely blocking the gangway and three or four men pushing and

Paul with Maud and Eyo, when their feet had been attended to.

pulling trying to release me, for quite a crisis to arise, and some of the suggestions we received from those waiting up the gangway were far from polite. Eventually I was wrenched free and, very red-faced, both Ted and I stumbled back up the gangplank and stayed on shore.

However, that was not the end of the story. Ted had agreed to drive me back home; when we got back I found that I was totally unable to walk on the rocker which was now loose and cracked. Ted, however, had a brilliant idea and he went down to the local garage and returned clutching a tin of 'bodyfiller' (this is really intended for cars). He spent quite a time mixing this up; it was coloured bright red, and with very great care, me lying on the end of the settee with my foot stuck over the edge, newspapers liberally spread underneath, he re-fitted my rocker by slapping the bodyfiller generously over the plastercast. This was a great success from the time it set, which took about five minutes, and I had no more problems.

Not until the day I went back to Wonford Hospital, Exeter. Whilst waiting in the queue of patients to have the cast removed, two men sitting near me were discussing their 'rockers', both of which were loose; one was saying it was his third visit back. I proudly showed them my bodyfiller cast and they were greatly impressed and in fact both left before going in to have their plasters reset, bound for the nearest garage to get some bodyfiller. When my turn came to have my plaster taken off I found a rather irritated elderly gentleman assigned to my cast. He took one horrified look at it and said, 'What on earth have you done to your cast?' I explained that the rocker kept coming off and that my friend had done it with bodyfiller. He snorted at me, 'In that case your friend had better come and take it off, because none of the equipment I've got here will do that.' With that he marched out of the cubicle. I waited rather pensively for about another twenty minutes and nobody came near, so I attracted the attention of a passing nurse and asked her what was happening. She said, 'You've really caused a stir. I don't think we've anything here that will get through bodyfiller,' and off she went. An hour later I was still sitting there. Eventually I asked one of the nurses if she would phone through to X-ray and ask June if she could spare some time to come down. I had never been so pleased to see her as when she walked into my cubicle. Apart from the fact that she was half convulsed with laughter at the furore I was causing in the department, she explained they were trying to get some special equipment down from theatre which was being used to cut through steel and that they would be down shortly to try and do something for me. For the next two hours June stayed whilst they tried circular saws and various other equipment, finally having to go down to the local garage to obtain some special cutting equipment which removed the offending plaster. I felt extremely guilty as I left the hospital and very grateful that it was all over.

But my penchant for accidents was not over; within two weeks I was pushed rather hard by an over-friendly donkey and in saving my right ankle, which was still very weak, I put all my weight on the left ankle and fell over, to my horror breaking my left ankle. I just couldn't believe it. It was especially disappointing as Clive was home for the weekend and with Sarah and June we had planned to have a really nice time. I was rather quiet as I was taken into the hospital, wondering who was going to be on duty and how they would react to my visit so soon after the previous disaster. I can't say I was encouraged when I sat waiting to be treated and found the two gentlemen who had been with me two weeks before, sitting proudly with their casts covered in red bodyfiller. This time I didn't even wait to go in, but sent a desperate call through to June and managed to get different staff to attend to me this time, keeping me well clear of what was a repeat performance of high-performance equipment removing plaster casts.

Fitted out with a new plaster on one leg and a still rather weak ankle on the other, I was gazing rather miserably from my bedroom window one day looking across the Donkey Sanctuary, when I saw what appeared to be a puff of smoke coming from the hospital. An incinerator had been installed in part of the building and at first I thought it was just this smoking, but I suddenly realized there was rather more smoke than one would expect. Despite being partially undressed, I stumped my way up the yard to see that all was well. To my horror, not only was the incinerator building on fire, but flames were creeping across towards the main hospital recovery area and it was quite obvious there was a serious problem. Our vet, Fiona Taylor, was there, and I shouted to ask if she had informed the fire brigade yet. She had not had time, having only arrived herself at that moment, and so I did a very hasty, plastered gallop to the telephone and dialled the fire brigade. Unfortunately we had a very sick donkey indeed in the recovery stables. Sammy had been taken in with a broken vertebra and was supported in a frame; Fiona and I had great difficulty in getting him out; the hospital block was fast filling with smoke and we knew we had little time. After we had finally got Sammy to safety, John Rabjohns and Brian Bagwell arrived, and they got out our fire hoses, keeping the walls of the hospital cool until the fire brigade arrived which was extremely quickly. Two appliances arrived from Sidmouth and they soon managed to control the damage; fortunately it was restricted to about two thousand pounds' worth, mainly to the roof. The other fortunate thing, of course, was that it didn't affect any operations that were due to happen – they were able to continue the next day.

In view of the ever-increasing numbers of donkeys coming in, Brian and I had been busy looking at new farms, as we realized that to keep the donkeys roughly at about two to the acre, which was what we recommended, we were yet again running short of land. We found a beautiful farm called Town Barton on the edge of Dartmoor, which would be most appropriate and Paul and Uschi came down to have a look at it. It was agreed that Paul would take on the management of it now that he'd had time to learn how to care for the donkeys and the basics of farm management. At this time John Fowler, a well-respected equine vet, joined our team and he and Fiona Taylor continued the increasing work for the care of our donkeys.

Just before Christmas we all had the great pleasure of seeing Paul welcome his 300 donkeys into Town Barton Farm. It's an absolutely ideal farm for them, facing south, with large airy barns for essential winter quarters. Run-out yards had already been built so all the donkeys could get some exercise as well as warm stabling during the winter. I know Paul was really keen to make his farm a success and build on the eighteen months' training he'd had.

I wasn't looking forward to Christmas at all. It may seem ridiculous but I still missed Niels desperately. I'd found the only answer was to bury myself in work and I was getting up earlier and earlier in the morning, sometimes being hard at work in the office before Sarah set off for school. Evenings were the same, and unless either Pat or June came and persuaded me to go out, I tended to work on. Although June had her own accommodation we often found after going out for the evening and coming back to my place for a coffee, she would stay the night, and it was really nice to know there was someone else in the house apart from Sarah and I.

Clive had made good friends with a girl called Grainne Slattery whose parents lived in Richmond. We decided it would be nice if she came away with us to St Lucia for Christmas, as I wanted all the children to see the new house. We really had a lovely time – Clive and Grainne came for one week with Sarah, and then, as they left, Lise and Jan with Mark and Kate came for the second week. It was supposed to be a complete rest for us all, but on our very first day, whilst we were all in the throes of jet lag, answering a knock on the door I found our next-door neighbour holding an extremely smelly baby at arm's length. He smiled at me, passed the baby over and said, 'Can you change a nappy? I don't know how to, and

'The ever-increasing numbers of donkeys coming in'.

my wife has just left me!' We were all kept pretty busy helping with his two children, but it certainly passed the time.

By the time Lise and Jan arrived our next-door neighbours had returned to Canada to sort out their problems, and so it was onto the beach with sand castles the order of the day. It was a delight to be able to spend some worry-free days with the family.

Chapter · 4

GREEKS BEARING GIFTS
1983

Shortly after our return to England I met Bill Jordan and his son-in-law, Don Bliss, who was an expert parasitologist and had offered to help me with my work in Greece, as I was getting increasingly concerned at the lack of control over our trials there. We met at the airport and stayed the night at a hotel, working out our plan of campaign for Greece and Turkey, discussing the problems and looking for solutions.

The following week there was a meeting of the trustees of the International Donkey Protection Trust, which we held in London, and they were delighted to hear that Don Bliss would write a paper giving recognition to the charity which would be published when the results in Greece were finalized. We agreed a payment for him for this work, and I agreed to go back to Greece in February to introduce Don Bliss to Dr Georgoulakis who had previously been working for us.

Pat had recently made a visit to Mijas in Spain, with Rosalind de Wesselow, another of our trustees, as we'd been very concerned by the condition of the donkeys used as taxis there. I was pleased to report that a special shelter for the donkeys was to be built, and also a water trough, and we were awaiting confirmation from the mayor that this would be done. Another of our trustees, Colonel Dodds, had reported that the US army were carrying out tests on radiation and its effect on donkeys, and I was delighted to be able to show a letter to the trustees showing that this had in fact been stopped in 1950 but there were some terrible accounts of the suffering, not only of donkeys but of other animals during these, to me, senseless trials.

All this time the constant problem of raising funds was present. I had to spend a great deal of time designing advertising so that each charity got the amount it required to keep running. Our newsletters were a tremendous source of income, as so many people loved to hear the genuine stories of the donkeys and to get a circular written from the heart – not appealing for funds but just trying to tell them what the funds they had already sent were achieving. The fact that so many donkeys were consistently coming in (we had by this time 1,500 donkeys in care) and cost an average of about £10 a week, made the fund-raising even more essential. Brian was by this time proving absolutely invaluable. Apart from looking after the farms and coping with all the building problems, he had taken over the legacy side of the charity's income and also the personnel side. The more staff we employed, the more human problems we seemed to get, and Brian was as determined as I was to keep the family atmosphere going and to make every member of staff feel important, as indeed they were. We both knew that by keeping this happy caring attitude the ones who would benefit long-term would be the donkeys, and this has proved to be the case. There was never a problem if I asked anybody to stay over in the evening to help, or at weekends when an extra pair of expert hands made all the difference to the donkeys' welfare and comfort. Together we all worked with the one aim in mind – to make our donkeys' lives as happy, peaceful and contented as possible. I do not know how I would have managed without the support of Julie Courtney and John Rabjohns; always willing to do the extra bits that were needed for the donkeys and frequently staying during the evenings and at weekends when problems arose. Their loyalty to the Sanctuary was immense and I know they were as proud as I was that we were able to continue taking in the donkeys, never turning any away, and giving extra help with the pathetic cases we were receiving.

I had used Ridge Advertising, based in London, to look after our advertising; it was run by Ken Birks, who had handled the advertising for Miss Philpin in the early days, and he had become a firm friend of mine. Placing advertisements is not as easy as it might seem; you have to choose exactly the right paper and you have to get the wording right, but ever since the start of the Sanctuary I had carefully coded every advert and by now knew exactly where to place them to get the maximum income. Ken one day invited me up for lunch to celebrate a particularly good campaign and Clive was at this time in his final year at Kings College, London, where he was reading Zoology. I asked Ken if I could invite Clive round for lunch, as I so rarely had the chance to see him, and I had to make the trip to London in one day as I was so busy at home. Despite the previous invitation I had received from Ken Birks, when he had invited my daughter Lise who was at college then, and which had ended in such a disaster as she managed to work her way right through the sweet trolley before becoming rather ill, he agreed. We arranged to meet at one o'clock outside the Sportman's Club. It is a very exclusive club and a beautifully attired doorman stands outside and quietly parks the cars of the rich and wealthy as they arrive. Ken and I waited a few minutes before Clive arrived, and in true student manner he was dressed in jeans and plimsoles, and was riding his bicycle. However Clive is never short of ideas of how to act in such situations and with great aplomb he stepped off his bicycle, handed it to the doorman and asked him very politely if he'd mind parking it, before walking into the club with us. His rather impressive entrance was, however, completely spoilt, as he wasn't allowed into the club in his current attire and had rather ruefully to go out, collect his bicycle from the pavement where it had been disdainfully left, and cycle back to college to put some more suitable clothes on. Eventually he got back and we all had a very pleasant lunch.

I got home in time to read with great concern a report to Roy Harrington from a lady who had been on a train and had seen two donkeys in a terrible condition in a field by a railway line. The stretch of line on which the lady had noticed the donkeys was over four miles long, but our local inspector managed to obtain permission from British Rail to walk valiantly along the railway line. Having done the four miles, he hadn't seen a single donkey. Roy rang the lady and she agreed to accompany the inspector, and together they walked the line. She was able to recognize the field in which the donkeys were, and what a good job she did. One donkey was a dark brown mare, obviously in foal and very lame, and the little stallion with her was her son. The reason they hadn't been seen was that they had now collapsed and were lying partly in water which had flooded the bottom corner of the field. The inspector left the lady with the donkeys and went around the area looking for the owner, who turned out to be a recluse. When the owner began to get agitated, and even violent, our inspector had to leave the scene, and he returned to the donkeys where the lady was still waiting. Together they managed to lift them up so at least they were standing out of the water, and move them across to the shelter of some trees. He was appalled to see the donkeys' feet; they were completely overgrown and obviously causing great pain. They had to agree to leave the donkeys until the next day, and our Chief Inspector was called in to return with them.

To their horror, when they returned to the donkeys the next day they found that the owner, realizing the feet were in terrible condition, had tried to saw off the overgrown hooves, leaving the donkeys in even more trouble. The owner, when approached, yet again became even more

(ABOVE) *Donkey taxi in Mijas.*
(BELOW) *A recovered Sue, with baby Cindy, enjoy a quiet chat.*

violent, but on being told that he could definitely face prosecution, he suddenly changed his mind and signed a relinquishment form to allow Sue, as we had named her, to come into the Sanctuary. She was too ill to travel for three weeks and we paid for a local vet to look after her and her feet were attended to at our inspector's home where she stayed. When she eventually arrived at the Sanctuary I was heartbroken to find the condition she was in; we aged her at thirteen years old and she was in foal to her own colt. She was an absolute darling, and thoroughly enjoyed the love and attention she was so rightly given. As the date of the arrival of the foal grew nearer she was given 24-hour care by the veterinary staff and we all popped in and out to see her regularly, as she was one of those donkeys that really loves company and seemed to need it. At last, on June 11th little Cindy arrived – the most charming little dark brown filly with the dearest little white nose. I was delighted when one of our contributors, who visited regularly, fell in love with Cindy and made a covenant to pay for her keep for life. As I carried the baby to another warm stable I couldn't help thinking of how both her and her mother's story could have ended without the work done by the Sanctuary. Happily the colt was also later taken into care.

I had a super phone call on March 28th from a delighted Paul; he now had a son – Simon. It hadn't been a particularly easy birth; despite all the latest technology, nobody had realized that it was to be a breech birth, and poor Uschi had to stay in hospital over a week recovering, before she was able to go back to Town Barton Farm. Being Uschi, she was soon back on her feet, and not only coping with Dawn and Simon but helping Paul on the record side of the Town Barton donkeys and answering the phone.

To keep in contact with his staff on the farm, which was very spread out, Paul had put in a CB system. I phoned Uschi to see how the donkeys were getting on, and she could hardly talk for laughing. Paul had got very technical over the quality of output from his set, and had found that anybody using the tractor had a job to hear clearly. So, unable to afford an echo chamber, Paul invented his own version, and Uschi found him in the corner of the kitchen with the coal scuttle over his head, talking through the CB system! I loved visiting the farm; apart from the family and the donkeys always being so happy, there was a peaceful atmosphere in the beautiful surroundings with the pure Dartmoor air. Dartmoor can be terrible for animals in the snow, when it is sometimes impossible to get food supplies to the ponies, donkeys and sheep by road. Paul was visited by representatives from the National Park to see if we would be prepared to supply emergency rations, which would be collected from Town Barton Farm by helicopter, and he was delighted to co-operate.

In May we held our first International Donkey Week. I don't think in my wildest dreams I had ever thought that it could be such a success! With Julie, Mal and Di Murray, who had recently joined our secretarial team, we had planned everything: everybody arriving at Exeter, either at the railway or coach station, was met by our staff and helped with their luggage to the coaches which then took them to the hotels. I had visited almost every hotel in Sidmouth and, instead of asking for a discount for our visitors who would stay, I had suggested that, rather than do a group booking, they treated each person as an individual and charged them the rate they normally charged, but then each hotel gave us 10% of the accommodation proceeds for the Donkey Sanctuary in lieu of a discount. We had eight hotels which had been very happy to join the scheme and to have visitors at a time when Sidmouth is normally very quiet. Julie and Di liaised with our supporters in making the arrangements and Di became almost a full-time Donkey Week organizer as everybody's worries or problems regarding the week landed on her desk. The first morning when the coaches arrived at the Sanctuary I managed to get on each coach and explain to everybody what we did, what we hoped to achieve and what we would try to do for them during the week, and as they got off the coach all my willing staff took over. It was apparent that there was an enormous rapport between the visitors and the donkeys and, indeed, the visitors and the staff, all of whom really appreciated the change from routine work to looking after the visitors and travelling round different farms. The donkeys loved every single minute of the week; so many people loved them, petted them and some just wanted to stand and groom the donkeys for the week, and it became a time of deep satisfaction for all those involved. About 110 people came.

The first day we spent at the Sanctuary, and then on the second day everybody got on the coaches and went out to Town Barton Farm. Here Paul had laid on rides on the tractors around the farm to show everybody the extent of the property and to see the donkeys in even the furthest quarters of the farm. Each day another farm entertained our visitors and each evening I went down to Sidmouth and had dinner at a different hotel so that I could see the guests and make sure that everybody was perfectly happy. I think one of the nicest things that happened was a gentleman coming up to me and saying, 'Mrs Svendsen, every Sunday I've had lunch alone since my wife died, and now I've found that Len lives only ten miles away and he and I have become great friends. In future we're going to meet up every Sunday.' This sort of comment was being heard all around as people found there were others as lonely as themselves, who had the same interests.

When the visitors came up to Slade Farm on the Monday for the final day we knew we would have to have another Donkey Week. So many people had enjoyed themselves; so the first Donkey Week ended on the most successful note, and we hoped to be able to hold one every year.

We had been approached by a film company to make a film of the Donkey Sanctuary; we felt this might be a good idea, as we could show it during the day to visitors coming round the Sanctuary; they would be able to see not only the other farms, the Slade Centre and the work that went on in the hospital, which they weren't allowed to visit, but also they could see some of the work abroad. So we agreed with the film crew that we would go to Greece and they could film the work we were doing on parasitology on the island of Kea. I had been working on Kea for the last four years with Dr Iannis Georgoulakis; we had now got the island almost parasite-free so far as the donkeys were concerned, and the change in condition of some of these donkeys was quite outstanding. Along with Bill Jordan came Don Bliss, Fiona Taylor and one of our nurses, Niki Latham, to help with the work. I was hoping that if everything was successful we could get the results from Kea published; the United Nations could then be approached and, hopefully, a subsidy would be given to poor people everywhere in the world to enable their donkeys to be treated for parasites regularly. The film certainly proved this; the difference in treated and untreated animals was obvious.

During the filming we went to Athens. As I have mentioned previously, the Agricultural Bank of Greece had been extremely helpful. Iannis Georgoulakis was seconded to the bank and had been working with their co-operation. During the filming Dr Panayotopoulos, Deputy Governor of the Bank, made the startling announcement that he had been so impressed with the work done by the charity that in future they would give over 150 million drachmas to be used for anthelmintics. This was the most fantastic breakthrough and on returning to the UK I spoke to the World Health Organization and arranged to meet their chairman the next time I visited Greece. When I met Dr Papadopoulos of WHO I found him most helpful, very impressed with the work and I mentioned to him a favour he could possibly do me. I was convinced that if we could get vets from other parts of the world to come to the Sanctuary and see the work we were doing, and put them on a special training scheme, then we could spread our donkey work much further afield. He seemed

(ABOVE) *A typical donkey and owner in Kea.*
(BELOW) *Big-eared Joey from Blackpool.*

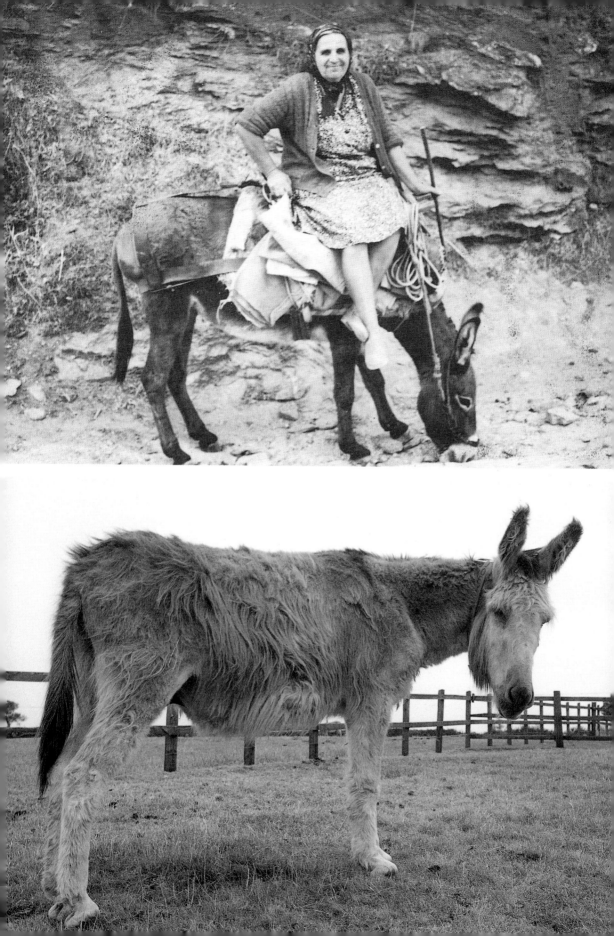

taken with this idea, especially when I pointed out that during the six-week training period, which we would fund completely, including fares to the UK, we would include a week at a veterinary university of the vets' choice in the UK and also a week at the Hereford Farriery College, in addition to all the training that would be given by our Veterinary Department. He became extremely enthusiastic. Thanks to Dr Papadopoulos we were sent a list of suitable vets who could come for training, and every single person he recommended visited in due course, which gave us a network of veterinary surgeons with donkey experience throughout the world, which was to prove absolutely invaluable.

I have previously mentioned problems back home on the beaches; the new inspectorate system was now working very well indeed. However, Blackpool regulations are slightly different from those in other parts of the country. This is because Blackpool has always been very conscious of the value of the beach donkeys to its tourist trade and over a hundred years ago they drew up their Donkey Charter. This was similar to present requirements of other local councils but in addition Blackpool has built some wonderful stabling where the donkeys can rest after their work in almost ideal conditions. Because of the length of the beach and the obviously popular sites for donkey riding, the operators are given a different site during each week in rotation, so each gets a fair chance. The Sanctuary has had a very good working relationship with the beach operators for many years and Inspector Matthews of the RSPCA liaised with the Sanctuary on many occasions to ensure that retiring donkeys came down to the Donkey Sanctuary. At this time, the owner of one of the donkeys, Joey Clews, decided to retire him as he had reached twenty years of age, and when he arrived we were pleased to see how well he had travelled. Due to the length of the journey Perry, the driver, had made an overnight stop to enable Joey to stretch his legs and have plenty to eat, and as he was so large he had been given two sections of the horse box. Unloading him was no problem, and he walked down the ramp in a calm and composed manner. We were amazed to see that he was almost as big as Buffalo, one of our donkeys who had also worked on Blackpool Beach and who, in fact, had known Joey for many years. Joey had an enormous set of ears and was very well built, with the kindest, gentlest nature possible, and he settled in very quickly. He was in good health; there were no special foot or lice problems and at the end of his isolation period Joey was ready to go and join a group.

Normally the donkeys that come in stay with the admission group they have been with during their isolation period, but we decided that it would be rather nice if Joey could join the group of donkeys from Blackpool that he had not seen for seven years in their little unit on Slade House Farm. One is always careful when introducing a new animal to a group as there can be some pushing or biting and so, as was our usual practice, we stopped alongside the enclosure and let the donkeys talk to each other over the wooden fence. It really was quite amazing. Although these animals had not seen each other for such a long time there was an immediate rapport. Buffalo and Bobby seemed to know that it was a friend who had arrived and there were the most enormous and delightful brays of welcome. After two minutes' talking over the fence, it was apparent there was to be no biting or kicking at this reunion, and so we opened the gate and let Joey in. The scenes that followed were almost indescribable. The donkeys appeared ecstatic and they all rolled together, kicking up their legs, trotted around the concrete enclosure, braying almost non-stop for nearly ten minutes. After this time, with Bobby on one side and Buffalo on the other, Joey was escorted round his new home, and the obvious pleasure the three took in being together was most touching.

We had been having a lot of complaints from visitors to Mexico on the state of the donkeys there, and I had met Dr Aline de Aluja at a meeting I had attended when giving a paper to the World Society for the Protection of Animals, and knew that she worked at the Veterinary University in Mexico. Bill Jordan also knew Aline and we decided we would make a visit to see for ourselves the situation there.

We decided first to go to Mexico and then from there on to the Galapagos Islands, where the feral donkeys were causing problems. We had the most fantastic response at the Veterinary University of Mexico and the Ministry of Agriculture. They were extremely helpful and, thanks to Aline, we managed to get them to co-operate in a joint project to help the donkey. Apart from suffering terribly from saddle galls and wounds, the donkeys' main problem once again appeared to be parasites. We managed to employ our own vet, Enrique Nunez, and arranged for him to come to the UK for his six-week training course, so that he could see our up-to-date hospital and how we cared for the donkeys here. Following this he would return to Mexico and we would employ him to work with the donkeys on our behalf. The Veterinary University agreed to do all the laboratory work free and to subsidize the remainder of his salary if we couldn't afford to pay him sufficient. We were appalled by the state of some of those poor donkeys in Mexico, and the general conditions for humans too. We visited one small village,

Capula, where the school had almost no equipment whatsoever and the children looked undernourished and unhappy. The small village streets were full of dust and sand and it was not only the animals in that part of the world that were suffering. I was determined to try and help on my next visit in any way that I could.

We then went down to the Galapagos Islands; here the feral donkeys on some islands were threatening to destroy the eggs of the giant tortoise found only in this area. On the way down we had to land in Peru due to engine failure and during our enforced stay at the airport we were fed on 'meat' sandwiches. A group of scientists from California were on the plane with us and by the time we arrived at the hotel in Guayaquil, the jumping-off place for the Galapagos, we were all suffering from extreme diarrhoea and vomiting. Sharing suffering such as this certainly brings people together and we became quite good friends with the scientists before we all left to make our way on different tours. The only way to reach the islands was by sea. Unfortunately Bill Jordan suffered badly from seasickness. Assured by travel agents that at the time of year we were travelling the sea would be flat and calm, we arranged to charter a small boat as this was the cheapest method of getting round the islands. However we were to learn that we could not depend on the agent's assurance. From the moment we boarded the boat we had a force-six wind blowing and, with the strong currents between the islands, the sea was extremely choppy and uncomfortable. By the second day Bill Jordan had endured enough and he decided that once he got off the boat at the main island there was no way he was getting back on board again.

It took him three days to recover sufficiently even to think of continuing our work and during this time we visited the Charles Darwin Research Station and spoke to their director, Mr Friedemann Koster, with regard to the donkey problems on Isabela and the other islands. The storms which had so upset Bill were, Mr Koster said, caused by El Nino, a strange weather phenomenon which happens every few years. When El Nino comes, so do the rains and the strong winds, which had caused the rough seas. However, El Nino and the rain had brought relief for the donkeys. Some of the team from the Research Station had been out to Isabela and found that, far from it being barren with just a few pools around the edge of the volcanic hole in the centre of the island, vegetation had sprung up in enormous quantities almost immediately on receiving rain, and the team, despite hacking their way through the undergrowth, had been unable to reach the rim of the crater. This, of course, in turn, meant there was drinking water everywhere for the donkeys, and the threat to the tortoises had receded. We spent some time discussing with them the ways that the problem could be solved in the future, and then began to rack our brains for a way to get round the islands that would be acceptable to Bill. We then had a real break-through, in meeting again the American scientists we had met in Guayaquil. They were on the only large boat that plies between the islands, and I thought this might be less unsteady and therefore better for Bill. They kindly agreed that we could travel with them. But despite this boat being much larger – it held 50 passengers – there was still a certain amount of motion. As we arrived at each island the scientists were very keen to be the first to get ashore; to be fair about it, they had split into three groups – the albatross, the boobies and the cormorants – named after birds on the islands. Day one, the albatross group would leave in the first rubber boat and land ashore, followed by the boobies and the cormorants. Day two, the boobies would go first, followed by the cormorants and the albatross group, and so on. Bill was finding the boat less than comfortable, and the first morning when he struggled up on deck looking particularly green around the gills, the team leader decided that we should definitely be albatrosses that day. On stepping ashore we were able to watch sea lions at the closest quarters I'd ever seen them. In fact one of the party had a rather watery experience as he mistook a sleeping sea lion for a rock. Apart from this mishap, however, it was absolutely wonderful. Being with such a knowledgeable group, includ-ing Bill who is an expert on wildlife, I learnt a great deal.

The following day it was the boobies' turn to step ashore first, but, once again, Bill's emergence on the deck, this time literally heaving, was enough to make us boobies for the day. For the rest of the trip we were automatically allocated to the first boat to go ashore, not only to Bill's relief but also to the relief of all the others who tactfully sat as far away from Bill as possible during the short trip to each island.

Clive had returned home having completed his university course and obtained his degree. It was lovely to have him back and I had been able to travel happily knowing he was living at home and able to look after Sarah, but on my return things didn't seem quite the same. My bathroom seemed different somehow – a radiator had miraculously changed position. It took quite a while for the full story to come out; it must have been quite a party in Mother's absence.

Grainne had come over for the Bank Holiday weekend and a party seemed to have started on the Friday and finished on the Monday with a real get-together of Clive and Sarah's friends. No one seems to know how the radiator became detached from the wall, but I understand the party participants took it in turns to keep their thumbs on the pipe to prevent the bathroom becoming completely flooded before the plumber arrived – not too happily at 2 a.m. on a Sunday morning! The flower border was not the same either, and the indent which was still apparent in the garden was where Sarah had apparently slept off the results of her first real taste of alcohol. Despite this, it was lovely to be home with the children and I had to make the most of Clive, as he had accepted a job at the Brain Bank in Boston, USA, and was leaving with Grainne in September.

I returned to a most enormous mountain of work. It's amazing how much paperwork gathers in three weeks, and how our numbers seemed to have increased even in that short time. We now had 190 donkeys out in good homes, being visited regularly, and much of the paperwork on my desk was with regard to requests to take donkeys in. Eileen Judge, who had joined me as my secretary many years before, was now Roy Harrington's Personal Assistant and was excellent in carrying out the day-to-day running of the Welfare Department. Eileen had dealt with many of the difficult welfare-related matters during my absence. Having so many donkeys out in homes to be checked, and dealing with complaints of donkeys in trouble, market surveys, and liaising with the inspectors, really kept Eileen busy. Roy, of course, had to spend a great deal of time out in the field working with his chief inspectors and he was setting up a trained team of voluntary welfare workers who could initially follow up cruelty complaints and regularly visit those donkeys placed out in good homes. We were also receiving complaints about donkeys on television being misused and I had to write several sharp letters with regard to the distressing habit of putting large adults on small donkeys. Particularly offensive were television broadcasts of *The Pirates of Penzance* with the major-general on a donkey, and Les Dawson on a beach donkey. Additionally there were several holiday posters and brochures featuring adults on donkeys. Through my newsletter I appealed to our subscribers to let me know if they saw any of this happening and to send in any newspaper cuttings from local events.

I don't know what I'd have done without Brian while I was away; somehow he'd managed not only to do his own job but to cover mine as far as he possibly could and I think without his help I would never have been able to get away again. Another big problem was our lorry; we were making so many long-distance journeys that it was beginning to wear out and yet it was crucial that the donkeys travelled in reasonable comfort. I put out a special appeal to raise some funds to purchase a new one.

I was just beginning to get into the pile of paperwork in front of me when I received a call from one of the vets asking if I would come out and have a look at Amos. Amos had come in during February 1978 and he had been such a gentle old donkey, but it was obvious as I stood there looking at him that he'd come to the end of his days. In earlier years he'd been shod and had pulled a cart in Ireland, and had been very badly treated. When he arrived he was getting on for thirty and in a very poor way, but he'd really enjoyed his five years of love, care and freedom. The vet and I stood looking down at him, his beautiful eyes clouded with pain, unable to get up after suffering what appeared to be partial heart failure. He seemed to know that we were there and managed a last nuzzle as I knelt beside him and said goodbye. His great friend was Daisy Knight and she was the oldest inhabitant of the Sanctuary at almost fifty. She'd had to be put to sleep the day before, and as I came out of the stable the first cold wind of winter touched me and I knew that many of my dear old friends would be passing on in the next few months. As I walked into the office the phone was ringing, and our Chief Inspector, Jack Turnell from Blackpool, soon cheered me up. Albert, a Blackpool beach donkey, was being retired and the owner was sending him to us. Memories of Blackpool tower and Albert 'wot was et by the lions' brought me back to the present, with so much work still to be done.

Chapter · 5

THE FIRE THAT SPOILED THE HAY BUT SAVED THE FOX
1984

B Y THE start of 1984 all three charities were really hard at work; each had its own set of trustees and the six-monthly meetings were full of interest, as we discussed what had happened in the past and looked forward to the next six months and the future. Each of the trustees had been carefully selected for their knowledge of the job in hand: for the Donkey Sanctuary the trustees were Pat Feather, Bill Jordan, Johnny Morgan (bank manager) and Rosalind de Wesselow (authoress). As June had retired, thinking she was going to take up a post abroad, we had asked Ken Rackham if he would like to join; he had enormous expertise as a business consultant, having been one of the partners of Arthur Young for many years. He agreed to join the team and strengthened even more those available to keep an eye on the charity, to ensure its future, should anything happen to Brian, Julie or myself. The Slade Centre trustees were George Hopkins (Headmaster), David Miller (Social Worker), John Lovell (Solicitor), Brian and myself. For the International Donkey Protection Trust we had Rosalind de Wesselow, Brian and Pat once again, and Bob Camac (Solicitor).

Just above the Donkey Sanctuary, a house called Highlands had come on the market and we had taken the opportunity to buy this, bearing in mind that taking in resident vets usually meant providing accommodation for them. John Fowler, our senior vet, had been living at Highlands since its purchase. However at our trustees' meeting Brian Bagwell had to report that the roof at Slade House Farm was gradually collapsing and that major repairs were desperately needed. For a while I thought perhaps Sarah and I could continue living there during renovations, but it became apparent as the extent of the repairs necessary was revealed, that it was going to be impossible. At first we tried to rent accommodation locally but when John Fowler announced he would be leaving Highlands, as he had purchased his own house, we decided to move up

John Rabjohns, joint Slade Farm Manager, with Crackers.

there. Life for me at Slade House Farm had been very difficult over the past two years; there were so many memories in the house and, with only Sarah and myself, I'd been gradually letting the office infiltrate more and more until really the house was no longer a home.

I looked forward to moving up to Highlands and as Brian and I were chatting one evening about our various problems – long after work and after everybody else had gone home – it suddenly struck me that with the number of staff needed to cope with all the paperwork, this would be an ideal time for me to move out permanently and let the Donkey Sanctuary have the full use of Slade House. I suppose both Brian and I had known this was going to be inevitable. Since the work required was so extensive, we might as well reorganize the rooms downstairs at the same time to get the maximum use out of the building as offices. Highlands was a very much smaller house than Slade House, but I didn't mind getting rid of my large bedroom furniture – in fact it was almost a relief to clear some of the memories of the past. By now Niels had married a girl called Sally and I realized there was no way I was ever going to get him back, although I knew I could never stop loving him.

June had bought herself a little bungalow in Honiton; she didn't have a name for the bungalow and as it was on Chestnut Drive I christened it Little Conkers but I wasn't sure how much she appreciated this, although the postman always managed to deliver the letters all right, so I think he must have had the same sense of humour as I had. We were seeing more and more of each other, as we were both alone, and it was great fun to have somebody to go out with in the evenings for a drink or just a chat over the day's events. June also had a busy life, so it was nice to relax with a good companion.

Sarah had by this time changed schools and to her great relief was no longer a weekly boarder at Paignton. She had settled very well at Sidmouth College and once again the house was full of noise and activity as her many friends spent time with us. Our house always seemed a popular meeting place as the girls could always slip down to see the donkeys, and I hoped that the other mums did not mind the extra washing after a day of mucking out the donkeys.

Sarah had always wanted a dog of her own, and to my horror she fell in love with Great Danes. After a great deal of searching we found a suitable litter and of course once Sarah had seen the basket of wriggling puppies there was no escape. One little pup threw itself at Sarah's feet, and so Hannah joined the family. Although Sarah had many friends, Hannah certainly became number one – Sarah was a keen member of the Venture Scouts and my only surprise was that Hannah didn't go potholing. She grew so rapidly you could almost watch her; at first as I would return for lunch I could just see a little head at Sarah's window ledge, pleased to welcome me, but hoping I was Sarah. Then, as the weeks went on, like Topsy, she grew, and grew, until she almost filled the window. Emma and Kate, two of Sarah's friends, would help at 'walkies' time, but I'm never sure who walked who. A great sloppy dog with humans, Hannah could not stand small dogs, and it was really tough if you were the one holding her lead when any small innocent dog dared to pass. Your feet could literally leave the ground.

I had recently written two more children's books, one about the children at the Slade Centre and how Eeyore helped them, all the royalties going, of course, to help the Slade Centre, and another about a poor little donkey called Crackers, whose past history had nearly broken my heart a short time previously. It had all started early in December, when we'd had a telephone call from a lady asking if we could find the owner of a donkey wandering about on waste ground near her home in the Midlands. Apparently the donkey had been wandering in and out of traffic in the town for six weeks or more and, despite requests to other welfare charities, nothing had been done. On this particular day she said he'd collapsed a little way from her home, and could we come and do something. Our local inspectors were immediately informed and set off with their trailer behind the car. The weather was freezing, there was a light covering of snow on the fields, and more was forecast. Our inspectors and some passers-by who offered their help were appalled by what they saw; the donkey was in a terrible condition. Very gently he was loaded into the trailer, supported by straps, and I'm sure you can imagine his feelings when put into a warm stable at the inspectors' home, with deep straw, clear fresh water and a small warm feed of bran, oats and molasses, the first real meal he had received in many weeks. The local veterinary surgeon found that Crackers was suffering from very bad anaemia, had lung noises which he said were probably due to a previous bout of pneumonia which had not been treated, and a very bad wound on the hind leg which had turned septic. In addition he had an injury on the left eye and he was heavily infested with worms and lice. Once he had got over his tetanus and antibiotic injections he was given special vitamin tablets, wormed, de-loused and had his hooves trimmed properly. Gradually his feed was increased until he was eating ad-lib hay and two meals of bran, flaked maize and oats a day. Every night he had a rug put over him to make sure he lost no body heat and energy, so desperately needed in his fight for survival during those early days.

It took nearly five weeks before Crackers was well enough to travel down to the Sanctuary, and he must have felt he was in heaven. What surprised everybody was the friendliness of this little stallion, who had received such bad treatment at the hands of human beings. Our inspectors were very sad when the Sanctuary lorry arrived to pick him up, but he had a great welcome when he arrived at the Sanctuary on January 13th. He gave a large bray of joy before walking down the ramp of the lorry to join us. Being a stallion, he could not be mixed with any of the other new donkey arrivals and, in any event, he was not yet well enough at this stage to even compete on a friendly basis for food.

Shortly after his arrival another little stallion called Daniel Chestnut came in. Daniel came into the Sanctuary as his owner had suffered several misfortunes. Despite being disabled and permanently confined to a wheelchair, Mr Bellamy had managed to cope not only with Daniel but also with driving horses; he had always loved his animals dearly. As well as having a handicapped son, his wife was taken ill, and sadly they had to agree that Daniel Chestnut should be taken into care. Mr Bellamy personally told us the donkey's delightful story. Apparently Daniel was born in Worcester, where his donkey family had been companions to horses. It is well known amongst horse and donkey owners that even the most lively horse can be quietened by the companionship of a donkey. Daniel lost his mother before he was properly weaned and so he decided that his mother was instead a 16-hand mare who also had a foal. Daniel got quite used to suckling and the horse mare was quite happy about this. Unfortunately the horse was sold and taken away. In a complete panic, seeing his milk ration leaving, Daniel managed to leap through the fence and gallop after the horse box. Luckily a police patrol car was nearby and the horse box was stopped, Daniel was loaded onto the box and driven back to the farm. He was put in a small shed with a window, but with one great leap, Daniel jumped through the plate glass window and once again galloped after the retreating box. Realising the tremendous distress to both the donkey and the mare, the new owner took pity on Daniel and he was put in the horse box and taken away with his 'mother'. His new owner, Mr Bellamy, weaned little Daniel as soon as possible, looking after him very carefully and putting up with continuous braying day and night for two days before Daniel finally accepted he was a grown donkey and quite old enough to eat his own food! As Mr Bellamy had always been interested in driving, he decided to train Daniel to pull a small cart, and spent many hours walking with him, leading him along quiet lanes, and gradually introducing him to traffic. By the time Daniel was two years old he was introduced to long reining, and by three years old was quite happy to feel harness on his back and a bridle with bit

Daniel Chestnut enjoying life at the Slade Centre.

in his mouth. When he was four he pulled a small log attached to a harness for the first time. Mr Bellamy had built a very light trap for him, running on two bicycle wheels. Patiently, Daniel was broken in, and he got used to voice commands as well as the shake of the reins and the gentle touch of the driving whip on his back. He proved very popular at the many fetes he attended, and thoroughly enjoyed giving rides; the money he collected went to charity and he raised over £500 for children's organizations in Bristol. When Mrs Bellamy was suddenly taken very ill and had to go to hospital, the Bellamys reluctantly decided that Daniel had to come into the Sanctuary, but they sent him in with one specific wish; he should be allowed to help in the Slade Centre.

On arrival, he was put next door to Crackers, and round the stable doors these two began to make firm friends. After six weeks it was decided that Crackers was fit to stand the castration operation which both our veterinary surgeons strongly advised, as they felt his recovery could then continue without interruption. Crackers was castrated on the same day as Daniel Chestnut and both the donkeys were then placed together to recover and make friends. Crackers's improvement continued at an even faster pace once he had a friend, and a very special bond quickly developed. When they had both been passed as fit and sound, a big decision had to be made. Daniel was earmarked for the Slade Centre, but due to Crackers's malnutrition, eye damage and chronic lung problem, he would never be fit to join the crème-de-la-crème. It was also obvious that they could not be separated and Crackers himself solved the problem by joining Daniel as the 'petting' donkey at the Slade Centre, as he loved being groomed, never fidgeted and at times leant on the groomer more and more heavily, eyes half closed and obviously enjoying every second! He just adored being loved and petted and the children worshipped him!

Readers of *Down Among the Donkeys* will remember the terrible condition of two little donkeys, So Shy and Tiny Titch, who arrived during the very early days of the Sanctuary in 1973. They had come direct from Reading Market and Tiny Titch had been so badly beaten that pieces of sacking were embedded in his splintered spine. So Shy had had almost every tooth broken by being beaten on the face. We had worked for months to get them restored to reasonable health and then came the opportunity for our very first rehabilitation donkeys. A Mrs Janet de Van Hogg from nearby had rung and offered to give a home to any donkeys in trouble. At that time I was desperate for stabling and so I had driven off and visited Mrs Van Hogg. She was just the sort of person I needed to give special attention to So Shy and Tiny Titch, with a lovely well fenced paddock, super stabling and a lovely family who were only too willing to help. I'd certainly made a good choice, because I had the pleasure of writing to Mrs Van Hogg to congratulate her on giving over ten years of happiness to the donkeys, and I quote from her letter back:

> Tiny Titch and So Shy, always called 'Sonny and Shy' now, are well and happy. Always friendly and curious, they are totally different from one another. Sonny is still gangly and immature, fussy and demanding and not very sensible! While Shy is well rounded and feminine, calm and patient, but not without a good measure of craftiness!! They are very much members of the family.

I think this description by Mrs Van Hogg of the donkeys sums up many of our inhabitants.

The Slade Centre had had a most unusual round of trouble some time ago, with the donkeys being so unlike their normal placid selves that I went with Pat to watch one of the sessions that seemed to be causing problems. These were with children from the Partial Hearing Unit in Honiton, and I couldn't understand why the donkeys were so nervy and jumpy whilst giving the children rides. Normally they are placid and biddable, but on entering the arena I put my ear close to one of the children's hearing aids and to my surprise I could just hear a rather high-pitched squeaky buzz. With the teacher's help we turned the hearing aids down and immediately Alfred, who was the child's mount, quietened down and got on with his normal routine work. Obviously the donkeys had been disturbed by the hearing aids.

During another session I watched quietly as one of our schools, which caters for the most seriously handicapped children, used the arena. Only three donkeys had been chosen for this class as the children were so severely handicapped. As the session ended Alfred and Wilma were taken out, but Harry, a very strong grey gelding, waited quietly in the arena, his volunteer handler just with a gentle hand on his neck. Then I heard it – yells and screams from the playroom, and a nine-year-old deeply disturbed boy was helped across the floor by two teachers and Pat. Suddenly the flailing hands touched Harry; the silence was uncanny. He stopped shouting and quietly the riding staff lifted him onto the donkey's back. The boy was so severely handicapped he couldn't sit upright, and when riding he had to lean back on his hands which were on the donkey's back, and as he passed, quiet at last, his fingers were gently rubbing the donkey. For the first time, the boy had a calm expression. Pat told me that the school staff said that this twenty-minute ride on Harry once a week was the only time that the child was calm – not only an achievement for the Slade Centre, but quite an achievement for Harry. It is not always easy for Pat but she must get immense satisfaction from seeing so many children gain so much pleasure, and the Centre is always so beautifully organized and well kept. It gives me real satisfaction to go up there.

We now had six full-time and forty part-time staff in our Inspectorate Department run by Roy. Conditions at markets appeared to be improving. I had always been deeply concerned about this, as I'd never been to a market which I felt didn't involve some sort of tension and stress for the animals being sold, to put it mildly. However, we were able to attend a meeting with the Ministry of Agriculture, where it was suggested that efforts were to be made to include equines under the auspices of the Farm Animal Welfare Council. We had recently received a communication from them asking us to supply information for their consideration, and so each of our full-time inspectors submitted a report covering the markets within their boundaries, which would be discussed early the next year. We were also carrying out an in-depth study of donkey derbys and hoped to draw up a Code of Practice which would be presented to the National Equine Welfare Committee to get its backing. There were still many flagrant abuses throughout the country, and many donkey derby operators were not licensed under the local authority. These had been reported to the local authorities concerned, but a Code of Practice would give the licensing authorities a basic understanding and a set of standards on which to judge those in their area.

Enrique Nunez, our Mexican vet, duly came to the Sanctuary as arranged, and June and I followed this up with a visit back to Mexico with him, along with Don Bliss, our parasitologist, to set up a trial similar to that which we had carried out in Greece so successfully. Accompanied by Dr Aline de Aluja, we once again went back to Capula, which I felt had sufficient donkeys to have a proper trial; there was a reasonable distance between their donkeys and those in the next village to prevent mistaken identities and infection from other parasites. As I have mentioned previously, I had been appalled at the conditions there, not only for the donkeys but for the children. There were absolutely no materials for the children to use for their education, no slates, no crayons, no paper, not even any desks or chairs, and the children sat around in classrooms with sand on the floor and on this they drew and did their lessons. The fact that there was no water into the village was obviously an enormous deterrent to improving conditions and so we had contacted the American Government as I felt they were the nearest neighbours and should be able to help. Senator Barry Goldwater wrote a nice reply to my request that they try to get water through to this village and, very much to our joy and surprise, on this visit we found that a water supply had been laid on. We took the opportunity to take a vanload of equipment for the school which consisted of all sorts of teaching materials, and even cleaning equipment, buckets and mops and so on, as they were now able to improve their primitive washing and toilet facilities with the use of running water. They had the equivalent of what we would call a parent/teacher association and the parents were so delighted with the help we had given them that, poor as they were, they decided to lay on a special treat for us.

Somewhat to our horror we found ourselves invited to a luncheon in our honour; we are always rather wary of eating and drinking abroad. All sorts of diseases, to which our systems are totally unaccustomed, are present in both the drinking water and a lot of the food. However, there seemed no way out of this. Aline told us that they had gone to great lengths and had all put up money that could be ill spared to provide a meal. We were shown into part of a small mill which had been converted for the day, the seats being sacks on which we sat, and five planks laid across piles of sacks to form a table. Don Bliss, who had vehemently declared that he could eat nothing that hadn't been made in the hotel at which we were staying, had at first refused to even sit down, despite pleading from Aline who was very afraid of upsetting the feelings of those who had sacrificed so much to give us this meal. However, he caught sight of an unopened bottle of whisky on the table and this seemed to persuade him to join us in the repast.

I don't really know how to describe the food we were offered. It was served in chipped enamel washing-up bowls and at first sight appeared to consist of a peculiar brownish liquid on which lumps of fat were bobbing and small bags were floating. Without any fuss a large ladle of this was spooned into the bowls in front of us. June and I looked round, hoping that somebody else would start to eat, so that we could try and sort out what we were supposed to do, but before we had time to give more than a cursory glance at the bowl in front, some bright yellow saffron rice was ladled on top and rapidly sank into the brown liquid. It was at this stage we realized that we were the only ones who were going to eat; everybody else was standing back looking, and Aline immediately took a large mouthful and then proceeded to pick out one of the little bags half submerged in the bowl. She carefully undid this and out of it took a small piece of gristly chicken. The bags were in fact made of the

outer skin of the cactus leaf; the chicken had apparently been ceremoniously killed and was regarded as the pièce de resistance for our
feast. We never really identified the other objects floating in our bowls;
suffice it to say that fortunately the taste of curry seemed to conceal the
other rather obnoxious tastes that one suddenly became aware of.

Don Bliss managed one teaspoonful and then said he wasn't feeling
very well, and sat hopefully waiting for the bottle of whisky to be
opened. This, however, was not to be; it was decoration, having been
obtained by the head of the village on a trip some years before, and
apparently was ceremoniously produced at any major function, although
never opened. We were all, however, treated to glasses of pulque. This
innocuous-looking, milky liquid, occasionally mistaken for skimmed
milk at first sight, was yet another product of the cactus plant and had
quite a dramatic effect on us all, in particular on Don Bliss, who hadn't
been able to eat anything to absorb the very high alcohol level. I was later
taken to see where they had cooked the food and, having watched what
they did, I can now give you the recipe for this feast and the methods of
cooking it:

1. Collect small twigs and pieces of wood, and add to the top four dried
   pats of donkey dung. These will ensure that the cooking is long and
   slow, and this use of donkey dung, flattened and dried, is prevalent
   throughout many parts of Mexico and Africa. The large cooking pot,
   which is slung over the fire, held by a tripod arrangement of sticks,
   should not have been washed, as it should retain flavours from
   previous cookings.

2. Catch the chicken to be prepared for the meal, and, having
   despatched it, use every single piece of the bone and flesh in the pot.

3. The water is used from the well (unless you have a supply which is
   nearer to hand), and does not necessarily need to be clean as you will
   be boiling it.

4. Place all the bits of chicken, including the entrails, into the water and
   cover, boiling as long as the wood and the donkey dung last.

5. Find a large cactus plant, take the outside leaves and, as they dry,
   strip off the surface which can be used as wrapping material. Once the
   stew has cooled, take out the pieces of chicken and by hand wrap
   them in the cactus leaves. Pop all these back into the pot, and this is
   then ready to serve when required. *Bon appetit!*

I returned home to find yet another problem from outside the UK. It had always been the policy of the Donkey Sanctuary to deal only with donkeys found in trouble in Great Britain, but we found ourselves having to make our first exception. In October 1983 a very worried lady wrote to our inspectors to advise that there was an abandoned donkey in Ireland who had been left for eighteen years on a very small island inhabited only by sheep. The original residents had been moved by the government, and the donkey had only received rudimentary care when shepherds visited, and it was apparently now in great trouble. Our inspectors, despite energetic searches, were unable to find a boat large enough to move the donkey during the winter tides; but they managed to trace the owner, who agreed that he would ensure that the donkey would receive as much help throughout the winter as possible. Our inspectors then arranged with a local fisherman that as soon as the weather permitted he would go across and bring the donkey back to the mainland; fortunately the sea crossing was calm and Islander, as we had named him, travelled extremely well. He was taken to a knowledgeable temporary home where he was cared for, although he was in such a terrible condition that we had to consider putting him down. However, despite his lameness, poor condition and extensive body parasites, the vet considered that with the right care he could improve. It was nearly four months before he was fit enough to travel to the Sanctuary.

He was due to arrive the day I got back from Mexico and I went out to meet Roy Harrington who had brought him back himself with a specially adapted box so that we were quite sure that the donkey would have every possible comfort. As Roy opened the door Islander stood at the top of the ramp. When any donkey arrives at the Sanctuary all the others seem to appreciate that a newcomer has arrived and they all go to the rails nearest to the box and usually they all bray in unison to welcome the new arrival. This time was no exception. He was greeted with an enormous bray and for the first time he lifted his head and looked round in wonder, to see not only green fields, but other donkeys which he'd never seen before, and we reckon that at this moment Islander decided that life was worth living after all, and he began to make the slow progress needed for him to recover. Just seeing him standing in his field surrounded by other donkeys made everything worthwhile.

Just after Islander's arrival Lady Di – the donkey – arrived. She'd been kept in a one-acre paddock with two other donkeys and was described by our inspector as very thin, with ribs and backbone only just covered by a thick coat. She was weak and dull-eyed, and obviously needed plenty of veterinary care. The owner was unable to afford veterinary bills and

asked if we could take the little donkey into the Sanctuary, and signed the necessary forms. Poor Lady Di could hardly move at all, and despite infra-red lamps to maintain her body heat, and regular feeding, she had to be admitted to the hospital. Thanks to the constant care and the skill of the veterinary surgeons her life was saved and she began to improve. She seemed to be a donkey who liked to be on her own but next door in the hospital was a little gelding called Samuel Pipsqueak, and very soon the most amazing relationship developed between these two, which gave everybody at the Sanctuary a great deal of pleasure. After a while, to try and catch Lady Di in the field was almost impossible – she galloped away full of energy, and our only chance now was to hold Samuel Pipsqueak, and then Lady Di, sooner or later, would come up to see that her little friend was all right.

At long last the filming which had been going on for the video was over. The film was ready to be previewed, and Town and Country Productions, the company which had made it, arranged for a venue in central London. It really was a most exciting day. We invited people from other charities and some of our supporters, and all enjoyed the first main showing of this film, which was to be such a tremendous help in spreading the word of the work that we were doing throughout the world.

One evening, just as I was getting ready to cook our supper, I received a desperate call from Charlie Courtney, our manager at Brookfield. 'Mrs S, we've got a fire,' he said, and put the phone down. Within seconds June and I had climbed into the car and were racing off to Brookfield. As we drove along the road approaching the farm we could see clouds of smoke billowing up into the air, and the only consolation that I had during the journey was the fact that I could hear the bells of the fire engines as they came up from Honiton. When we drove into the yard and shot out of the car it was quite obvious that one of our largest barns of hay was well ablaze, and Charlie, Julie and their staff were desperately trying to pull bales away to safety to stop the flames spreading to the next barn. Our fire equipment and hoses were being used and the biggest relief of all was to see that the fire was going to be well clear of any donkeys, who were all out safely grazing and watching the proceedings with not a little interest. The fire brigade stayed for five hours, by which time most of the hay in the barn had been ruined. Charlie and Derek Battison, Manager of Paccombe Farm, helped by Tim Mason, farm hand at Brookfield, had defied the smoke and flames using the tractors to try to salvage all they could. It was very late that night before we all got to bed

(ABOVE) *Islander on arrival . . .*

(BELOW) *. . . and twelve months later.*

but that wasn't possible without a bath first; I couldn't believe the sight in the mirror when I saw myself covered in smoke, smut and dirt, and I shudder to think what the others had looked like after their magnificent efforts on the tractors.

The following day Brian and I went to Brookfield to see the extent of the damage. Brian of course had the job of arranging for insurance, one of the many tasks that he had taken on. We were reasonably happy to find that the main damage was confined to one barn, with only minimal damage to the next barn, and we realized that we had been extremely lucky. As Brian did the more technical inspection I wandered round the fields to talk to the donkeys, trying to take my mind off the loss we'd just suffered (although we were insured), and whilst gently talking and strolling through I noticed a whole set of fox holes which had large rags protruding from them. I couldn't understand what this was, bent down, and with great difficulty managed to drag one of the rags out. It was soaked in a horrible smelling oil, probably diesel oil, and I looked in dismay at all the other holes around me, all of which were stopped up. I went back to the farm faster than I'd walked down, and, with Charlie accompanying me, went round examining the different fields. Charlie of course knew immediately what had happened. Apparently the local hunt was due to ride across the area the following day and they'd trespassed on our land to stop the holes to prevent the fox escaping. I was absolutely furious, and so was Charlie. We removed every possible rag in sight to allow the fox a fair chance and my first job when I got back to the Sanctuary was to ring up the huntmaster and tell him that in no way could he trespass across any land owned by the Donkey Sanctuary, as we were not prepared to allow hunting on our ground. I don't think this made me the most popular person locally; I was already in trouble with many farmers for taking so much land for the donkeys, but at the managers' meeting the following week everybody else agreed with the action that had been taken and we agreed to write to the hunts in every area in which our farms were located, pointing out that our land was private property and they were not to trespass.

On the health side we were gradually learning more and more about the donkey's physiology. The comparison I was able to make with donkeys abroad and those here showed some amazing differences; for example, donkeys abroad rarely seem to suffer from hyperlipaemia or laminitis, which were causing great problems here at the Sanctuary, and I spent a great deal of time with our vets discussing the various symptoms and helping to analyse the reports and careful veterinary records that were being made. I've always found vets extremely kind and considerate to me, as, having had no professional veterinary training, I'm obviously at a disadvantage. Wherever I've been in the world people have been helpful, and gradually, with the practical information that I was able to give them, a picture was being built up of the donkey, not only here, but throughout the world. The information that we were putting on our computers would, I knew, be of the greatest value at some time in the future and whilst visiting Glasgow Veterinary University to discuss donkey problems with Professor Jimmy Duncan, who had helped greatly in our parasitology projects, I was asked if I would like to give a lecture to the veterinary students on my next visit.

I accepted this with some trepidation, but was given the most enormous reception by these students and we had an extremely lively hour of questions and answers after the lecture, as they were so interested in the work being done and the knowledge that was being gained. Many students wrote after the lecture and in fact many came down to the Donkey Sanctuary to have some practical experience with our vets during their training. I could only feel that all this veterinary interest was going to be of the most immense value to the donkeys in the future; it seemed beneficial to get as much information to the profession as was possible.

By this time our income had become substantial and every Monday morning my first hour was spent in discussion with Boo, our accountant, ensuring that we gained the maximum interest from any monies that we were holding on deposit. Rates vary greatly and it often meant contacting Jersey as well as London to get the best bank rates, or contacting building societies to see what special rates they were offering to charitable institutions. According to the official figures from the Charities Aid Foundation we were now the 81st largest charity in the UK from over 100,000 registered charities. We still managed to keep our administration overheads the lowest of any animal charity quoted and this made up for the very long hours and the job strain that we were all experiencing. My evenings had certainly been filled lately, as I'd written a new book called *In Defence of Donkeys*; having been approached by Annabel Whittet of Whittet Books, I had decided to have a professional publisher again, so that our donkey news could be spread as far as possible.

Following up my idea of informing veterinary surgeons throughout the world of the work we were doing, and to try to get vital information on the donkey's physiology out, I'd decided to produce *The Professional Handbook of the Donkey* and to ask some of the best authorities in the world on various subjects each to contribute a chapter. This proved more time-

consuming than I had thought, but I was quite convinced that, once produced, we should circulate this free to as many veterinary universities in the world as possible.

Once again we were beginning to run out of land; we held a special meeting with the vets and farm managers to discuss a new idea which Paul had been trying with great success down at Town Barton. Strip grazing has long been known in agriculture as the ideal method for grazing cattle so that they don't take too much fodder at one time, but it had not been tried before for donkeys. Paul's trials had proved that within a very short space of time the donkeys respected the electric fence, and this enabled Paul to use his land better by using a double range of fencing. He moved one fence ahead of the donkeys each day, with a strip of new fresh grass, and put another strip of electric fencing further back down the field. As he gradually used up his field, he moved up the back fence so that the grass could be recovering for when the donkeys had got to the end of the field. This meant the donkeys always had some clean fresh grass to eat each day, and this met with approval from the vets as they were concerned that some donkeys were in fact eating far too much; apart from being obese – which is a great health hazard for donkeys – it was making some of them prone to laminitis, a very painful disease of the foot, one of the causes of which can be the over-consumption of fresh grass. It was agreed that the farm managers would all try strip grazing as this would reduce the acreage required per donkey and would give us much greater control on feeding.

Following the fire at Brookfield, Brian had been putting a lot of extra time into having the electric wiring checked on all barns throughout the Sanctuary, getting the wiring put in conduits and putting extra protection around light bulbs. He invited the fire chief to inspect all our farms and his subsequent recommendations were complied with. In his report to the trustees, Brian explained that he thought the fire had been caused by combustion. He also pointed out that the pond at Brookfield, which had supplied most of the water for fighting the fire, as Brookfield is not on the main water supply, needed to be extended to provide additional water should there be a future emergency. All the trustees were very happy to agree with this.

Also at the trustees meeting our rehabilitation policy was discussed. In the past we had never allowed mares to go out, as we felt that they might be put into foal and we feel there are enough donkeys without breeding more. Most of the donkeys suitable to go out on rehabilitation had already gone, and there were many good homes in the pipeline where donkeys could benefit. Our strict policy of not splitting pairs of donkeys

(ABOVE) *Lady Di with my grand-daughter Dawn.*

(BELOW) *'The donkeys always had some clean fresh grass to eat each day.'*

was now rebounding on us slightly, as all those donkeys left, and suitable to go out on rehabilitation, had mares or fillies as their companions, and this of course prevented either from leaving. However, after a long discussion, it was decided that we would try it on a limited basis, and, provided over the next twelve months none of the donkeys got in foal or had any special problems, we would relax the earlier rule. This allowed about forty more donkeys to take advantage of the excellent homes offered, and worked out fine.

The International Union for the Conservation of Nature was holding its annual meeting in Madrid and, along with Bill Jordan, I attended this, not just because of my interest in that particular congress but also because the World Society for the Protection of Animals (WSPA) was going and I'd been in discussion with them regarding the many trekking centres where donkeys were being used in Tenerife and on the mainland of Spain. During our trip to Madrid, Victor Watkins of WSPA and I went together to see the Ministry. They were fairly co-operative when they found that we weren't going to try to get involved in bull-fighting which seems to be a stumbling block for any animal welfare improvement in Spain. We managed to keep off this subject so that they could concentrate solely on the problems we were concerned with, and together we drew up a very good code of practice which the government agreed to enforce throughout Spain after a twelve-month trial period.

Suddenly Christmas was upon us yet again, and this time June and I, with Sarah, enjoyed a quiet Christmas at home. Christmas always seemed a sad time, but we did manage to make the best of it. It's always an especially trying time for Julie, and I was rather glad this Christmas to be able to be there to give her a hand. On Christmas Eve Sarah, June and I all went down to Paul and Uschi's house, where they had made the most marvellous Christmas preparations: we all danced round the tree in typical Danish fashion, and I did my best to keep cheerful and keep memories of other Christmases with all the family to one side. Together we phoned Clive, who was now living with Grainne in Boston. He was enjoying his work at the Brain Bank, which was part of Harvard University and was doing research on Alzheimer's and Parkinson's diseases. We then phoned Lise and so, apart from speaking to Niels, our little family was complete.

Chapter · 6

FIRST AID IN LAMU
1985

NEW YEAR was spent in Denmark with Lise; I did enjoy spending some time once again with my grandchildren. Mark and Kate were growing to be real little people – they were great fun to be with – but I only had three days to spare, and then it was back for our managers' meeting to try and discuss the problems we were now having during the winter.

In very cold weather, one of our problems with the donkeys was to provide warmth *and* ventilation, the need for which was constantly emphasized by the vets. However, alterations made to one of the barns were all very well until the first very heavy falls of snow, when we suddenly found ourselves having to evacuate the donkeys, their backs covered in snow where it had blown in through the ridges. Managers were as concerned as I was over this problem, as we felt that cold, wet donkeys were certainly not contented donkeys; although perhaps they may have been healthier, they certainly didn't appear to be happier. After long discussions with the Veterinary Department, a compromise was reached and the gaps were reduced. Although I still felt the donkeys were colder than I would have liked, this was a definite improvement, and we set up trials with maximum and minimum thermometers so that we could see what extremes of temperature range the donkeys would experience during the night. I spent an enormous amount of time worrying, especially during cold nights, as I couldn't bear the thought of the donkeys not having the best possible conditions. Fortunately before there were any more cold nights the spring had come and the donkeys were able to be turned out into the fields. Before the next winter, the draughty barn was partially boarded. At our trustees' meeting, the trustees were very interested in the ventilation problems and my concern that the donkeys hated the cold so much; they appointed Bill Jordan, our Consultant Vet, to go into the matter fully and also to look into the ideal weight for each donkey.

With the increasing workload I realized that another secretary was needed, and Marie Long joined Mal in the office. Marie's main responsibilities were to take on the legacy work which Brian was dealing with. I remember going into the office one morning to relate a funny story I had heard the night before. Apparently a young man went through the car wash and as he stopped to pay at the end the attendant said, 'That will be one pound, Paddy.' The young man asked how the attendant knew he was Irish. The attendant smiled and said, 'Oh, we don't get many motorbikes through the car wash!' We all roared with laughter and then Marie said in a quiet voice, 'I'm Irish, Mrs Svendsen'!

At the Sanctuary things were getting busier and busier; we'd offered a special referral service to veterinarians throughout the country. This was to make full use of our operating facilities and the specialist skills that our vets had now attained, having looked after so many donkeys. Donkeys are not the easiest animals to treat and are extremely difficult to anaesthetize successfully unless you know the tricks of the trade. We had taken in a little donkey called Eeyore; she'd almost been crippled by thugs the previous August, and she came to the Donkey Sanctuary for operations and intensive treatment, and I was pleased to be able to say goodbye to Eeyore when she was cured, and send her back to her home in Balcombe, Sussex, and to her owner Mrs Maggie Kear, who had desperately feared Eeyore would have to be put down when her hind leg had been broken in the attack. Apparently when Eeyore got home there was an enormous welcome from the villagers. Mrs Kear put an article in the papers saying, 'She's a lovely donkey, adored wherever she goes. The Sanctuary is an amazing place; she had full-time attention from vets, central heating and proper accommodation. We might retire her there.' Mrs Kear said that Eeyore would have no trouble remembering her old friends, and was used to all the publicity she'd attracted. Our local inspector, Jimmy Gough, said, 'Eeyore was treated round the clock from September until March. We then kept her for a few weeks for further rest, and she'd been a great favourite with the hospital staff.'

By now we had over 2,000 donkeys in care, and were seriously thinking of our next farm purchase. It was suggested we might like to move to Norfolk as, although it was very cold in winter it was dry, and donkeys could, apparently, tolerate the cold weather as long as they didn't get too wet. Although I wasn't too sure of this, we went ahead with looking for properties in the Norfolk area, much to the delight of the national press, who seized on the reasons for moving, and came out with large articles stating that we had to move because the West

Country climate was too damp. According to our vèts we'd be able to let the donkeys out all the year round instead of keeping them in during the winter months, although they did have big outside run-out areas where they could get plenty of exercise on a daily basis. However, as is often the case, wherever we looked property prices seemed to be too high and we decided to put off the move until we'd seen how we got through the coming winter.

The Sanctuary has always been open to the public completely free of charge. I've always believed that, as we are a registered charity, people making any donations, however small, should always be made welcome and be able to see the work that the Sanctuary is doing. If I feel that something is going to happen that will distress people, such as when a lorry comes in loaded with donkeys in trouble, we quietly advise the people in the area so that, if they wish, they can leave. It's surprising how many stay to watch the donkeys unloaded, and then take a particular interest in the case they see. They like to come back again and again to follow the donkey's progress as he is gradually restored to health. Many of these people, and many of our contributors, very kindly make provision in their wills for something to be left to the donkeys when they no longer have use for the money. For very many of us these days, almost every penny of our money is needed but of course there does come a time, after death, when it's possible to do what one would have liked to have done much sooner. The legacies we receive are one of the main lifelines of the charity; I felt it would be very nice if everybody who left us a legacy, no matter how small, had their name put up on a board on what we would call 'the Memory Wall'. This wall has become a very much visited area of the Sanctuary. Families derive great comfort from coming and seeing the names of their relatives on the wall, and the knowledge that the generous help their loved one has given the donkeys is being used to such good effect. Many people ask to dedicate stables to a loved one, or even just a seat on one of our lovely donkey walks, so that they can sit and remember, and give pleasure to other people, by being able to take advantage of the peaceful surroundings and beautiful views.

Talking of bequests to the charities, we had a slightly different one in 1985, in the form of Poppy and Mary. In his will their owner had left his two donkeys to the Sanctuary. His solicitor immediately took them into care until they could be transferred, and we enjoyed reading his letter. In the midst of technical legal comments regarding probate, etc., came the comments about the donkeys: 'The donkeys are in robust health and are rather apt to stalk one round the fields and attempt to kick. Fortunately the writer had some experience with mules during the 1939/45 war and realises that one must not present a target.' I'm sure the solicitor was extremely pleased to be able to get the donkeys safely into the Sanctuary, and maybe it will reassure some people that we can do this.

Although many of the donkeys create a peaceful impression, it wasn't so with Dobbin! We received an urgent call for help on his behalf. This two-year-old gelding had been permanently shut into a small stable, and had become totally unmanageable. There was no question of Dobbin not being fed well enough; in fact, to quote the inspector, 'He'd been fed like a racehorse.' Full of oats, he became steamed up and constantly kicked his stable door or kicked anybody who approached him. Perry, our driver at that time, was warned how dangerous he was when he called to collect him, but fortunately for all concerned, Perry was extremely experienced at handling donkeys, and Dobbin's owners were amazed at the apparent ease with which Dobbin allowed himself to be loaded onto the lorry. Many people don't know our secret trick here; donkeys have an enormous love of peppermints, and of course if you want to spoil a donkey, you give him a polo mint! Obviously when picking up donkeys this isn't always possible, but if you yourself suck a polo and then breathe on the donkey, he'll follow you as docile as any little lamb. Our drivers use this trick to very good effect when picking up difficult donkeys. Many owners have had their pain at losing their favourite donkey eased by the apparently immediate rapport between the driver and the donkey. They've dreaded having to see him pushed or pulled up the ramp of the lorry and are completely comforted when they see the donkey trot happily into the lorry on a short rope halter. It does ease the stress and it is an extremely useful tip when filming with donkeys.

Talking of mints reminds me of Stella, Eddy and Minty, who came in almost immediately following Dobbin. Stella and Eddy were mother and son, and unfortunately Eddy had not been castrated. Having served his mother, little Minty was the result. The owner, who loved them dearly, was desperately concerned because their grazing field was grazed absolutely bare and had become waterlogged. He had nowhere else to put them. Even though he was a stallion, Eddy was a very gentle father, and when his turn came to be castrated I know you'll be pleased to hear that Stella and Minty stayed with him until the last moment, when his anaesthetic was administered, and were there when he came round in the recovery box. It is Sanctuary policy to keep all donkeys together as they come in.

Donkey Week this year was the best ever; it was an established event by now, with more people coming back for a return visit; they helped with the new visitors by showing them around. The atmosphere seemed to build up even more quickly than before. I usually gave two lectures on the Monday; one was supposed to be for new people to tell them some of the funny stories from starting the Sanctuary, including my stallion St Paddy of Kennetbury mistaking the BBC cameraman and his long fur coat for another visiting mare, to the not-so-funny story of the legacy of 204 donkeys which so changed my life. I was always surprised to see supporters who had been on previous years were laughing just as heartily as everyone else. The lecture in the afternoon was to bring everybody up to date, and the reaction was always so kind and considerate that really it has become quite an emotional experience. The terrible thing is that if I try to recall some of the tragic cases that come in, particularly those that haven't made it, my voice begins to falter and it doesn't help when, looking up, I can see everybody else crying. However, there are many more cheerful stories to tell than sad ones. A total of 239 people attended and, once again, the tractor rides were one of the favourite pursuits. During the year we had the most exciting event in the birth of a little foal we named Stepping Out. We named her that after a show in the West End. One of the cast, Josephine Gordon and her friend, Maureen Flenley, had both been at the 1984 Donkey Week, but as Jo was involved in the show, only Mo Flenley had been able to come this year. The cast adopted Stepping Out and up until Donkey Week over £150 had been sent for her care.

On the Sunday of Donkey Week we held our special luncheon, and as I stood up to make a speech the genuine feeling of love and sympathy coming from everybody around the tables suddenly overwhelmed me – that so many people could help our donkeys and could take such an interest in the work we were doing, was almost more than I could bear. As I turned to thank Brian and Julie and give them the praise they deserved, and to thank all the staff who were asked to stand up so that they could be seen, I was overwhelmed with emotion. As the tissues were passed around my only consolation was that almost everyone else in the room was crying as well.

The Slade Centre continued with its work and we had some particularly marvellous help given by the Friends of the Animals Group in Jersey. You may remember I had been over there to give a talk, and Mrs Sheila Dormand and her team of ladies worked extremely hard organizing raffles for the Centre at hotels and holiday centres in Jersey. They raised the magnificent sum of £650 this year. During my visit I'd also very kindly been taken back to the beautiful house of Mr and Mrs Massey, which overlooked the bay; Kitty, Eric and I have kept in touch since and they have been able to help quite substantially with the funding of various projects in which they had a great interest.

In January I had written to Arthur Negus asking if he would again give his tremendous support for Fiesta, but I was upset to hear that neither he nor his wife, Queenie, were at all well. We were all so sorry when we heard that Arthur had died; he was greatly missed, having been such a supportive and loyal patron of the Slade Centre. Very sadly, by the time the Fiesta took place we had lost not only dear Arthur but also our patron Dorian Williams, who had always given us support in our work. This year's Fiesta was a half-day event, as it had been felt that the whole day exhausted everybody to such an extent, and having to provide lunches cut down the desperately needed profit required to keep the Slade Centre running.

Knowing Her Royal Highness Princess Anne's interest in handicapped children, we invited her to come down and visit the Slade Centre and the Donkey Sanctuary. It was like a dream come true for myself and all the staff when she accepted. Knowing that local children would love the chance to see Her Royal Highness, we invited all the schools to come up for the afternoon, and each was allocated a separate area with a different coloured flag, so that their children could get the best possible chance of seeing Princess Anne. The immediate area around the Slade Centre was, of course, restricted for use by the handicapped children, and I think every child that rode the donkeys had the opportunity to see her. Her arrival was extremely exciting; she landed in a bright red helicopter right in the middle of one of the fields. The Assistant Chief Constable of Devon and Cornwall arrived, as did the Chief Lieutenant of Devon and Cornwall. All the VIPs joined in the fun with the children, and Wilma, one of our favourite donkeys, drew a cart with its driver, an eleven-year-old child suffering from muscular dystrophy, thrilled to be wearing the Assistant Chief Constable of Devon and Cornwall's hat. Having spent much time with the handicapped children looking round the Centre, Princess Anne then toured the hospital, with which she was greatly impressed, and she fell in love with Buffalo, one of our favourites, who received a royal pat. All the managers were presented, and had displays of their farms on show. Roy Harrington explained his work with the inspectorate unit and 20 of his voluntary staff, with 42 Donkey Sanctuary staff, lined her route. Brian Bagwell, Pat Feather and Julie Courtney had a very special introduction and a wonderful time was had by all. Whilst Princess Anne was touring the hospital and part of the Donkey Sanctuary, we'd arranged for clowns and entertainers to come and keep the children amused. As Princess Anne finally began the last walk back

HRH The Princess Royal at the Slade Centre with my sister Pat, Principal of the Slade Centre, and one of the Slade Centre children. (By kind permission of HRH The Princess Royal)

towards her helicopter amongst the cheering children, we had a final surprise in store for her; two of our staff were dressed up in a pantomime donkey outfit and gambolled alongside her, trying their best to curtsy and nuzzle her as she left. It was such a happy day, and one that we sincerely hope we'll be able to repeat at some time in the future.

Shortly after Princess Anne's helicopter took off the Sanctuary lorry arrived with five donkeys on board. They had been kept in appalling conditions by gipsies near Hatfield. They'd been found by an Animal Liberation Group in Leighton Buzzard, who had desperately tried to effect the rescue. They called our inspector, who went with them to the site, and after much arguing the owner signed them over to avoid being prosecuted. When they arrived they were very malnourished, wormy and anaemic. The group included one emaciated pony who we named Mrs Merrylegs. She was accompanied by her week-old baby mule, the most enchanting little black foal that we'd seen for many years. There was another mule in poor condition as well as two donkey stallions. Merrylegs, the little foal, soon began to behave more like a normal foal and was a very lively little chap. He led us all a terrible dance. We never thought that any of the little group in the nursery could jump the post and rail fence, but Merrylegs proved us wrong! They're 3ft 6in high and normally donkey-proof, but now we knew they were not young mule-proof.

We had a rather sad telephone call one morning from one of the London City Farms. These farms are usually extremely well run and provide inner city children with an opportunity to see and touch large animals, possibly for the first time in their lives. Frequently a city farm takes on one or two donkeys for the children to enjoy. This particular farm had previously sent in a little donkey called Fury. Apparently very well named! He had been at the farm with another donkey called Primrose, who came from a pub in Bilston, Suffolk, and who was extremely good with children and could be ridden. Unfortunately Fury had proved a very different kettle of fish, becoming quite ferocious at times and tending to bite or kick at the staff without any warning. Fury had also bitten several children. In all our years at the Slade Centre or the Donkey Sanctuary we have never had donkeys bite children; normally they have an enormous rapport with youngsters. In the end, Fury was sent in to us and they hoped Primrose would carry on being good with the children but unfortunately, as is very often the case, the city farm completely underestimated the strong bond that develops between donkeys. Primrose refused to eat and, in desperation as her condition deteriorated,

(ABOVE) *Mrs Merrylegs and her little mule foal.*
(BELOW) *Bob Marley, rescued from South Wales.*

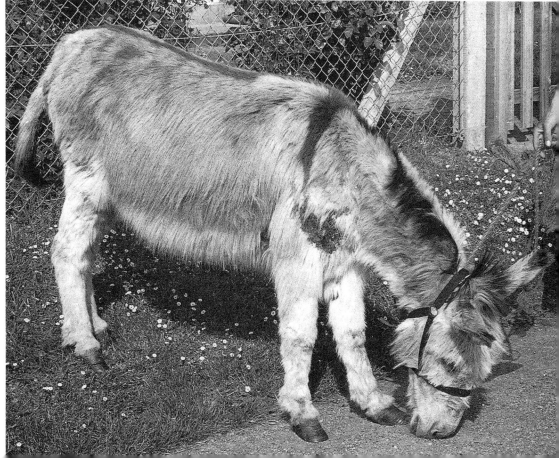

they asked if she too could come into the Sanctuary. They were having many problems at the city farm as alterations were under way with fences removed for roadworks and workmen all over the site. So we arranged to collect Primrose.

This particular morning as I watched the lorry being unloaded, there was a dejected little chocolate coloured donkey called Primrose. I was really rather concerned when she came off the lorry as she looked so miserable and sad, although there was a surprise in store for her. Fury was waiting in one of the boxes and as we led Primrose towards the Isolation Unit there was suddenly the most enormous braying of delight as Fury's head shot out over the stable door and Primrose immediately became fully alert and tried her hardest to get to meet her old friend. In the event we had to put both of the donkeys together; Fury having to go through another six weeks' isolation period to be with his friend, who from that moment perked up and began to eat again.

When the donkeys had finished their isolation period they both went down to Town Barton where Paul gave them a great welcome and they joined one of the groups of donkeys. Both then became very happily settled and I am pleased to say nobody got a bite or a kick from Fury whose temperament changed dramatically once he and Primrose were able to gallop around their large fields and have the company of so many other donkeys.

Poor old Bob Marley! What a life that poor little donkey had until one of our supporters made a desperate telephone call on his behalf. Our inspector for South Wales was actually on holiday when he received the call but it sounded so terrible that he jumped in his car and rushed off to the town of Newent. He had been told a donkey in desperate trouble was in the car park at the rear of the shopping area.

Quite a sight met his eyes. The supporter who had telephoned was there with her husband, endeavouring to detain a man who was determinedly holding on to the donkey. He had tied him to the car park fence and there was an enormous load on the donkey's back held on with a makeshift harness made out of an old car seatbelt and sashcord which had actually embedded itself into the donkey's flesh. The owner, who was extremely abusive, was a travelling man and had used the donkey to carry all his belongings.

Under pressure from our inspector and the large crowd of people who had now gathered around, the travelling man was persuaded to remove the large load from the donkey's back. As soon as this was taken off a gasp came up from the crowd. The poor little donkey's back was covered with sores. Our inspector immediately called a vet who agreed the donkey pack was totally unsuitable and was causing severe distress. The vet started to treat the sores and said that the donkey needed further treatment and rest. Our inspector, Iwan, then told the traveller that the donkey would need at least three weeks' daily treatment and several months of further rest before being fit for work again. He threatened to prosecute if the donkey was moved in its present condition with the load and, after some arguing, the donkey was passed over to the care of the Sanctuary.

Iwan and I had a long conversation on the telephone and we took veterinary advice and decided that as the donkey was in such terrible condition – he was tired, footsore and in pain – we should try and home him in the Newent area until his condition had improved. Luckily the lady who had reported his plight lived locally and she offered a free stable at her home. The donkey had been named Bob Marley by his owner. So Bob was moved to this new comfortable environment. He was given a warm bath in a solution provided by the vet and antibiotic cream was applied to the severe sores, cuts and ulcerated areas. It took four weeks of loving care before Bob Marley was fit for the journey to the Sanctuary but it was really delightful to see him happily settled and having a well deserved rest after his long ordeal.

My daughter, Sarah, had finished school. I don't think anyone could have looked forward to the day more than I. I was really proud of her: apart from a string of CSEs she had gained an 'O' level in cookery, and perhaps even more important, had passed her driving test, which gave her a real taste of freedom. She had been doing a holiday job at the Salston Hotel as Assistant Chef and I'm sure this helped in her interview at the Pru Leith School of Food and Wine in London, where she was accepted for a year's course. I knew once Sarah had gone I was going to be even more lonely at home and June and I were finding more and more evenings were being spent together, and 'Little Conkers' was in fact being used less and less. It seemed sensible to us that when Sarah had left, June would move into 'Highlands' with me. Although I could still see the donkeys from my window, I felt isolated up there, and I really missed being close to the main yards. June duly moved in and put 'Little Conkers' on the market.

We settled into 'Highlands'; it was great having June as a companion now that Sarah had left for London. One night a week June did night duty at Exeter Hospital and in a weak moment I asked if she would like me to come in and give a hand sometimes, as she often explained how desperately busy they were when there was an emergency. June readily accepted my offer and so every Tuesday night, having finished work and had a quick tea, I left for Exeter Hospital and the radiography department. I must say I thoroughly enjoyed working my nights there; it would usually be pretty busy until about eleven o'clock and then things would start to quieten down. I manned the reception desk and, as I grew more experienced, June used to let me do the developing in the very complicated machines, which allowed her to continue doing the X-rays. I was able to register the patients in; I soon found out how to go to the record room and find their past X-ray films if they'd been X-rayed previously, and thoroughly enjoyed playing with any little children who came in, placating their fears and having time to console the parents. I often heard June's agonized yells from one of the rooms where she was trying to X-ray a particularly difficult patient, and gearing myself up in the heavy lead aprons, I was also able to lend a hand. One evening a stretcher was wheeled in when we were quite busy, and on it was an elderly lady who had been involved in a traffic accident, and they thought it possible she had some fractures. She lay on her trolley and I lined her up outside the next room, where I knew June would X-ray her. The poor lady was only semi-conscious and I suddenly realized she was staring at me as I manoeuvred the trolley around.

In a weak voice she said, 'I'm dead, aren't I?'

I said, 'No you're not, You're all right. You're in hospital and going to have an X-ray.'

'No, I know I'm dead, because when I died I wanted to go to the Donkey Sanctuary and I know you're the lady who looks after it,' she said, gazing at me, 'I must be dead.' It took me quite a while to convince her that she wasn't, and I'm very pleased to say she'd suffered no serious injuries.

One night at about 9.30 p.m., we thought we had finished with the rush of the day, when suddenly it was apparent an emergency was about to break upon us, and four or five porters came rushing in with laden trolleys, each one with a helmet sitting on top of it. There had been a fight following the local football match and unfortunately many of the police had come off worst. I felt so sorry for them all, lying there politely with their helmets on their chests, and we started to get them in for the X-rays as quickly as possible. What particularly delighted me was that the Chief Constable of Devon himself came down to check how his men were, and to have a quiet word with each of them. Many of them had sustained fractures and it was quite a busy night for us.

Sometimes June would be called up to the wards and I'd go up with her. This meant taking one of the mobile X-ray units, which are placed on each corridor, and June soon taught me how to collect up the unit, put it into gear and steer it along to the respective ward. I would then be able to help her, manoeuvring the unit around, putting the plates where June advised me on the patient so that she could take the X-rays, and then I would gallop off and develop them to bring back to June so that she could check that the job had been done in a satisfactory manner. Sometimes we were called down to the emergency room and into the casualty unit, and there was always a great deal of urgency. Special doors were fitted here and I soon learnt that I could keep my machine at full speed and go straight through the doors, which were specially adapted to open on contact. We would try our hardest to keep out of the way of the working staff as we X-rayed the parts requested by the doctor and, once again, I did my long run back to develop the films. June, as Superintendent of Radiography, was one of the best radiographers there, and we rarely had to take a second film, but sometimes a patient moved at the wrong moment and the whole procedure had to be repeated.

In addition to June there was one other technician on duty, and on one particular night it was Tony Dempster. Whilst June was in the middle of taking a difficult X-ray we got an emergency call from the renal unit, and Tony said, 'Can you come, Betty, and get the mobile for me as quickly as you can.' The renal unit was a long way from X-ray and I'd got quite a good speed up by the time I got onto the corridor where the renal unit was. Tony went through the door first, motioning me to follow him. They were double doors and I suppose I automatically expected them both to open, and charged after him at full speed. To my absolute horror, half the door was in fact fastened and there was the most resounding crash of glass and splintering timber as the impetus carried us both through. Apparently the patient, who had been semi-conscious and had not spoken to anybody for the previous five days, rose in bed, rather like Lazarus, and fully came to life. I also heard a few words I hadn't heard before from various staff who were around, but everybody seemed to take it extremely calmly, and without any fuss the staff started picking up the broken glass and shattered door, and we just got on with our job of X-raying. I must say I got my leg pulled rather hard after that every time I was asked to bring a mobile, and the hospital staff would spread in alarm as I came along the corridors!

I never stayed the whole night; usually it had quietened down enough by one or two o'clock in the morning for me to go back home, but of course June had to stay on duty; she'd start work in the morning, leaving home at 7.30 a.m., and would not get home until the following day after

6 p.m. I take my hat off to people working in the National Health Service; they certainly earn their money.

On a daily basis I saw the problems of handicapped children at our Slade Centre, and I was delighted when I received a letter from the headteacher of a school in Scotland asking me to write a few lines in our newsletter to prove what donkeys could do for children. She ran a special school and she said that reading and writing held no interest for James when he was sent there at the age of twelve, but the donkey in the field did, and, skilfully using his interest in Jenny the donkey, the staff found the key to success. After visits with him to the library, they followed up snippets out of books about donkeys, and this persuaded James of the need to read. Then from someone came the address of the Donkey Sanctuary and letter writing took on a new meaning for James, as he wrote and received replies giving information on donkeys. With the knowledge he'd gleaned from reading his information sheets from the Sanctuary, Jenny became James's first experience in caring; he made sure her drinking water wasn't frozen over in the winter, and that she had extra feed when the frost was on the ground. He moved her from one paddock to the other when he felt the grazing was poor, and demanded they call in a farrier when her hooves needed attention. He was far more fastidious about her sleeping quarters than his own. A short time before, however, Jenny had become very ill and James agreed she should come to the Sanctuary for the cause to be investigated. As the headteacher noted, Jenny's final lesson to him was that of unselfish love in letting her go, and I'm pleased to say that two rehabilitated donkeys were sent to the school. James loved them immediately and Jenny, having done such a wonderful job, settled in happily with a group of friends, completely recovered from her illness. The headteacher pointed out that the only time in James's life they had ever seen him smile was when he was with Jenny.

We get a lot of strange stories in the Sanctuary; one was particularly interesting. Christine and George Tardios and colleague, Andrew Graham, had left London on January 14th, 1982, to try to retrace on foot H. M. Stanley's 1871 journey in search of Dr Livingstone. They had been accompanied by four donkeys: Livingstone, Stanley, Burton and Speke. They'd had incredible adventures on their 1,200 mile safari from Bagamoya through the African bush to Ujiji on Lake Tanganyika. The donkeys were in a very poor state when they were purchased originally as pack animals and George Tardios wrote to us saying that, after all they'd been through together, it would be a tragedy if Livingstone, in his advanced years, was to die from overwork, and if the others were again to be mistreated. The letter arrived as a plea for help – could we give the donkeys a home following their quarantine period if they got them back to England. We immediately cabled to Tanzania to tell them we would accept and keep the donkeys for life, provided they were returned to the UK. Obviously we would make no charge for their keep. We received a letter from Dar es Salaam saying the team were overjoyed at our response, and they were hoping that Lufthansa would fly the donkeys to the UK. After their isolation period we looked forward to their arrival, opening the door and being able to say 'Dr Livingstone, I presume? Welcome to your well-deserved retirement.' As it turned out, the donkeys did not arrive at the Sanctuary, but were re-homed in Africa with our help.

The world is such an enormous place, and sometimes I would lie awake at night trying not to think about the enormity of the task that I had undertaken in trying to help donkeys in other parts of the world. We received the most awful complaints regarding Matabeleland, Zimbabwe, where, apart from the most terrible working conditions, they had decided on an identification system which consisted of chopping off donkeys' ears at different lengths. This was a terribly cruel practice causing deep distress and pain, even infection and death, and we felt we had to act to stop it. In addition, we were told of barbed-wire muzzles being used on donkeys. We had also been told of equally bad conditions and cruelty to the donkeys in Nairobi. I planned to visit with Bill Jordan later in the year, hopefully to liaise with the two charities trying to work out there in appalling conditions. The work we had been doing in Greece and Mexico was continuing very satisfactorily.

Our work in various parts of the world was beginning to make an impact on the veterinary profession, and I was asked if I'd go to Rio de Janeiro and give a paper at the World Association for the Advancement of Veterinary Parasitology Conference. It was, of course, quite a formidable task, and I spent ages writing my paper and speaking to various people to get as many tips as I could. Meanwhile John Fowler and I had also been invited to a meeting in Newmarket with regard to the British Equine Veterinary Association's projects for the coming years. Various papers were given, and, as far as I could see, most of these were concerned with racehorses or eventing and how to improve performance – there were also papers on multiple births and other projects I personally felt to be intrusive and which I didn't particularly like. The association was also trying to find more ways of raising funds and as I had been asked to represent welfare groups I stood up and made my points fairly clearly, and pointed out that I was quite sure that many of the general public would be willing to subscribe to BEVA if something practical was done with regard to horses being injured in racing and jumping. I often felt that having to shoot a horse because it had a broken leg was unnecessary, as in some cases I was quite sure the horse could carry on to live a happy life, although of course, he would no longer be commercially viable. After the meeting I felt rather ostracized, and was quite sure this was the case when we went in for lunch and I found myself sitting at a table on my own, but a very nice gentleman arrived and sat opposite me. We began chatting, and he happened to say that he would be going to Rio de Janeiro to give a paper at the conference later in the year, and would be delighted to make mention of my work for the donkeys whilst he was there. I was still slightly tensed up from the previous meeting and rather spitefully replied that he didn't need to bother as I was going there myself. It was at this moment that John Fowler joined me and managed to whisper in my ear that I was speaking to Lawson Soulsby, one of the foremost world experts on parasitology. However, Lawson Soulsby took it all in good part, was very sweet, and said he really looked forward to meeting me down in Rio.

On arriving at the hotel in Rio I went down to dinner and thought I would have a glass of the local wine. I asked for the wine list, and I was casually glancing at it to see the prices, and just couldn't believe my eyes when I got to Moet et Chandon Champagne, which worked out at £4.80 a bottle! I couldn't believe this was right – even a bottle of Beaujolais was £30, as of course it had a very long way to travel, but just for fun I asked if I could have a bottle of champagne. To my surprise the most beautiful bottle arrived – a very early vintage, and in absolute perfect drinking condition. I managed two glasses and then with great difficulty replaced the cork and bore the bottle away to my bedroom. The next day everybody else arrived, and one of the first people to come and greet me was Lawson Soulsby and his charming wife. I said, 'Why don't you come for a little party this evening outside round the pool?' and they immediately agreed. I went inside and ordered four bottles of champagne, which duly arrived on the table and caused a great impression on everybody present. I paid cash, so that there could be no dispute at a later date if we found the champagne had been wrongly charged. How wise I was! After that lovely party Lawson invited us all to a party at another time, and he burst out laughing when I came down and there was just one bottle of champagne on the table. He said, 'Betty,

I think they've found the error of their ways – the bottle should be priced at £48,' and to this day we often joke about our first champagne party in Rio de Janeiro.

The conference started the following day and I was giving my talk on the very last day of the session. On the day before, I frequently walked into the small room that had been allocated to the equine lectures, and made myself feel comfortable at the podium, speaking to what I knew could not be more than a maximum of 100 people. During the conference plenary lectures were given in the enormous hall which could seat over 1,000. Each paper was automatically translated into four different languages and of course the speakers were all fluent and practised. Having not slept much the night before, I arrived to give my paper in the morning, and was surprised to find the lecture room completely empty and some of the chairs removed. My first thought was, 'At least I'll only have a very small audience,' but then Don Bliss came up and said, 'Did you know, Betty, you've been put on in the main hall,' and there on the television circuits which were on all the corridors showing where the lectures were being held, was my name for the main hall. Apparently a fair number of speakers had failed to turn up and gradually sessions had been whittled down and extra sessions slipped in, so there were in fact only four speakers left to give their papers that morning, of which I was one.

I don't think you can imagine how terrified I was when I had to get up and stand on this enormous podium and face an audience of hundreds of professionals. I think I was the only one who was not a vet, and I could feel my knees trembling as I looked out over this very highly educated audience of over 500 vets and veterinary parasitologists. I knew I had to make some impact on them, as obviously a paper on donkeys, the very first in the world to be given on this particular species, I think, was of no obvious interest to many of them. So I started off by asking them all a question. I said, 'Now I'm not a qualified vet, and I do thank you for giving your time to listen to me today, but you're all qualified vets or parasitologists and I want to ask you two questions. The first one is, 'Can anybody here tell me the average temperature of a donkey?' There was a rather startled silence and I had no takers at all, and so I said, 'Would you think it's the same as a horse, and would you treat the donkey the same as a horse? Those thinking this please put your hands up.' Almost immediately, nearly every veterinary in the hall raised his hand, and I was able to say to them, 'Well, if you are treating a donkey with the average temperature of a horse, that donkey is probably going to die.' The average temperature of the donkey is 98.8° – slightly above that of a human, and that of the horse 101°, and the fact that no research into the donkey has previously been done to even tell veterinary surgeons this most essential basic needed to treat the species gave me the courage to go on.

I then gave my full paper, encouraged frequently by nods from Jimmy Duncan and Max Murray, two of the professors from Glasgow University, who were sitting in the front row, and by the wide grin appearing on Don Bliss's face, as it was obvious that the lecture was going down really well. Afterwards, following what I can only call an extremely good reception, I was absolutely inundated, as was Don Bliss, with questions from many of those present. Representatives of drug companies came up and started offering supplies of anthelmintics for me to use in the Third World, as I was absolutely convinced by now that even two strategic doses of anthelmintic a year would greatly improve the donkey's physical condition and its lifespan could be considerably increased. Some American veterinaries came and asked if I would be prepared to give a paper in Atlanta early the next year, and I readily agreed, as I knew the more we could spread the word to these professional people, the more hope the donkeys were going to have in the future.

Back home again to reality, I continued my weekly visits to all the farms, and walking round Town Barton with Paul one day, I received the most undignified butt in the backside. I turned round to admonish the miscreant, and to my amazement it was little Lady Di. She was almost unrecognizable now – a complete contrast to that poor little shattered, desperate donkey, who had arrived early in 1984, unable to lift her head, dull-eyed, almost a skeleton, but it was one of the nicest butts I'd ever had, I decided as I continued on my rounds!

Many of our donkeys that go out to rehabilitation homes really find their niche in life and this has certainly been the case with Barney. He was sent in by one of our supporters, who had already sent two donkeys into us in the past. Although she had desperately tried to keep Barney, her grazing rights had run out and there was just nowhere for him to go. He seemed an ideal donkey to go out to a family and an extremely good home was found for him in Cumbria.

The new owners were absolutely delighted with Barney and he settled in really happily. We were pleased to receive a beautiful picture of Barney taken at the Christmas Eve service at St Luke's Church, Soulby, where he apparently behaved impeccably. His kind new owners were extremely thoughtful and did not just send us one photograph of Barney in all his glory carrying Mary, but sent a spare one to send on to his previous owner so that she could see how well he was keeping, with the message that if she would ever like to visit him she was more than welcome. It is a joy for us to see our rehabilitated donkeys in such lovely family homes and we get very few failures indeed, mainly due to the fact that our inspectors are so selective in the homes that we choose. Our inspectors also visit regularly giving advice and they make sure that problems that arise are dealt with simply, with a little help from the Sanctuary.

Barney has certainly fallen on his feet and is really loving his new family life.

Whilst on a short break I met an extremely good photographer called Len Shepherd, who worked for British Aerospace. Len was a kind and pleasant companion and we'd enjoyed some time together in St Lucia, and when he rang me and told me he was going for a holiday in Malindi, Kenya, I decided I'd go with him (on a purely platonic basis!), as I wanted to go up to the small island of Lamu where I'd heard there were a lot of donkeys, and there had been reports recently that, because of the health hazard caused by donkey droppings, all the donkeys were going to be put in nappies! Following this holiday I was going to meet up in Nairobi with Bill Jordan and we were going to check the general conditions for donkeys in Kenya for a week before I returned home.

Len and I had a pleasant few days in Malindi and then we took the plane on the first leg of our trip to the little island of Lamu. As we stepped off the plane a young man came rushing up and said, 'I am one of the local guides. I would like to take you to see all the sights. We can see the museum and the market . . .' I broke in and said, 'No, I'd love you to show us round, but I don't want to see any of the sights. I want to see as many donkeys as I can.' Though he was obviously perplexed, he agreed, and leaving the little airstrip, we climbed aboard the boat to take us across to Lamu island itself. Having arrived at Lamu, we had to climb over three or four other boats anchored there, through masses of people, and up the very steep steps onto the jetty. The first thing I was aware of was the enormous number of donkeys visible. They looked in very poor condition – thin, obviously overladen and very hard-worked. The island has no roads for vehicles, apart from a small strip from the Governor's office to his house, and he has a jeep, which is his official vehicle. This is the only stretch of road on which the jeep can travel, and everything else arriving at the village going to any of the houses has to be carried by donkeys. I was most interested to see the special panniers they had on their backs, which I learnt were called 'soggies', made out of local rush. These seemed to fit very well and the skilled owners could load these up with a large number of coral blocks which could then be taken by the donkeys to building sites. The general condition of the donkeys was poor – many had injuries, and to me they certainly looked full of parasites. As we walked past the museum with Abdalla, our guide, desperately trying to interest us in the ancient cannons standing outside, he began to realize that we really were serious and that Len, who was busy photographing the donkeys on the waterfront, and myself, had eyes for nothing but the donkeys.

I was appalled at the numbers wandering around the town, foraging from refuse dumps and litter bins, and with apparently no home or stable to go to. Abdalla took us up over the back of the town; it was boiling hot and we were already wet through with perspiration. 'If you want to see donkeys,' he said, 'have a look at my uncle's, because I think he has one that's in trouble.' He threw open the door of a small shack made of makuti and there inside were eight or nine donkeys, some in a very poor condition. The one which immediately caught my eye had the most terrible wound right down its flank and into its belly. This was lying wide open and blood was still seeping out.

'Whatever has happened to this donkey, Abdalla?' I asked.

'Oh, he wandered into somebody's garden and the man hit him with a panga,' explained Abdalla. I soon found out that a panga was a curved knife, rather like a smaller edition of a scythe, which was used by the local people for cutting crops and generally for working in the fields.

'This has to be stitched up immediately,' I said to Abdalla. 'Is there a vet on the island?'

Abdalla laughed, 'Not only is there no vet, there is no doctor here,' he said. 'We only have a witch doctor.' I couldn't believe the state of the donkey and I knew I couldn't leave him, as he would be dead in the morning, so I sent Abdalla off to get some plasters, and pulled the wound together as best I could. 'What's the matter with the ones that can't stand properly?' I asked Abdalla, and he explained that it was probably tetanus; there was such a lot in the village, as so many donkeys cut their feet on tins left lying about whilst foraging; the wounds became infected, leading to tetanus. I knew I would have to come back, and I told Abdalla, 'I shall come back next week with Bill Jordan, our vet, and then he can look at this donkey and treat it properly.'

I was heartbroken at having to leave the island with all those donkeys in desperate need of help. Len and I had a quiet ride back, and as he went home to England and I went on to Nairobi I knew the first thing that Bill Jordan and I had to do was to go back to Lamu, and this we did. Poor Bill thought he would be having a few days quietly going round the city and looking at the other welfare organizations, and he got quite a surprise when I told him we were getting straight on a plane and flying back down to Lamu. But, of course, as always, Bill was deeply disturbed at what I'd told him, and was as eager as me to go and see the donkeys. He'd brought out some anthelmintic with him and we decided we would do a few trials on the island to see what sort of condition the donkeys were in, and how many parasites they had. Once again the little plane was met by the group of tourist guides, but Abdalla immediately recognized me and came rushing forward. 'Your donkey does very well,' he said, 'my uncle is very pleased.' I introduced Bill to him and without any more delay we were off on the boat, clambering onto the jetty and up to the top of the village to see 'my donkey'. To my absolute amazement the wound seemed perfectly clean and had begun to heal and Bill decided I'd done quite a good job. He of course had medical equipment and was able to give the donkey a much-needed shot of antibiotic. Like me, he was very distressed by the signs of tetanus and we asked Abdalla where we could stay for three or four days so that we could carry out some surveys on the parasite infestation of the donkeys. Without hesitation Abdalla said, 'You must go to Peponis.' He took us down and we got on a little boat to chug up the estuary, and there at the mouth of the estuary we saw one of the most beautiful hotels I think I've ever seen. Set right by the sea, Peponis is a real dream. Little individual cottages are placed around, all with a beautiful view of the sea; it is run by a Danish family, whose first priority is for their guests' comfort. I think they were a little amused to find a very dirty Bill Jordan and myself checking in – most of their visitors were of course tourists. They greeted us warmly, and we were each given a small cottage where we could stay for the next few days.

Until Lamu, I don't think I'd really realized how many mosquitoes there are in the world, and how easy it is for a mosquito to get inside the net when you're sleeping. With the heat and humidity, I found sleep almost impossible for the first two nights, and tossed and turned, praying for a breath of fresh air, and for the mosquitoes to lose interest in me and attack somebody else. Each day Bill and I went into the village early in the morning and we'd asked Abdalla if he could get as many people as possible to bring their donkeys to us so that we could give them some special medicine to get rid of the worms. Abdalla did this, and our first morning we had a queue of about ten donkeys waiting when we set up our little clinic on one of the streets running directly from the sea. We were regarded with great suspicion for that first day, but we managed to treat many wounds and, once the local people realized that everything we were doing was free, they became much more co-operative. Every donkey we saw, we dosed, and the following morning, when we returned, we hoped there would be many more donkeys waiting. Alas, only two or three turned up on the second day and we were beginning to despair when we heard a great shout up the street. A young man came running into sight, and on a newspaper were several pats of donkey dung, each one absolutely crawling with live worms. 'Dudus,' he shouted, 'dudus.' We couldn't believe it! This was the word for worms, and he dashed up and down the jetty, showing all the groups of men who were busy loading their donkeys, and all the handlers, what he had found in the dung from his donkey the day after we'd wormed it! Within half an hour, we had 30 donkeys waiting, and by the end of the day Bill and I had dosed over 100 donkeys. Abdalla, we could see, was extremely impressed. I told him, 'Look, Abdalla, we're going to come back to Lamu, and dose a lot more donkeys and hold a proper clinic here. Would you like to help us when we come?' His face broke into a grin and I knew we had the right person to help us in Lamu when we returned.

When I got back to the Sanctuary and recounted what had happened and showed everybody the distressing pictures that Len Shepherd had taken, we all decided that Lamu must go on our list of areas where the IDPT should work in the following year.

Brian Bagwell and myself also made a quick trip to Greece to visit the World Health Organization and also Dr Panayotopoulos at the Agricultural Bank of Greece, to ensure that the money promised was in fact going to go into anthelmintics for the donkeys. We also hoped to go on to Kea so that Brian could see the work that had been going on there, but unfortunately it had to be postponed, as Iannis Georgoulakis failed to turn up for the meeting to arrange the trip.

We had also been helping with the Richard Martin Restfields in County Cork which I had visited for many years, when it had been run by Mr Barrett and his wife, partly on behalf of the Irish Society for the Protection of Animals. After his death, his son, Paddy, had taken over but there was a desperate shortage of money for shelters and farriers and there was no system of castration of the colts and stallions – these therefore were having to be put down. We agreed to send £500 immediately to help with the necessary building of the shelters, and then Roy Harrington and Bill Jordan would go over to see the situation for themselves and meet their local vets. We decided that as soon as it was practically possible we would bring Paddy Barrett over to the Donkey Sanctuary to give him some special training, and I rather hoped that perhaps the Donkey Breed Society might be able to help, as they had some money in the Wiesen Trust which could only be used for old and sick donkeys.

During a weekend in the winter we woke to find a covering of snow, making the Sanctuary look like fairyland. Having checked with the night staff that all the donkeys were well, I went up to the office to deal with the never-ending paperwork. I could see the yard from my window, and spent more time than I should watching. Sarah, home for the holidays, loved working with the donkeys – it must run in the family – and was helping out over Christmas. She and John Pile were busy giving the geriatric donkeys their breakfasts; each one had his or her own individual bucket, and the yard was full of contented donkeys who seemed rejuvenated by the snow and only too willing to come out of their big cosy barn for an individual feed. Despite their ages, woe betide anyone who trespassed near their feed, and I nearly cried as I watched Rosie, elderly, and almost crippled by arthritis, aim a half-hearted kick at Timothy, who was showing too much interest in Rosie's breakfast! I tore myself away to concentrate on my work, and the next time I looked the yard was cleared and all the donkeys back under their infra-red lights. All was peaceful – in fact, too peaceful. Where was everybody? By the time I'd finished I decided to walk up the yard to see what was going on. Tearing down the hill in the snow, using empty feed sacks to toboggan on, were Sarah and John! I couldn't stop laughing, and crept away so as not to spoil their fun, but later a very sheepish John apologized, saying, 'Sarah persuaded me, saying that you wouldn't mind.'

Chapter · 7

ME TARZAN – YOU BETTY SVENDSEN
1986

I HAVE TO be in the office before eight o'clock in the morning, otherwise the day never seems to go right. My first job, however, is to walk round the yard and say good morning to all the donkeys. It's amazing how cheering it is on even the most freezing January mornings, the sound of all the donkeys braying in welcome warms me up. Having said hello to all my great friends I then go up to the hospital and check that those under special care are improving and there have been no emergencies during the night about which I've not been informed. Having assured myself that all the donkey matters are in hand I then go back to the office where the postman is frequently waiting.

Taking in the mail can be a time-consuming project! After the newsletter goes out, there can be over 2,000 letters in the mailbag, and registered envelopes and recorded deliveries all have to be signed for. I then go through every letter, picking out those that I think look official, legal or are personally addressed to me. The balance I then carefully sort into the different departments, and, as soon as the staff come in at 8.30 a.m., the postroom girls come up and collect their mail bag. Next I open all the post that I have sorted out and fortunately, having a photographic memory, a quick glance at most of the contents allows me to store the contents away for future use if necessary. I always pick out some of the general letters to look at, because it's just so heartwarming to read letters from so many people who share my love of donkeys. Many old age pensioners regularly send us a pound a week, and you get to know the writing on the envelopes; as they pick up their pension, one pound always goes to the donkeys, and we never fail to write back to thank these faithful supporters because we know how much it means to them. I think the letter also means a lot, as many are on their own and don't get much correspondence, so they love to hear of the latest donkey episodes. I then have Boo down, and together we go through the cheques and have a look at the financial position.

On this particular morning in January I was quite desperately concerned. Purchasing a new farm had now become absolutely essential. We had been offered some land immediately adjoining our Sanctuary, consisting of 82.7 acres and also some farm buildings with two acres in the little village of Weston itself. Obviously this would be absolutely ideal for the Sanctuary, but I was only too well aware that it was going to drain our resources. The vendor was already planning to put a new barn on the site and this would of course increase its value. My staff think I've got a 'prayer mat' because, whenever I desperately need money, something turns up, and fortunately this morning was no exception. The very first letter I opened contained a legacy from Miss Bailey for £14,700! I knew then that the money situation was going to solve itself and we should go along with the purchase. I rang round all the trustees to get their agreement for an official valuation on the property, and Brian began the painstaking job of checking the land and negotiating with the vendor. Brian, having had so much experience as a house agent, was highly skilled at this, and many of our purchases have been made at most advantageous terms thanks to his knowledge.

The rest of my day passed in attending meetings with various staff, doing interviews, writing articles, discussing future projects with Brian and Julie, visiting the farms, and of course doing my 'rounds' which I feel essential to the smooth running of the Sanctuary. John Rabjohns, our farm manager, always watches with a wary eye as I do my rounds, because as he says, 'Mother always finds something whenever she goes round,' and it always seems true. (Many of the staff call me 'Mother' or 'Mrs S'.)

Knowing the donkeys so well, I could always see if something wasn't quite right with them, and if it wasn't the donkeys, it was a water trough that wasn't clean or a fence that needed repairing, but of course we have such a marvellous staff at the Sanctuary, that there were seldom any serious problems. I think their cheerful willingness to work any hours necessary has contributed greatly to the success of the Sanctuary. I'm always extremely keen to allow our own staff to better themselves, and so every now and then I invite any members of staff who would like to come for a special interview, with a view to progressing to management, either on the agricultural or the office side. This particular week I'd arranged an interview and twelve staff were coming. We take the boardroom for these events and tell the staff they should dress as if they were attending an official interview for a new job. It's quite delightful to see them turning up dressed immaculately, some of them carrying small briefcases, when you're used to seeing them in their Sanctuary uniform (tee-shirt or sweatshirt with the Sanctuary logo) on a normal daily basis. What I always do is get all the potential managers sitting round the big boardroom table and Brian, Julie and I sit at the end. I then explain to them the state of the Sanctuary at the moment, as many of them are unaware how many actual donkeys we have in, and our situation amongst other charities doing similar work. I always like to update them on the charity before we start the interview properly. Having done this I ask each of them to introduce themselves in a few words, as if they were unknown to the others present. This takes quite a few minutes and it's interesting to see how they cope. Brian then gives a little talk about what the future holds for staff, and then comes the bit that really sorts the men out from the boys!

I previously prepare a list of subjects, which include the following: cats, firemen, laundry, school, the weather, travel, hospitals, cars, newspapers, haymaking, gardening, boating, dogs, etc. Each candidate then has to draw their subject out of a hat and speak for two minutes on the given topic. At the end of this time we take a break for coffee and have each interviewee up to our main office where we hold a private interview of 15 minutes with each member of staff. Those awaiting interview are busy completing a small test to find out what they know, not only about the care of donkeys, but the set-up of the Sanctuary. In between, a lunch is provided and we take the opportunity to chat socially with the staff, which once again gives a good indication to us as to who could possibly make future managers. As a result of the day's work our staff feel they've been given a fair opportunity to better themselves and we, as administrators, have a very good idea which members are suitable to be promoted.

It seems 1986 was the year for receiving groups of donkeys. I had a call from a very concerned farrier in Cornwall who knew about the Donkey Sanctuary. He was worried about the plight of four donkeys who would soon be in trouble as the owners had been told they could no longer use their two-acre field. The owners managed to get another small field but in trying to transfer the donkeys found that one of them, Dusty, would not come out of the field. The reason was that she was totally blind.

They moved the others and left Dusty on her own but then, of course, the donkeys began to bray for each other across the fields, causing a noise problem to the local residents. The little blind donkey, Dusty, was obviously heartbroken and distressed at losing her friends.

The owners managed to place one of the donkeys in a good home but were unable to find homes for the other three. The situation had become

(ABOVE) *Rob Nichols, Woods Farm Manager, with Dusty, Amigo and Eros.*
(BELOW) *The therapeutic value of a donkey.*

critical by the time we were informed. Our inspector immediately contacted the family and visited and within days the three donkeys had arrived here. It is extremely difficult settling a totally blind donkey into new surroundings, as you can imagine, but Dusty was so delighted to have her friends back that nothing seemed to bother her. Unfortunately, Amigo was a full stallion and we hoped that he had not put Dusty into foal as obviously this would not be good for her. We decided that once Amigo was castrated the group would be kept together although Dusty would need special treatment on a permanent basis.

Every year on my birthday the family seem to think up a different surprise, and on this particular occasion all sorts of threats had been made by Paul and Uschi, and as Sarah was home looking for a job and I had a conference in London, I decided to take her up with me, so that she could keep me company on the actual day. We stayed at the Mount Royal Hotel, and as my birthday morning dawned, I decided it would be a nice treat to have breakfast in bed. Sarah, however, was quite obstinate, and determined that she wanted it downstairs in the dining room, so somewhat regretfully I got up and we both went down together. The Mount Royal is a large hotel and the breakfast room was very full. However we got a nice table and began to enjoy a leisurely breakfast. I think I'd just put my knife into the bacon when I heard the most enormous commotion in the doorway. I looked across and started to giggle, because there stood a half-naked Tarzan! He was banging his chest, and his Tarzan cry resounded throughout the dining room, with everybody as startled and amused as I was. Then to my absolute horror he shouted, 'Me Tarzan – Me want Betty Svendsen,' and started leaping up and down, to the great embarrassment of the maitre d'hotel, who was standing, red-faced, and not at all pleased to have his peaceful breakfast routine disrupted. My darling little daughter (bless her!) stood up and waved, and Tarzan advanced in a series of leaps and jerks amongst the startled foreign tourists, right to the table, where he swept me off my chair into his arms, yelling, 'Me Tarzan – You Betty,' and tried to bear me out of the dining room. It was here, however, that I decided the joke had to come to an end. The bacon was too good to leave! So, breathing in Tarzan's ear, I said, 'Tarzan join Betty for breakfast.' He happily agreed and came and sat at the table. Eventually peace was restored, and we had quite a pleasant meal whilst I managed to wrest from him the information that, of course, Paul and Uschi had been behind this little 'birthday treat'! I've never stayed at the Mount Royal since, much to the relief of the maitre d'hotel.

We had been thinking very seriously about the move to Norfolk, but the offer of the land next to the Sanctuary had been one factor in causing us to hesitate; another far more important factor had been the attitude of the donkeys during the winter. It had indeed been an extremely cold, but dry, period and we had been able to experiment with the idea that the donkeys would, if it were cold and dry, enjoy being outside taking exercise. The donkeys appeared to have a different view and, despite every attempt to encourage them into the cold but crisp air, they very much preferred the warmth of the large airy barns. So we all came to the conclusion that, so far as the donkeys were concerned, the trip to Norfolk would be a disaster rather than a pleasure! The trustees at our meeting suggested that perhaps Brian and I could look for land in another direction, and so we set off on a tour up to the Lake District and to the south of Scotland, where properties were very much cheaper and we could buy land at a very economical rate. The trip was not a success – the land we were offered was bleak and bare. Brian, having been born and bred in Devon, found the very thick Cumbrian and Scottish dialects almost impossible to interpret. I think had I not been born in Yorkshire I would have been as confused as he. He obviously wanted to ask all the technical questions on which he was such an expert but he was totally unable to understand the answers. I found myself trying to interpret as we bounced along in the back of a Land Rover over the most inhospitable ground. At one stage the Land Rover in which we were being shown round was driven almost vertically down into a quarry which left Brian and I quite white and shaken.

We got back into our car to go to the next farm, which was down in the Lake District and became even more confused as we tried to navigate our way around the countryside. The book Brian had brought with him, proudly saying that this would solve all our navigation problems, when investigated thoroughly on one of our coffee stops on the motorway, had proved to be *Country Walks in the Lake District*, so this did nothing to help us in our current dilemma. Eventually, when I was absolutely convinced we were going the wrong way for Carlisle, although the village signpost pointed firmly in that direction, we decided to stop and ask the way. Brian leaned out of the window and asked an elderly resident who was walking past, the way to Carlisle. As I'd thought, he pointed in the opposite direction to the signpost. Brian said, 'But the signpost says Carlisle is that way' in an irritated manner, to which the resident replied 'Aw, 'tis always turnin' round,' went up to the signpost and turned it round to face the other direction! We both came back to Devon thinking that perhaps we'd better stay in the West Country!

Being rather lonely at nights, and feeling rather vulnerable, June and I decided that it was time to replace our dogs, both of which sadly had died the previous year of old age. We decided we'd go for a standard poodle, and went to a well known breeder near Brent Knoll, who had a very good reputation, and there I met and fell in love with my little 'Winnie the poodle'! Although only a puppy she was absolutely full of fun, jet black, and would grow to be quite big, as standards do. No sooner had I fallen in love with my Winnie than her sister came into the room, and June, I'm afraid, went exactly the same way as me. We decided we'd buy the two together, to be companions to each other, and so we agreed to buy Winnie and Gemma. I'm not sure if it was an accident or not, but, having just signed all the paperwork for our two new dogs, into the room came the tiniest, cutest little black poodle I think I've ever seen. The owner was very loath to sell her; she had apparently been bred specifically for the export market, and would have been worth thousands of pounds had her teeth not been genetically deformed. I couldn't resist this little tiny bouncing thing, and June and I ended up at home with three dogs! They really were such fun; they took our minds off all our worries, but of course we found Tinkerbell, as I named the tiny one, rather cowed by the two larger gambolling puppies. So we went back again to the kennels, where we bought Bubbles, a cheeky little apricot poodle, to keep Tinkerbell company. I now seemed to have three dogs, and June had one, but this wasn't to be the end of the story. June had always loved dachshunds and she was determined to buy her own miniature wire-haired dachshund. It took six months before she found the right one, but eventually Zara completed our good team of house dogs.

Looking back on earlier years the first hour of my morning had been so peaceful; as soon as I started taking Tinkerbell into work things changed! She was a lovable little puppy, absolutely full of life, and insisted on helping the postman in his early morning routine in my office. All our 'posties' are quite wonderful, and on arrival at my office they tip the post out onto the floor and then, generally in a kneeling position, pass the letters up to me. We have laughed about them kneeling at my feet many times. As Tinkerbell grew she wanted to take part in the proceedings and the postman was almost licked to death on many occasions, and would leave looking rather dishevelled to go on to his next port of call. No sooner had the postman left than John Rabjohns would come in to report officially to me on the state of affairs around the Sanctuary, but unofficially it was because he always liked to throw a ball for Tinkerbell, and the next ten minutes would resound with Tinkerbell

Tinkerbell helps the postman.

dashing back and forth like mad and John encouraging her with, 'Go on, Lad. He's a good boy!' John could never accept that Tinkerbell was a girl. Pat would then arrive to discuss the Slade Centre and John and I would stand back waiting for the inevitable to happen. No matter how many times Tinkerbell had spent a penny during the morning, or how excited she got playing with John, she always managed to spend a little penny when Auntie Pat arrived. Every morning Pat managed to show the same horror and shock as if it was an unusual occurrence as she wiped up the carpet with the pile of tissues I always kept at the ready at this time of the morning. Brian and the vets' arrivals in the mornings did not seem to bring out the same response in Tinkerbell fortunately. There is no other part of the day when visitors to my door are so blessed.

I was delighted with the progress Paul had made at Town Barton Farm. He was very interested in farming and the donkeys always looked so happy and content there. He was producing a haylage for the donkeys. Haylage is a good feed for donkeys with respiratory problems, as it is moist and dust free. The Sanctuary aimed to produce a low protein haylage rather than a high protein one. Great care needs to be taken not to feed too much as it does have a higher protein value than hay. A silage tower was adapted to Paul's requirements and erected on the farm, and once the haylage was made and ready for feeding it was carefully monitored to ensure it was not too rich. The main problem was that the donkeys enjoyed it but too much was definitely not good for them and it had to be strictly rationed. Whilst battling to get the haylage exactly right, on one occasion Paul spent nearly all day in the tower. As soon as he went into the house the personal results became apparent. Uschi took one look and one sniff, and rushed up to run a bath whilst Dawn and Simon held their noses and opened all the windows. Paul had become immune to his terrible aroma and it was only when Sapphire, his faithful Old English sheepdog, crept away whining, and refused to come out of her kennel, that Paul decided perhaps he *had* better have a bath.

A cereal crop had always been grown at Town Barton Farm, and when the farm was purchased some of the farm equipment was also bought. Paul decided to continue growing oats partly in order to provide as much as was required for our groups of donkeys on special feed at Slade House Farm, the balance being sold, and partly to give the land a break from grass ley. In addition Paul had taken over the buying for the Sanctuary so that from Town Barton Farm he could keep a link with head office.

Paul had been running the farm very successfully but I had been feeling that he wasn't altogether happy there, and one day he came to see Brian and myself and explained that he would like to go more into the administration of the Sanctuary, but felt he didn't have any of the necessary experience. For this reason he thought it a good idea to leave the Sanctuary and start his own small business, to gain business experience which could be useful for us later. Obviously I was very upset at the thought of losing Paul, and so were the trustees, as he was such a valuable asset to the charity. I would miss him, especially as he was always so cheerful and such a marvellous help in times of stress, but I did see his point of view, and so did Brian. Paul had previously trained as a chef and he and Uschi and the two children moved to Moretonhampstead, where they opened a little restaurant. It really was a unique type of cooking and proved immensely popular. Much of the food was cooked on marble slabs, and fondue was the speciality. June and I found ourselves driving to Moretonhampstead more and more, not only to see Paul, Uschi and the children but also to enjoy the food. Paul did, however, continue the buying on our behalf, which kept up his contact with the Sanctuary. One of the aspiring managers at our interview had been John Pile, and he replaced Paul as manager at Town Barton, Paul staying a while to ensure the farm was running smoothly before leaving.

By this time we were being inundated by people wanting articles written on the Sanctuary, for *This England*, *The Splash Annual*, *Animal Crackers* and many other magazines and periodicals. These take little effort to organize, but whenever a television crew arrives, it's always quite chaotic. John Craven's *Newsround* was no exception; the team moved from farm to farm and demanded the donkeys in different places for different shots, all of which our staff complied with as amiably as possible. The one shot that television crews always seem to want is for me to be surrounded by an enormous number of donkeys, and although this looks pleasant and placid when it appears on television it isn't as easy as it seems. Our donkeys are not used to being organized and we like them to have as much freedom as possible. So to get them altogether in one place means putting some food down on the ground so that they will congregate, but once again, donkeys can at times be slightly difficult and this is the time they usually choose. I normally stand in the middle of a nipping, pinching, kicking group, all trying to get to the small amount of food on the ground. It's not easy trying to smile bravely and to remember what I'm supposed to be saying, whilst receiving little butts in the back, having my feet trodden on and getting the odd very affectionate nip. No sooner had John Craven's *Newsround* team left, than Pebble Mill decided to come down, and this was when I decided that enough was enough, and in future all television programmes were strictly limited. I think everybody agreed with me that time must be spent with the donkeys and for the donkeys, and the enormous interruption made by the television crews had to be carefully restricted.

I was delighted with all the contributions I had received from specialists for the *Professional Handbook of the Donkey* and finished compiling the book this spring. I had also written a less technical book, *Donkey's Years*, and to my delight both of these were ready later in the year. We sent a copy of the handbook to each veterinary practice in the UK and also to each veterinary university. As you know, I'd been horrified that there was no clinical information available to vets regarding the donkey and I was delighted to be able to give this information from the specialists regarding anaesthesia, operating techniques, management, feeding, foot care – even down to training donkeys. The response which came in over the next few weeks was quite amazing; the universities wrote to ask if they could have books for their students, to be used as teaching material, and we had many requests for the book from members of the public, which we sold at the price of £3.85. The money from the books I had written was already making a significant contribution to our funds and, on checking with the Accounts Department, I found that already £48,000 net had gone to the donkeys as the result of the books that year alone.

In March we visited Kenya. I wanted June to film the Lamu area so that I could show the trustees exactly what the position was; once again Abdalla was there, smiling and helpful, and beginning to realize that this visit of ours was to be one of many in an effort to help the donkeys on the island. He introduced us to the local vet, Dr Mzungu, who came from the mainland, and we invited both Dr Mzungu and Abdalla to visit us in the UK so that we could train the doctor further on veterinary needs for donkeys, and assess Abdalla and give him the working knowledge that he would need if he was going to help us with the donkeys in Lamu. I had already decided in my own mind that this would be an ideal place to set up a small Sanctuary, as donkeys would always be needed on the island and I could see there was more than enough work for IDPT to start a project. Provided Abdalla proved himself while at the Donkey Sanctuary I thought he would make an ideal manager. Whilst in Lamu, June and I were fortunate enough to meet Dr Fegan who happened to own a property which would be absolutely ideal for the new premises, as literally hundreds of donkeys passed its door every single day.

(ABOVE) (from left to right) *Niels, myself, Clive, Grainne, Dennis and Betty Slattery.*

(BELOW) *Working in Ethiopia.*

We were staying at Peponis once again. Just past the hotel began a walk to what must be one of the most beautiful beaches in the world. About three-quarters of a mile up the estuary, the sand suddenly opens out onto a seven-mile-long beach. There are beautiful sandhills at the back and quite often you can see dolphins playing in the water. It is an extremely lonely and deserted beach and on my previous visit I hadn't liked to walk along and have a swim, but together June and I decided we would have a good walk down the beach and find a place where we could have a quiet swim. We duly left our clothes safely above the tide's reach and swam in the beautifully warm sea. As long as you keep an eye out for sharks, swimming in the Indian Ocean is usually a joy, but on this occasion things changed rather rapidly. June of course had left her glasses on the beach, but not needing glasses myself I was aware of two large Africans walking along the sand towards the spot where we'd left our clothes. Bearing in mind there was no one else in sight I kept rather a close eye on them while leaping over the waves and enjoying myself. To my horror they stopped by our pile of clothes. The smaller one of the two walked on, leaving the other one standing at the edge of the water. Horrified, I watched as he suddenly took off his shirt, and then trousers, and then his underpants, and – completely stark naked – came bounding across the waves to join June and I! I must remind you that June, without her glasses, was not aware of the approaching obviously highly enthusiastic gentleman, who wished to join in our pleasures! With a horrified yelp I struck out for the shore. June was still oblivious as he bounded closer and closer to her, and shouted to her in Swahili a message, which neither of us understand – perhaps thankfully. Before he actually reached June I was able to shout, 'June – come in quickly.' Looking slightly bemused, she came in on an approaching wave, doing one of her very best crawl strokes. When she got to me she said, 'Betty, what on earth's the matter? Why did you call me out so quickly, and why was that black man coming out waving a flag!' When I'd explained the situation I can tell you it didn't take us two minutes to grab our clothes and set off back towards the safety of Peponis.

As I mentioned earlier, I had been to the British Equine Veterinary Association in Newmarket, where I felt I'd put my foot in it, but to my surprise Mr Owen, the President of the Association, came to visit to ask how best I thought they could raise funds to increase the work of the association. I was delighted to meet him and very proud to show him around the Sanctuary, and I could see he was as surprised as most people who visit. Everybody seems to think, until they come here, that it's just a dotty little old lady with a number of empty railway carriages housing dirty smelly donkeys, and to come into this beautiful part of Devon and to see the sweeping fields all neatly fenced, and the hundreds of happy, grazing donkeys, gives them quite a shock. I helped as best I could, as I have an enormous amount of time for the veterinary profession, and through them I hoped to get our message about donkeys out loud and clear.

We were delighted when Clive announced that he and Grainne, with whom he had been living in Boston, were going to get married. It was wonderful to have all the family and children come to Richmond, Surrey, for the wedding in June. However for me there was one very difficult problem; I could cope with Niels being there but, of course, he was bringing Sally as well, and I knew this was going to make the day very difficult for me. I was, however, determined not to spoil it in any way for Clive and Grainne. I really can't say how lucky I've been with my daughters-in-law and my son-in-law. I don't think I've known a kinder, more considerate man than my son-in-law, Jan, and he'd always protected me from the start, called me Mother, and in fact treated me as his own mother. Uschi was a tower of strength in all the family crises, and again I felt she was as much my daughter as Lise and Sarah. Now I was to have an Irish daughter-in-law, Grainne. The wedding was absolutely wonderful – Grainne was a picture, and Clive, tall and handsome in his topper and tails. Grainne's father gave her away, and then we all attended the reception, the highlight of which was Grainne's father, Dennis, leading everybody out for an Irish reel. It wasn't easy for me, but it did all go well, and nothing spoilt the day for the bride and groom.

We had been having trouble finding the funding for the new bus for the Slade Centre but, once again, my prayer mat worked and we had the most marvellous donation of £25,000 which we received from the Sheila Jordison Estate. It was way back in 1985 that I had been in contact with this trust, and had told them of our need for a new bus, and then suddenly out of the blue a cheque appeared, and yet another big problem was solved.

Just before Christmas June and I arranged to visit Ethiopia and Kenya. We had received many requests to help the donkeys in Ethiopia, but we hesitated because to help donkeys when so many humans were starving could be criticized. The work done in the early days by Jimmy Duncan in introducing us to the University and setting up the parasitic trial had brought forth results, and we received an official invitation from the

University to start work with the full support of their staff.

I don't think any of the work I had done abroad – and I thought I'd seen the most terrible places in Mexico – had prepared us for what we found in Ethiopia. The donkeys were in an appalling state, covered in terrible sores, carrying the most enormous loads, and so pitifully thin that all their bones were prominent. This became apparent on our long journey from the airport at Addis Ababa to Debra Zeit itself, where the university had booked us into a local hotel. I think we had our second cultural shock here. The room was very dark and dingy; there was a bathroom but, on turning the taps, we found no running water, and when we turned down the covers of the bed we could immediately see that it was already occupied by many minute creatures. Jimmy Duncan had warned us of the mosquitoes as well, and we tried on our first evening to close the window to prevent them coming in; there were no curtains and the one light bulb hanging from a cord in the middle of the room was attracting a vast array of winged insects. To our horror, the window proved absolutely impossible to close, as there was a five-inch gap between the sill and the actual window. Our first night was extremely uncomfortable; we doused the beds with some of the insect powder that we'd brought for the donkeys, and hoped to sleep, but it was quite definitely not to be, and we got up in the morning covered in bites and suffering from lack of rest.

The Veterinary University staff turned up in good time to take us down to meet the Dean, and we were given a marvellous welcome. We were shown round the buildings and were amazed at the equipment, not only in the X-ray room where June admired their beautiful Chinese X-ray machine, which on a closer examination she found was totally inoperable due to rust, but also an operating theatre, well equipped with everything in a spotless condition. I couldn't understand why, with such marvellous facilities, a group of students were standing outside in the dusty compound, carrying out an operation on a cow. Dr Feseha explained that at the moment there was no electricity at all to that part of Debre Zeit, but they'd accepted the gifts which had been showered upon them from various other countries in the knowledge that one day electricity would become available and they would then be able to make full use of all the facilities. He then took us round one of the local markets, and I will never forget the sight that met our eyes. It wasn't just the donkeys in such terrible trouble and in such enormous numbers, it was the number of women and children dressed almost completely in rags, crouched on the muddy ground trying to sell perhaps four pats of donkey dung which had been dried out and to which a little straw had been added. This they

With Daphne Sheldrick in Kenya, treating a baby elephant.

were trying to sell as fuel. For this they would perhaps get one birr, their currency, and as it took three birrs to buy a loaf of bread, I realized the pitiful level of their existence. June had brought her camera with her and while she started taking photographs, I did my best to start dressing some of the terrible wounds that I saw, June joining me as soon as she had the footage she required. Gradually the vets who had taken us to see the market began to help; I think up until then they had never thought it necessary to actually treat the animals, and the people had never been able to afford a doctor for their children, let alone the luxury of a vet.

We both decided that, although this was only a short visit, we would come back with a full team and do our best to help the donkeys in Ethiopia. Every night since, before going to sleep, I have counted my blessings as I lie in a comfortable bed and think of the poor of the world – trying to rest on dirt floors, with little or no bedding. How they can survive so cheerfully I do not know.

From Ethiopia we travelled to Kenya to save expense, and once again I visited the KSPCA. We also met Daphne Sheldrick, a great friend of Bill Jordan's. She was having a problem with a small orphaned elephant that she had rescued, and asked me if I could possibly help to solve severe sunburn problems on the baby elephant's ears. Normally baby elephants hide under their mothers, where they get plenty of shade during the heat of the day, but in this case, this poor little elephant's mother had been shot and the baby had stood for days under the blazing sun, suffering acute sunburn which had almost taken all the skin from its ears, feet and forehead. Luckily I had plenty of pots of Dermobian on me. This we call our 'magic ointment', as it seems to heal every known wound a donkey has. It's thick, green and sticky, and one would imagine that if you put it on an open sore, the sore would stay open for ages, but in fact the opposite is the result, and the skin heals from inside. So I found myself treating a baby elephant with sunburn.

We then returned to Lamu; I had agreed to meet Dr Fegan again to see if I could negotiate to purchase the building which I knew would make a superb sanctuary. He already had somebody else interested in the property, and I felt myself lucky to be able to purchase it at the price I did, after a great deal of bargaining. We both shook hands on the deal, and we met again that evening to finalize details with our lawyers. At the end of our meeting I passed him my autobiography *Down Among the Donkeys*, which he said he would read. The following morning I met him on the little narrow street in Lamu while walking up towards our proposed new property and, to my surprise, he rushed straight across and put his arms around me. 'Mrs Svendsen,' he said, 'I sat up the whole

Helping Belinda to recover psychologically.

night reading your book and I really have the greatest admiration for you and all the work that you are doing. I realized I don't really need all the money I've got and I would like to take £3,000 off the price that we both agreed as a contribution towards your charity.' With that we both burst into tears as we stood on that hot little street in Lamu.

We stopped in Nairobi for a night on the way home, and there was a message waiting for me from Daphne Sheldrick. She said, 'Could I please have some more Dermobian? The baby's ears are beginning to heal already. Bless you and the donkeys.'

During the year we also visited Atlanta, where I'd been asked to give a lecture at the American Veterinary Parasitology Association Congress, which was extremely well received.

By this time we had taken our 2,900th donkey. We never buy donkeys; all are relinquished to us either by owners parting with a loved pet for necessary reasons, by the public who have rescued donkeys from slaughter or by other welfare organizations; and those donkeys relinquished as a direct result of our checking up on cruelty allegations. Belinda was a donkey who came through another welfare organization but we were called in by the RSPCA to help in her rescue. They had the terrible job of sorting out many animals on a farm which had been abandoned. Belinda was found amongst dying poultry and starving cattle, and she was immediately moved to one of our holding areas in the north. She was there given the care and attention she needed. It was easy to attend to the physical problems and her feet were trimmed, she was de-loused, treated for worms and fed nourishing food. However, there can be psychological damage when an animal has been neglected in this way. Belinda stayed in this safe home whilst the legal battle ensued, and was finally 'our property' after a court case brought about by the RSPCA in which her previous owner pleaded guilty to a charge of neglect and abandonment. The owner was fined £50, had to pay costs of £350 and was ordered to relinquish Belinda.

On Christmas Eve I rang all the children and had the most hilarious conversation with Clive and Grainne in Boston. As Clive was speaking, Grainne was unwrapping the Christmas tree he had just bought that day, and Clive was telling me how very inventive the Japanese were, as he had bought a five-foot tree which they had been able to pack into a two-foot box. I suddenly heard a shriek from Grainne and roars of laughter as they found it was only a two-foot tree in a two-foot box!

It was the end of a very hard year, but I had one more sad job to do. I decided I would have to sell the little house in St Lucia, as I just wasn't having time to get there enough.

Chapter · 8

ARRIVAL OF A GIANT AND A STAR
1987

I'VE GIVEN many talks for the donkeys – I think the biggest have been the ones to veterinary professionals; now I was asked to give a talk to the Rotary Club of Great Britain in London at the Café Royal. Although it was quite a frightening experience they were all terribly kind and seemed really interested in the work, not only of the Donkey Sanctuary, but of the Slade Centre and the IDPT. Although these talks are very time-consuming, it's difficult to assess their long-term results, and I'm sure that many of the wonderful surprises that we receive at the Sanctuary have been triggered by somebody hearing of our work and appreciating what we are trying to achieve.

By now arrangements for the completion of purchase of the land opposite the Sanctuary were well under way, and I walked round with Brian and John Rabjohns. I felt it would be delightful if we could have a track around the perimeter of the land which would extend to approximately two and a half miles, and that trees should be planted along this track to make it pleasant for visitors to walk right around to see all the donkeys. I found from one particular spot on the walk I could see Dartmoor in one direction and Portland Bill in the other. It would also save having to use any of the main roads for moving donkeys from one field to the other, and everybody agreed that this would be a good plan. Brian got to work to put it in hand. We decided to make the barn that had been erected by the previous owner the base for a new isolation unit, and set about altering the inside to suit our needs, with the help of the Veterinary Department. We all felt it would be better if new arrivals to the Sanctuary could be on a separate piece of land, as there was the ever-present risk of an infection spreading from our new arrivals to our resident donkeys. Many of the donkeys at Slade House Farm were, of course, now getting very elderly, and the geriatric group in fact had more than 140 residents, all over the age of 35! Despite their age, this 'grannie group', as they were affectionately called, seemed to enjoy every moment of life and it was surprising how many times during the day we would see them break into a trot or even a sedate gallop, as they enjoyed their well deserved retirement.

Every donkey coming in automatically goes into the Isolation Unit. For the first three weeks these donkeys are gradually integrated into groups of a maximum of ten, and during this time they receive full veterinary treatment and get all the necessary inoculations; for many of the donkeys, this is the first time in their lives that they have received the tender loving care to which I feel every donkey is entitled. Those who don't have names are given them, along with their Sanctuary number, and this is put on the collar which every donkey wears. The collars are coloured differently – white for stallions (this is the 'danger' collar, and all stallions are normally moved to the hospital block to await the necessary operation to allow them to join the main herds and be gentle to one another instead of retaining stallion tendencies). Red collars are for the gelded donkeys, and yellow for the mares. After this first three weeks the donkeys are moved to large airy shelters with run-out yards, and have the choice of being either in or outside, and once again they are carefully observed and allowed plenty of time to make friends with their group.

The administration work and the buying was becoming a more full-time task and Paul and Uschi decided to sell the restaurant; Paul would come back to the Sanctuary to help me with this, as well as the advertising and publicity. He was also very concerned on the welfare side, and began taking an interest in the rehabilitation of the donkeys and their care by the voluntary staff. Although we had five full-time welfare officers strategically placed in the UK, many, many more were needed to provide instant response to desperate calls for help, and so 67 voluntary welfare officers had been appointed. They were trained by the Sanctuary on donkey welfare and paid a small fee and expenses for each call out. They regularly visited the rehabilitation donkeys to check all was well and liaised with owners.

Having the new land had made life very much easier, and we were able to split the donkeys into even smaller groups with their own friends, and give them more space to enjoy themselves. Rosalind de Wesselow, one of our trustees, was especially anxious that all the donkeys should be given a special facility which at the moment was only provided by Three Gates Farm. John Fry had what he called a special 'galloping field', and during the winter months, if there was a cold, sharp, dry day he would let all the donkeys out onto this one field to have a really good gallop and stretch their legs. The Veterinary Department was concerned about the spread of parasites, which is of course a constant problem on all the farms. However, John used to keep this field separate when he started his routine summer management, and was therefore able to control any problems. On the other farms, however, we hadn't been so lucky – particularly at Slade House Farm, where land was at such a premium. Rosalind was absolutely delighted that with the new land it was a possibility that a galloping field could be provided at Slade House Farm.

Having completed her cookery course, Sarah had worked at Buckland-Tout-Saints Hotel at Kingsbridge, Devon, during the winter season, and on February 12th she started with them full-time as commis chef. She was very happy there and although the work was hard she enjoyed being independent and got on extremely well with the Shepherd family who ran the hotel.

We had some very disturbing news from a Spanish welfare society called ADDA (Asociacion para la Defensa de los Derechos del Animal), who informed us that in a small village in Spain called Villanueva de la Vera a donkey had actually been crushed to death during an annual Fiesta. They had sent us full details of this Fiesta which apparently lasted three days, finishing on Shrove Tuesday with the donkey, ridden by the heaviest man in the village, being dragged by local youths on a long rope with over 50 knots in it through the village street. This was apparently to celebrate an event which had happened hundreds of years before and involved a certain Pero Palo, a notorious criminal who was caught in the village and executed there. According to ADDA, and indeed they sent us the most distressing photographs, the donkey used in the procession was actually crushed to death by the crowd at the end. We had been absolutely appalled to hear this, but had hoped that it was a one-off occasion. However, in January we received a desperate call from ADDA to say that, once again, the Fiesta was to be held and that a donkey was again to be tormented.

The day of the Fiesta unfortunately turned out to be the day that we were due to leave for our second trip to Ethiopia, and the enormous difficulties involved in getting our visas and transport arranged to go there precluded us from cancelling. So, when Vicki Moore, who was a member of the RSPCA in Southport, contacted us, and offered to go on our behalf, we gratefully accepted. She had been unable to get any funding so we gave her £500 to attend the Fiesta, and on the day we left for Ethiopia Vicki Moore, accompanied by the *Daily Star*, the *Sun* and other British press, attended the event. Apparently everybody there was absolutely appalled at the treatment meted out to the donkey, which had been named Blackie. After a quite spectacular and well-publicized row between the *Daily Star* and the *Sun*, Blackie was in fact purchased by the *Star*, and at the suggestion of Vicki Moore it was decided that he should be sent to the Donkey Sanctuary. Whilst my team and I were on our way to Ethiopia, Brian Bagwell had to deal with perhaps one of the biggest publicity outcries that the Sanctuary had ever experienced. The phone never stopped ringing, representatives from television and the press almost camped on the doorstep, as they tried to find out what the Sanctuary was going to do to get Blackie back to England. Brian managed to cope with it all and, taking advice from our veterinary surgeons and from the Ministry, he realized that the donkey would have to be put into some sort of quarantine in Spain before he would be allowed into the UK. So he made all the necessary arrangements to solve the problem until I returned from Ethiopia, and the plans needed could be put into action.

On the last visit to Ethiopia, in an effort to get visas, I had personally gone up to London and had to sit it out in the Embassy. The delays were really unbearably long; I'd had to sit there for five hours, with a very bad-tempered girl on the desk refusing any of my pleas to speed the matter up, and becoming extremely angry with me as I persisted in my efforts to get our visas through. This time I had what I thought was an excellent idea; before I went to the Embassy I went to one of the flower sellers in Kensington and bought an enormous bunch of flowers. I entered the Embassy full of hope and, walking up to the girl's desk, said, 'I've brought you a present for being so helpful in the past.' To my absolute horror the girl had been sacked two weeks previously and it was a completely new receptionist. For a short time I thought all my efforts had been wasted. However, the flowers did do the trick and on this occasion I managed to get the visas within one hour.

June and I were this time prepared for Ethiopia; she had been given leave of absence, glad to get away from the hospital atmosphere, which she was finding more and more difficult as the administration became more obtrusive in the running of her department. This time when we went, we had a few tricks up our sleeves. We both took our duvet covers which we absolutely saturated in Keatings powder; we also took two pillow slips, as we'd found out by now that the bedding was completely full of not only bed bugs but lice and fleas. Once we got to our room we stripped the beds and at night just slept inside the duvet covers. We found the Keatings powder lasted for three days, and it certainly saved washing – we just got up out of bed and shook, and a cloud of powder came off! We'd also solved the problem of food, which we had found totally inedible. We took our own little water boiler, which we used in the bedroom, and we lived on a diet of oatcakes, sardines and shortbread biscuits, topped up with Marmite and condensed milk. We found we could live on this quite comfortably for the time we were working in such terrible conditions. On this particular trip, however, we hadn't bargained for one other problem, which was the closure of the bottling plant. In the past, although the tap water was totally undrinkable, we had been able to buy bottled water or lemonade, and live on this; now we found there was no bottled water to be had at all, and so we had to take to the local wine! This caused a few problems; we couldn't really explain to Dr Feseha why we were just drinking Gouda wine, as we didn't want to be rude to him or his country, but he was so impressed with the fact that we obviously liked Ethiopian wine that when I met him at Heathrow Airport some four months later on the way out to Montreal to give a lecture, he brought me a present of half a dozen bottles.

It was on this occasion also that June had a rather unfortunate experience at the hotel in Addis Ababa where we had to stay a night. This hotel in Addis Ababa is the only place in Ethiopia where we can be sure of getting water and this gives us the chance to clean up and get ready for the days ahead. Whilst getting ready, June had washed her underwear and hung it out over the balcony. We were horrified later to find that her knickers had vanished. Peering over the ledge we saw that they had fallen down behind a very high wall and appeared totally inaccessible. We sought out the only receptionist who understood any English. As we stood in the hotel foyer, I carefully and slowly explained that my friend's knickers had fallen off the balcony and were down below our room in the enclosure. 'What is fallen? Please tell me . . .?'. By this time I had run through the gamut of 'pants', 'underclothes' and 'knickers' and did a little mime of trying to pull knickers on and take knickers off!

'Ah,' she said, smiling. 'Now I understand.'

We both smiled at each other. 'So, please, will somebody find them and bring them up to our room?'

Her reply was not what we expected, and left us completely flummoxed. 'Yes, I will replace the shower curtain immediately!'

This time we had taken Charles Courtney, farm manager, and Fiona Taylor, our veterinary surgeon, with us and it was indeed a very, very hard ten days spent working in the most terrible conditions. We did, however, manage to dose over 1,000 donkeys and treat the most appalling and serious injuries.

One morning we had been out to one of the markets where we had a distressing time treating the most terrible injuries and back sores I think any of us had ever seen. Added to this there was a loose rabid dog running around the market and we were all concerned every time it came into the area where we were working, as it was yapping wildly, saliva dripping from its mouth and threatening the heels of all the donkeys in the market and in fact all the humans as well. We were relieved to be returning to Debre Zeit after a hard morning's work. Fiona had her camera on her lap and as we drove along in the Land Rover she picked it up and looked through the viewfinder to the hills in the distance. At this moment June noticed a group of soldiers standing under a tree and nudged Fiona, saying, 'I don't think you ought to do that at the moment, Fiona. There are soldiers.' But it was already too late. The soldiers sprang up shouting, and within seconds had jumped into their own Land Rover and took up chase. Our driver stopped as soon as he realized what was happening and, to our horror, two of the soldiers jumped into the back of our vehicle pointing their guns at us. Despite protestations by Yilma Makonnen, the veterinary surgeon accompanying us from the Faculty of Veterinary Medicine in Debre Zeit, and the driver, we were forced to turn around and follow the soldiers' vehicle up a rough track into the hills in the distance. The two soldiers in the back kept their guns trained on us the whole time, and the lurching and bumping along the rough track made the journey fraught with danger. Eventually we drove into a large well concealed army camp and Fiona, without ceremony, was hustled out of the Land Rover by the soldiers. At this stage I insisted on accompanying her, as I had no idea what they were going to do and couldn't allow her to be taken away on her own. Yilma joined us and together we were pushed and shoved into one of the army barrack buildings which was just like the type of interrogation room one sees in the films. We were all sitting on a narrow bench; there was a naked light bulb above us which was switched on, as the room was very dark and dim, and a desk facing us. The soldiers took up position at the door, still with their rifles pointing at us, and we waited there for some half an hour before an officer marched in with two more soldiers, both carrying guns.

We were interrogated for over an hour. Fiona's camera was taken away and our passports were seized. Yilma had to work very hard on our behalf and told us afterwards that it was only because we were British that we weren't immediately put in jail, as they had assumed Fiona was

Yilma Makonnen, now Assistant Dean of Veterinary Medicine at Debre Zeit, with Charles Courtney, and a veterinary assistant, working in our local clinic in Ethiopia.

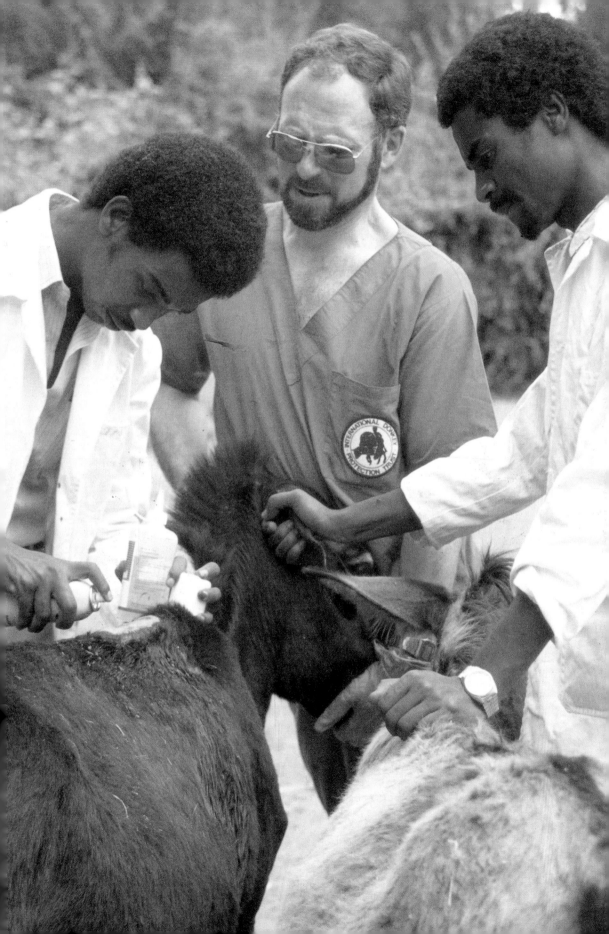

trying to photograph the concealed camp on the hill, which in fact none of us had even seen. During the interrogation I noticed that behind the officer's back was an outline plan of the whole camp showing where all the buildings were and I felt that we probably learnt far more of the layout of the camp during our hour's interrogation than we would ever have done if Fiona had taken a photograph from the road. We were eventually released and allowed to drive back but, of course, were now without our passports, which weren't given back to us until the last day of our stay.

On departure from Ethiopia they refused to give us boarding cards at the airport, and we spent an hour arguing to be allowed to board the plane. We had no idea why we were being kept, as nobody seemed able to explain why they would accept our air tickets and take our luggage but wouldn't allow us to pass the departure desk in the main hall of the airport. When the flight was due to depart in only half an hour we still hadn't got as far as the immigration or customs departments and I went back in desperation to the desk. I offered them a copy of *Down Among the Donkeys*, and four leaflets describing our work. To my surprise they all smiled happily at getting this small gift and issued us with our boarding cards. I can tell you, it was a very grateful team who got on the plane for our visit to Kenya.

In Lamu, Abdalla advised us of donkeys on various other islands near Lamu where nobody had ever visited to treat the donkeys, and they obviously were in need of help. We rented a boat and set off at six o'clock in the morning to help the donkeys as much as we could. On the first island, Pate, nobody had told us that we would have to walk almost 10 miles to the village on a rough sandy track, carrying all our equipment, with the temperature gradually rising to over 100° by the time we'd eventually struggled back to the jetty! Looking back on it, we all wondered how we managed to do it; Charlie said, 'Well, if you and June could do it, I knew I should be able to,' but it certainly took it out of us, and by the end of the trip going round other small islands giving much-needed anthelmintic and first aid to the donkeys, we were all completely shattered when we got back to Lamu. We had met the most dedicated young man on one of the islands, and he promised to go back to dose the balance of the donkeys we were unable to treat. He'd tried to better himself with the little education he was able to receive and told us his heart's desire was to be a veterinary surgeon. Not promising anything, we offered to look into the matter for him and see if we could help with the sponsorship when we got back to the UK. On our return to England he wrote to us as follows:

I would like to inform you that I have presented your medical gifts to 258 donkeys, the remaining doses are just waiting for any donkeys with great luck. And how I would like to inform you that by the time you were telling me you would try to do something about my scholarship I was about to drop with joy, just by the mention of your willingness to try the scholarship for me was as if you removed from my flesh a thorn that has pricked me long ago of which I was unable to operate it. Besides relief and joy has stayed with me since, knowing at least and at long last someone in a far corner of the world could help me have what I long for i.e., having sound veterinary knowledge to help animals and particularly donkeys . . .

I promised to try and send him to college, followed by veterinary training in Nairobi. He was so dedicated and without our help had no chance of improving himself.

I visited the KSPCA in Nairobi. They work very hard in Kenya and I had previously visited and corresponded. We had given them money to build a small hospital block for donkeys. On this particular occasion I had the great honour of opening this for them.

Our return journey was, as usual, very anti-social; the flight left Nairobi airport at ten minutes past midnight, which meant flying from Lamu and then hanging about for eight hours with nowhere to go before we could board the plane for the journey back to the UK. Unfortunately Charlie became very ill during the flight, and we were increasingly concerned as he went greyer and greyer and began rocking up and down on his seat with pain. It was a very relieved team that eventually got back to Devon, and Charlie was whisked away for medical treatment.

At the Sanctuary, Donkey Week this year was even bigger than we'd anticipated; it was lovely to see so many old friends, and the week seemed to pass in a dream. It's very hard to name those who stood out, but Mo Flenley and her little party, who always stayed at the Torbay Hotel, with her immense love of the donkeys and her tremendous enthusiasm, was certainly making her mark. She worked for Mobil Oil and her constant harassment of the company for them to donate towards the Sanctuary had certainly brought forth results. We'd had two large cheques already, for which she was totally responsible. Blanche Alexander was another lady who regularly arrived, brisk and cheerful – I couldn't forget her, as she'd run to tell me on one occasion that somebody had fed a baby donkey with a carrot that was stuck in its

throat. Thanks to Blanche's information I was able to remove the carrot, possibly saving the donkey's life. During our Sunday lunch, Blanche had received the shock of her life when she received a small certificate thanking her for her prompt action. We couldn't forget Nick and his mother, Marjorie, either. Nick, who suffers from multiple sclerosis, and has some difficulty in walking, absolutely loves his trips to see the donkeys, and his constant cheerfulness and the amazing care given to him by his mother are always a source of inspiration to us all. One can't forget Barbara Abercrombie and her friend, Tom Evans – always tremendously generous to us, and so fond of all the donkeys.

I'd always wished to expand the work of the Slade Centre, and had been very interested in the Queensway Trust, which had been set up in the Birmingham area. For some years we'd been involved in this and Bert Duncan, our Chief Inspector for the Midlands, kept a very close eye on all their operations. They were using donkeys to give rides to children from various hospitals, hospices and children's homes, and I was honoured to be asked if I would take a seat on the Queensway Trust Board so that I could help with my knowledge and information on the donkey. I was always surprised at how interested the press were in our work and various articles kept appearing. *Donkey Work*, our new film, had amazingly been shown on New Zealand television and this resulted in a letter from the New Zealand Donkey Breed Society asking if I would consider visiting them some time in the future.

At this time we offered a home to a giant: even having been prepared for the arrival of the largest admission to the Sanctuary, we were absolutely stunned when Jubilee walked out of the horse box. She stands at 16.2 h.h. Jubilee was in fact the largest mule in England and had been specially bred by a man who happened to love mules, which he had dealt with whilst in the army. He had decided to breed the biggest mule in England and he'd chosen the mother carefully, a sister of the famous racehorse called Rubstic, who had won the Grand National. He also chose a very special donkey from France to be the father. This was a lovely Poitou donkey called Eclair. Jubilee was born in 1977, the Queen's Jubilee Year, and that's how she got her name. Unfortunately her owner became very ill and Jubilee was sent to a horse stable to be trained to pull a cart, but she didn't take to it at all, and became very difficult to handle. Various people offered to give Jubilee a home, but the owner decided that he'd rather she came to the Donkey Sanctuary where he knew she would be looked after for the rest of her life. I decided that this would make a nice story for children and so the book *Eeyore Meets*

(ABOVE) *Giving anthelmintic in Kenya.*

(BELOW) *Faza island, where we met Adow, the 'most dedicated young man'.*

a Giant was written. It was a great success, and, yet again, brought donkeys and their needs to the attention of children. Many schools purchased the book for their libraries. We think that this side of the work is extremely important.

Another new arrival was Donna Kalepp, who came from the New Forest. We do have many problems with the donkeys allowed to roam in the forest but our Inspector, Gill Preston, has managed to make an arrangement with the verderers whereby donkeys that fall below a certain standard can actually be moved and returned to their owners to be specially cared for, or sent into the Sanctuary if permission is obtained. However, Donna was a different story altogether. Donna's owners, Mr and Mrs Kalepp, were not in good health and had decided that Donna was likely to outlive them. Her age was eighteen, and theirs a little higher! Donna had always been on her own but had actually been treated as their own child, as the Kalepp's had no family or close relatives. Donna was their pride and joy. They were advised to move to Spain for health reasons, and really hoped they could take Donna with them, but on reflection they decided it would probably be better for her to come into the Sanctuary. They approached us on a non-urgent basis, but said they would like her to be picked up reasonably soon so they could see her settle before they continued their plans for a move. So in February Neil Harvey set off in the lorry to pick Donna up.

You can imagine how difficult it was for them to see Donna go, and in fact they were so concerned that, having loaded her, they followed the lorry down in their car, and were there to help her off the lorry and settle her into the Isolation Unit. They even went further than this, and rented a house locally so that they could stay for the next few weeks to make sure that she had settled down properly. This was, of course, a great advantage to Donna, who would otherwise have missed her owners terribly, and could have pined to the extent of totally refusing to eat, and perhaps even dying. The Kalepp's eventually decided that they would move down to the area permanently instead of going to Spain. When Donna was moved to Brookfield Farm they continued to visit her regularly, and still do so. It's really heartwarming when owners love their animals so much, and continue to care for them whilst they are unable to keep them themselves, and we hope that all three have a happy retirement together.

By April, Blackie had finished his isolation in Spain, and we decided it was right to bring him back to England and the Donkey Sanctuary. We already had a horse box in Spain but it was a rather small vehicle in which to bring a donkey such a long journey and I was concerned over this. I did get on to the Spanish Embassy to see if there was any way that they could help me in transporting Blackie back to the UK as I felt it might improve relations between our two countries if they were seen to be helping in his journey. I give them all credit; they really did try and Air Iberia spoke to me on several occasions. Unfortunately, the largest plane they brought over to England was the Airbus at that time and the access into the Airbus was not high enough for the crate size we would need to transport Blackie. LEP Transport were also very helpful and offered us a special rate of £3,000 for the air journey for Blackie and ourselves but only on one certain day and, unfortunately, the Spanish authorities were unable to complete his health tests by that time. If we couldn't take their offer on that day then the cost would be £10,000 to fly him home and I felt we couldn't spend all that money. We were awaiting the results of the tests but our Spanish agents told us we wouldn't get the final ones until 48 hours before he could leave the country and so, in the end, we had to fix a date when we would go over to pick him up after the thirty days' isolation period was up.

This meant we had to go during the Easter holiday, but there was no way out and my team, which I named the A-Team, agreed to go without hesitation. During all the time Blackie was in Spain we had been pestered constantly by phone calls from the press, particularly the *Sun*, demanding to know when we were bringing Blackie home. We were hoping to keep this secret to prevent any problems between the *Sun* and *Star* newspapers yet again. We had agreed to take the *Star* reporters with us as they had purchased the donkey and passed him over to us, so they were the only ones in the know when Brian and I finally made our arrangements. We hadn't told them, however, how we proposed to bring Blackie back, only the date we were going to Spain. Brian and I agreed that we would send our best lorry, specially equipped for transporting donkeys, over on the ferry to France with Perry, the senior driver; he would then drive down to Madrid and meet me there. John Fowler and Roy Harrington would drive over the Shogun to bring the horse box back and I would fly over with the *Star* newspapermen, be there two days earlier, clear all the paperwork with the agents and then we could all, with luck, set off together. The idea was to drive from Madrid to Santander and get the ferry from there to Plymouth which would arrive on the Friday night at 6.30.

As arranged, I flew over with the *Star* newspapermen, Don Mackay and Stan Meagher, and we spent two frustrating days in Madrid whilst I tried to get the paperwork cleared. The agent did not want to be associated with Blackie in case of reprisals after we left and so he refused to put the species 'donkey' down on all the veterinary forms and every other form I required, insisting on calling Blackie a horse. As you can imagine this caused innumerable problems both at the docks and back in the UK, but anyhow I had to accept it in the end. We had been told on booking to be on the docks at Santander at 4 p.m. on the Thursday, but when I picked up the final papers in Madrid at 5 p.m. the evening before we were going to set off, they then told me we had to be at Santander by 9 a.m. the following morning, so all our plans had to be changed again. Luckily by this time the A-Team had all arrived and we were together at the same hotel in Madrid. The lorry had travelled over incognito, with its Donkey Sanctuary signs inside, and the *Star* news-papermen had travelled with an enormous suitcase carrying a very thick, red donkey rug with 'Blackie Star' written on it, which they hung on to, grimly determined to use it when the time came.

We left at midnight to pick up Blackie and carefully loaded him onto the lorry. It was a long drive throughout the night to Santander and nobody slept; we were all very tired when we arrived on the dock. We were concerned that the press would spot us on the dock and so, having registered our arrival, we moved a short way off and hid the lorry under some large cranes which would give it shelter from the sun and keep Blackie happy. He had travelled extremely well and seemed totally unconcerned by the events which had taken place. We then spent nine hours trying to find the papers which hadn't arrived at the shipping agent's office and it was only at the last minute that we were able to relax and accept that we had actually got Blackie onto the ferry and could settle down for the 24-hour journey.

Our problems were not yet over, however, as, by accident, the bookings made on our behalf had not gone through, and whilst the men got a cabin for four, I was left with no accommodation. Blackie travelled far better than I did that night. Fortunately the sea was completely calm and the donkey box had been put right at the front of the ferry ready to off-load; eleven polo ponies were in the box next to us, which meant that the deck was left open and we could visit Blackie throughout the night and day as required. Brian and I had arranged that a press release should go out early Friday morning to say Blackie was coming home and would be here at the weekend, without revealing our travel arrangements, which could bring the reporters and upset Blackie. Brian also arranged for someone to phone Vicki Moore to let her know that Blackie was coming back in case she wanted to come to the Sanctuary to meet him on the Saturday morning. We all knew it was going to be very late on

Friday when we arrived and had hoped that our return would go unnoticed. Our hopes were quickly dashed, however, for as the ferry drew into Plymouth we were informed that the press were 'all over the docks'. Blackie didn't like the last bit of the journey, there were a lot of banging noises from the seamen unlocking the chocks holding the lorries down, and the sound of the reversing engines disturbed him and I spent some time calming him down in the box. The two *Star* reporters were quite determined to put his blanket on, which they did, but not without cost – one had his finger bitten and the other had his foot trodden on!

However, we were all smiling and delighted to be back as we drove down to the customs area. The police and customs men had done a marvellous job and had managed to get all the reporters off the docks and behind the wire. One, however, had crept through and jumped up in the cab with us and started doing an interview. He was very quickly removed by the police but I made quite an error when two more people climbed in and said they wanted to see Blackie and I said, 'Absolutely no way, we are not going to open the doors,' to find they were, in fact, the immigration officials who had to see him. However, all was sorted out and they realized why Blackie had been called a horse and not a donkey, and eventually we were waved through. The pandemonium that broke out when we went through the gates was unbelievable. I had told the reporters that we would stop the lorry and open the back door for five minutes but we were not going to allow Blackie to come out and they could just photograph him there as he needed a good rest and we were going to take him home. However, one of the *Sun* reporters jumped up into the lorry and actually started a punch-up with Don Mackay which was duly recorded on both television and camera. Quite a return for Blackie, who thought he had got away from all that. Within moments we had closed up the back of the lorry again and then drove Blackie home. Many of the staff were waiting at the Sanctuary to welcome us. He was happy to be introduced to his new warm stable with an infra-red lamp and something that wasn't moving for the first time in 48 hours, and we were all extremely pleased by the way he had travelled.

I was horrified when I returned home to find June deeply distressed; she told me she had resigned from her job.

Of course Television South-West wanted some pictures of Blackie and they were fortunate in that, on the particular day they came, Blackie had finished the normal isolation he had to have at the Sanctuary. Shortly after he arrived we had introduced him to a girlfriend called Lola, who had come from Wales, having herself had a fairly tough life, and they had already become firm friends. TSW were delighted when we opened the gates and for the first time the two little donkeys trotted out into their own private meadow and enjoyed the lush grass. As the TSW team left happily with their films it was just coming up to 2 p.m., and almost on the dot arrived Ena Kendall and Christopher Cormack, the photographer, from the Sunday *Observer*. That afternoon Christopher Cormack walked around, finding his way round the Sanctuary and in fact photographed a small operation on one of the donkeys, while Ena Kendall spent two and a half hours doing her interview.

I always find it very difficult being interviewed; there are so many sides to the Sanctuary to talk about, and sometimes those coming down have no idea of the wide range of our work. However, Ena Kendall was completely different. She had done a lot of homework and knew exactly what she wanted to find out and proved a most pleasant person to talk to. She and the photographer were staying the night in Sidmouth so there was no hurry to complete our work and she finally pronounced herself satisfied with the interview at about 5 p.m. That night I only had time for a brief round of the donkeys in the yards; it had seemed such a busy day and yet I felt I had achieved very little, but everybody was happy and settled and as far as the donkeys went they had had an idyllic time.

During the year June and I went out to Cyprus to meet Dr George Efstathiou, a really marvellous vet who had visited us on a training course organized by the World Health Organization. He had already started a trial to rid the donkeys of parasites, and we visited the donkeys with him. Nothing was too much trouble for him, and we drove right round the island, being introduced to donkey owners and agricultural officers. At the end of the trip, to our joy the government decided that owing to the good results we'd obtained they would dose all their donkeys at their own expense. They were really grateful for the help and advice we had been able to give them, and we left Cyprus confident that George was going to look after the donkeys in our absence.

Our next trip was to Lamu again. Earlier this year we had made one of our regular visits to the village of Matondoni on the island, and had been appalled to find one of the most emaciated and sick-looking donkeys we had seen on our trips. This donkey was about eight years old and was brought to us by an obviously heartbroken, caring owner, who was extremely elderly. A medical examination of the donkey showed that she was not only riddled with parasites but had been affected by trypanosomiasis (sleeping sickness) and it seemed almost impossible that she could survive. The donkey's name was Bahati and the owner was almost in

Blackie and Lola in their new quarters.

tears as we explained that her chance of survival was very slim. He asked if there was any way we could help. We told him that if he could get the donkey to Lamu town, we would take Bahati into our premises and see what we could do for her. We imagined that he would bring her by boat, because of the distance involved, and were very surprised two days later to find the old man walking into the Sanctuary alongside a completely exhausted Bahati. Although Bahati's chances seemed poor, we immediately set to work and she was given the necessary injections, vitamin supplements and much needed food. We had to be very careful worming her, as too large a dose in her weakened state could have killed her, so this was done with the greatest possible care.

On this visit to Lamu we were to perform the official opening ceremony of the Sanctuary, and on arrival I was absolutely delighted to find the immense change in Bahati. She had already put on weight, and instead of looking so desperately sick and without interest in life, she was much brisker and quite obviously well on the road to recovery. I invited her owner to the opening ceremony and then had the joy of seeing him and Bahati set off on their walk home. The old man said goodbye and kissed me with tears in his eyes. It was a very moving experience.

The opening ceremony on July 4th – Independence Day for the donkeys – was also a very emotional occasion, particularly as it was our first Sanctuary abroad. We got the local chief to perform the actual ceremony of cutting the ribbon and we then had a Muslim celebration on the property, which was probably just as well, as consuming alcohol at 11 o'clock in the morning, in that heat, is not really to be recommended. The following morning we tentatively arranged a clinic, not sure how many donkeys would turn up on this first morning but, to our surprise, over 90 attended and of particular interest to myself was the use of the new water trough which we had placed in the end wall of the corral. On previous visits we had noticed donkeys so desperate for water they had to go down to the sea to drink, but the new water trough was accessible to the working donkeys as they passed and they made great use of it.

The Montreal Conference of the World Association for the Advancement of Veterinary Parasitology, where I had been invited to give a paper, came up all too soon. I was accompanied this time by Pat, my sister, who took care of the display stand, and Bill Jordan, who was also giving a paper. Once again our work was received with great enthusiasm and I was delighted that so many people were now becoming interested in

(ABOVE) *Typical Cypriot lady with donkey.*

(BELOW) *Finding Bahati in Matondoni.*

donkeys, and for the first time someone else had included the word 'donkey' in their paper! I really felt the tide was beginning to turn in our favour.

At the end of the year June and I visited Egypt and had a most enthusiastic reception. We had a good contact in Dr Ragheb, who had also been on one of the special training courses at the Sanctuary, and after a tour of the Veterinary Departments and Public Health Departments, we visited various sites within a 60-mile radius of Cairo; we wanted to set up a proper anthelmintic trial, and needed to determine the best time to dose the Egyptian donkeys to get the maximum benefit. The trial was to commence in December and last for twelve months, after which we would return to assess the results with the authorities. I hoped that this would be the start of a larger project in Egypt, a country where the donkeys and mules were in tremendous need of help. Working in the markets was not easy but, once again, the reception from the owners was overwhelming and the cause of great surprise to the senior Egyptian veterinary staff who came with us, who I think had assumed we would meet with some resistance. We treated over 200 donkeys in the short time we were there; their needs arose from sores caused by ill-fitting harnesses, ill-fitting bits and general debility of the animals due to heavy parasite burdens.

Back at the Sanctuary, during one of our managers' meetings, we discussed the possibility of growing a new type of grass using the hydroponic method. We were assured by the manufacturers of the units that, with very little problem, we could grow fresh grass in trays without soil throughout the winter, which of course our donkeys would absolutely love. With the support of all the managers we decided to give it a trial at Paccombe Farm, and Derek Battison undertook the day-to-day running of this project, with Brian and the Veterinary Department delving into all the problems. I was delighted to visit and see our first grass appearing. The donkeys certainly loved the product but we soon became aware of many problems. Firstly the whole procedure took up the entire time of three of our employees, and secondly the seeds formed themselves into a very hard mat which was inedible. After six months' trial we had to drop the project, as it was too labour-intensive.

Contact between Niels and I over the last few years had been very strained but in September Sally, his wife, left him and at long last we were able to start talking to each other. Niels decided he would like to go into the yacht chartering business and bought *Leopard Normand III*, a twenty-metre yacht, to work in the Greek and Turkish waters. Although I still loved him, I had settled down with June as my companion, I had my beloved donkeys and could work every hour I wanted without distractions. Niels had his own interests, and at least we could now contact each other when necessary.

Just after Niels set off I received a phone call from our lorry driver, Neil Harvey. He told me he had had a terrible trip, and asked if I could be at Isolation to meet him when he arrived at 8 p.m. that night. I do not think I have seen any driver so shattered as Neil when he returned from Bognor Regis. He had been caught in the severe October gales. He told me the story of how the lorry had rocked, nearly tipping over, and how he had to drive around live electricity cables, fallen trees, etc. However, thankfully he had returned safely with the donkeys, and as we unloaded them they seemed completely unaware of the danger they had been in.

We also got a desperate telephone call from the owners of a donkey very aptly called Joe Mischief. They were finding him impossible to cope with. Joe arrived here and duly lived up to his reputation. All the best tender loving care we could give him made no impact and he spent the days braying and kicking at any human or donkey nearby. We were beginning to despair when one of the little mares who arrived at the same time as Joe decided to step in. Bonny too was known to be rather free with her teeth and heels and they must have recognized each other as kindred spirits. Miraculously the braying, kicking and biting stopped and peace fell over the Sanctuary once more. They had quite literally fallen in love and from that day were quite inseparable.

Not all outcomes, however, are so happy. Our voluntary inspector, Jimmy Gough, in Brighton was called by a family who were emigrating to Spain. They wished their three donkeys to come into the Sanctuary. On visiting to collect the signatures releasing the donkeys, he was not too happy with the conditions, and found one donkey, Lolly, missing, although her foal was there. The emigrating owners, insisting she had been there a short while previously, signed over the donkeys and, the next day, they left. Our inspector returned to find Lolly still missing. He reported it to the police and RSPCA and searched the woodlands and fields around in the snow and ice, getting more and more desperate as he could not trace her. He even appealed on the local radio, but no trace could be found. The new owners of the house moved in and to their horror, as the ice on the swimming pool melted, the frozen body of poor Lolly appeared. Her foal settled down after intensive care and attention, but, sadly, we were too late for Lolly.

Chapter 9

A FAIRY-TALE ENDING
1988

FOR some time we had been getting worried about Buffalo's health. He was such a favourite with everybody, with his enormous long, floppy ears and his extremely gentle and placid nature. He had a lovely habit of leaning on you, and if you decided to groom him and stood against his shoulders, gradually more and more weight would descend upon you, until you had to move very quickly, otherwise I think both would have been on the ground. His health had been quite obviously failing, and one of the saddest days of my life was when we had to agree to put dear old Buffalo down. He had also been a tremendous favourite with our Donkey Week visitors, and we decided that we would erect a Memorial Barn, to be called the Buffalo Barn, and this was built entirely with contributions from his Donkey Week friends.

One of my jobs is to ensure that all departments keep in touch with each other. We hold regular management meetings at Slade House Farm and occasional meetings on one of the other farms. The first meeting of 1988 was at Brookfield Farm, and I was absolutely delighted to see, not only how immaculately Charlie Courtney was keeping it, but also how happy and contented the donkeys were. On that particular farm he had the donkeys known as 'Big Boys Group'. These were donkeys who had recently been castrated or geldings that were particularly difficult and had been causing problems, upsetting groups on our other farms. This group was always a pleasure to watch and Charlie explained how a 'pecking order' had been established. It amazed us all to see that the smallest donkey, called Treacle, who had a very humped back and who I well remember coming in from Miss Philpin many years previously, was in fact 'The Boss'. He kept all the donkeys in order and it seemed that as long as Treacle was around, everybody behaved impeccably.

Brian had now taken over the weekly visits to the farms, as this fitted in well with his work in making sure that all the buildings were kept up

(ABOVE) *Lamu Sanctuary.*

(BELOW) *Looking for wounds in Egypt.*

to scratch, and that the voluminous problems from the donkey dung were kept under control. Brian had always been very careful to ensure that proper dung pits were built, as almost all our farms are near rivers and we were always very conscious of the problems of materials of this nature getting into the river system.

Without the superb back-up of Brian and Julie and all the staff, the work would certainly not have continued at the pace at which it was going. I was very aware of the promise I made that every donkey coming into the Sanctuary was entitled to the best possible treatment, conditions and the right to life until it was decided that a donkey had no quality of life left, and then in its own interests, and its own interests only, it would be put down.

At this time one of our inspectors, Ian Hodges, got an almost hysterical telephone call one evening from a lady in Wales. She could not stop crying on the telephone. All she could say was that her husband was going to shoot the donkey as the children had lost interest in it and nobody was bothering with it. She managed to tell him her name and address and Ian set off immediately to go to the donkey's aid.

After a great deal of talking and argument he was able to persuade the husband that the donkey deserved to live and that the Sanctuary would take it and arrange all the transport. The donkey was called Patience and that must have been what she had needed over the past years. She had been kept with a herd of cattle and fed on whatever the cattle were getting, which was mainly silage and cattle cake. Although perhaps the cattle were wormed, Patience had never had that advantage and was full of parasites and in a very poor condition. In addition to this her feet were a most terrible shape; the owners had never had a farrier but had attempted to trim the hooves themselves; it's a job difficult enough for a farrier, never mind an amateur. Ian's report was dated January 18th and by January 19th Patience had been received into the Sanctuary.

We really do have the most magnificent drivers; on hearing of an emergency like this there is never any hesitation in their setting off whatever time of the day or night and I know they gain great satisfaction from being able to pick up donkeys from these situations and bring them back to somewhere so different for the donkey.

Mules can be quite difficult to catch and can lead their owners quite a dance. This is fine when the owner is young but as the mule outgrows its owner things tend to get a little more difficult. This was the case with Daisy the mule and her donkey friend, Topsy. An elderly lady had been trying to help animals in trouble by taking them in and by allowing local

Our darling Buffalo.

people to use her land and grazing free in exchange for their looking after her rescued equines, but unfortunately the plan did not work out. Apart from never being handled the animals had not seen the farrier for many months, long before they had been rescued by her and by the time our inspector saw them they were in a very serious condition indeed. In this instance some pressure was needed for the animals to be released to the Sanctuary but the local vet was a great help and with our inspector managed to get the relinquishment documents signed so that Daisy and Topsy could take advantage of the Sanctuary facilities. Topsy's feet are now improving rapidly and she is able to walk again without pain but I still find it terribly sad that our inspectors keep finding similar cases despite all our continued efforts to educate donkey owners. Daisy and Topsy settled in happily.

Despite letters of protest to the Spanish Embassy, to King Juan Carlos, to the Pope and to anybody else we could think of, it appeared that yet another donkey was going to have to suffer as Blackie had the year before, and, along with Roy Harrington and Neil Harvey, and accompanied by the BBC, we left with some trepidation for the village of Villanueva de la Vera in February. The situation was just as bad as I'd imagined; I was absolutely horrified and appalled at the tremendous noise of gunfire in the enclosed town hall where the poor donkey was waiting, shivering and terrified; almost completely drunken crowds leapt on the donkey as it was pulled out, dragging it to the ground before it had even left the town hall. We followed its progress as best we could through the narrowing streets, being deafened ourselves by gunshots and frequently bumped and hassled, as people realized we weren't local, but we were able to get to the donkey at the end, to prevent it being crushed to death. We moved poor Beauty away, and managed to get her up a side street, which gave her time to collect herself and for her respiration to return to a more normal level.

Before the event we had spoken to the Mayor, and he had managed to keep a group of men around Beauty, which had protected her to a certain extent, and we were so grateful that the donkey had indeed come through alive that we invited the Mayor and his wife to come to our next Donkey Week. We also suggested to the Mayor that we could make a full-sized model donkey on special wheels to be used in future fiestas instead of tormenting a live donkey. We said that if the villagers liked the idea, we would present it to them so that they could use it for the future, but he didn't seem very keen. We returned to the UK to find Brian having to cope yet again with the blaze of publicity that seemed to surround this fiesta, and were very grateful indeed to be able to report that the donkey had come through alive, although very shocked and shaken.

It was lovely to have Paul back at the Sanctuary again, and he was picking up the threads of general administration. He had decided that he would rather have his own property and, having lived for some time in a caravan on John Rabjohns's land, he and Uschi bought a house at Dalwood, where they were within easy commuting distance of the Sanctuary. Clive and Grainne were settled in Boston; Clive was doing very well in his job and my visits to Lise and Jan in Denmark had shown how well and happy they both were. Sarah was, of course, at the hotel in Kingsbridge, and so, from a family point of view, everything seemed to be going well.

On the housing front, things were not quite so smooth. The repairs to Slade House Farm had been completed and we now had plenty of space to move our office staff. Highlands, the house that we had bought for veterinary use, was really too far away from the Sanctuary for emergencies. I got many calls during the early hours of the morning due to various problems, either a donkey seriously ill, a foal being born or one of the very many fire alarms. When people invented fire systems and smoke detectors, it seems they didn't take into consideration the fact that on a frosty night a donkey 'spending a penny' under a smoke detector causes a cloud of steam that sets all the fire alarms off. I was getting tired of running down the hill to the Sanctuary, sometimes twice a night when the fire bells went, as I knew that the one time I didn't go down, it would prove to be a real fire. We had already had two disasters – I wasn't prepared to have a third.

Between Highlands and the Sanctuary was a lovely big field, owned by Mr Tucker, our neighbour, who ran Stoneleigh Country Club and Holiday Camp. Brian and I approached Mr Tucker and asked if he would like to exchange Highlands for the land with, of course, a cash adjustment, and he became extremely interested, as he and his wife were both finding it difficult living right over their shop. Having a house just next door would prove far more satisfactory. Eventually a deal was arranged, and as the office staff had moved into the main house from Little Slade, we adapted this to become our new home. Once again, I dug into my reserves to carpet and curtain the new house, but I knew on the first day June and I moved into Little Slade that I had made the right decision. From my bedroom window I could see the geriatric group, the blind group and the special care group, and I could answer emergency calls within two minutes instead of having to run the five minutes previously necessary to get to the Sanctuary.

I particularly loved the little blind group. It never ceases to amaze me how these totally blind donkeys' partners look after them. Each one has its own minder, and as the blind donkeys come out in the morning the minders will gently move in front of them as they come to the fence, and guide them round it, and if the minder goes to have a drink of water, he always makes sure that he takes the little blind one with him. By now Dusty had joined this group with her new friend Eros. Amigo still had stallion tendencies and could not be bothered with his two earlier companions once he had made friends with some of the larger geldings. Dusty and Eros had settled in extremely well. I could stand for hours just enjoying the peace and tranquillity of the unit and the immense feeling of concern between one animal and its partner. Also in the group was a little donkey with the strange name of Icabod. She was with her son, Souter, and had been sent into the Sanctuary by her owner as totally unmanageable. Nobody had realized that Icabod was blind; no wonder she was unmanageable.

The blind group had grown rapidly and now included Jessie, Rainbow, Connie, Demetra and Poppet in addition to those already mentioned. I have noticed many of our visitors stop for a long time in this area, and I sometimes think if we only we humans could help each other the way many of the animal species do, life would be much happier.

During my last trip to Ethiopia I had been approached by Dr Aberra Ayana at the University, about a young girl he knew called Meron Tsegaye, who was suffering from a brain tumour; the Black Lion Hospital at Addis Ababa had recommended that she should go abroad for further investigation and possible neurosurgical treatment. Dr Ayana explained to me that there was no chance at all of Meron receiving any treatment in Ethiopia, as the girl had no money and the facilities were just not there. She was going blind and it was even possible she might die. Though, of course, the Donkey Sanctuary and the IDPT were restricted from helping in any way by their charitable objects, I had personally managed to arrange to bring Meron over, and June and I had met her at Heathrow Airport with her aunt, Senait, and she had spent some time in Exeter hospital as a private patient. She had then been transferred to Plymouth for an operation. During that time, brain scans were carried out and I'm delighted to say that Meron had improved dramatically; with the proper medication her sight had improved and we'd been able to send her back to Ethiopia after three months, well on the way to recovery. But I now began to get letters from Meron, who was back safely, asking if we could possibly help her to get a job in the UK when she grew older. At our marvellous Donkey Week that year I told our visitors about Meron's plight, and was overwhelmed with the response. Her drugs were still costing a great deal of money and one of our visitors offered to pay for a year's supply, which offer I most gratefully accepted. Niels's stepfather, Sven Iverson, who I mentioned in my earlier book and who took Lucky Lady for so many years and looked after her so beautifully for me, had re-married and his wife, Nora, a most wonderful woman, was heavily involved in the Catholic Church. Together they had built a hospice for patients in Torquay and when I approached Nora with regard to Meron she immediately offered to do all that she could for her. I think there is a very good chance that if Meron can improve her English, she could get a job training as a nurse in a Catholic hospital in London.

On a recent visit to Lamu I'd had a really good look at the way the soggies were made. These were the carrying panniers that the donkeys used to transport almost every item they had to carry through the village, and, despite the tremendous weight of the coral bricks and the heavy wet sand which was piled high on each side of the soggie, the donkeys in Lamu hardly ever seemed to have any saddle galls. In Ethiopia, however, we'd been absolutely horrified by the terrible sores on so many of the donkeys' backs. Usually the sufferer would be a very thin, pathetic donkey, and when the owner brought it to us for treatment, its back would be covered by a sack. We would lift the sack and a cloud of flies would rise from a piece of dirty brown pus-covered paper, which again on removal, revealed yet another set of flies and maggots and the most terrible open wound. In almost every case these saddle galls were caused by full sacks being slung straight across the donkeys' backs, and as they walked perhaps 15 miles to the market, these rubbed and rubbed, and must have been absolute agony for the donkeys. Abdalla told me that the soggies were made by the local villagers, and I gave them an order for a thousand, for which the villagers would receive the equivalent of one pound for each soggie. We then managed with great difficulty to transport them by lorry overland to Ethiopia, to the Veterinary University in Debre Zeit.

On visiting Ethiopia again, we were delighted to find that the soggies had all arrived safely. There are over 3.5 million donkeys slaving away, all full of worms and lice, and a third of these had the most ghastly back sores, which we really hoped the soggies would help to alleviate. Hopefully the Ethiopians will make their own soggies in future. The

anthelmintic trials had been an outstanding success, and the results relayed to agricultural officers and veterinarians. I was pleased to be asked to lecture at the Debre Zeit Veterinary University, to a large audience of specialists, and the message certainly got across.

One agricultural officer stood up during question-time and said, 'A strange thing recently happened – a large organization offered fifty poor farming communities the gift of either an ox, a donkey or ten goats for their village. Everyone chose the donkey and now I understand why, as the donkey is used for all the most vital aspects of village life, carrying water and goods, and doing the ploughing.'

Visiting one of our project areas, where we had been dosing the donkeys, June and I received a rapturous welcome. The donkeys were amazing by Ethiopian standards, fit and strong and full of energy. The head of the village, Ato Yeshaw Kassat at Dembi said, 'The donkey is the key to survival for the poor farming communities in Ethiopia.' I feel this sums it up. Hopefully, appeals to world organizations will bring help in the form of anthelmintics now we have proved our point beyond doubt. Whilst in Ethiopia I was able to meet Meron Tsegaye once again. She had recovered her sight, and was now studying English ardently, hoping to work in the UK when eighteen years old. It was lovely to see her again and see her enormous improvement.

Paddy Barrett had come over from Ireland as arranged to receive some training; he was now reporting back from Cork about the tremendous problems, mainly financial, that he was experiencing. I had always kept in contact with the Barrett family. They certainly shared our love of donkeys. We were impressed by Paddy's genuine concern and his determination to help, and after discussions it was agreed that we would become financially involved: the Irish Sanctuary became part of the Donkey Sanctuary. I knew of some of the problems in Ireland. Donkeys were still being used for work but unfortunately when no longer required they were simply turned away to fend for themselves and there was no law to prevent this. There were indeed a great many donkeys in dire need. Having left the ISPCA, Paddy became our Chief Inspector for Southern Ireland and his donkey rescue centre in Liscarroll, County Cork, at long last had the much needed finance.

Brian and Paul were both very involved in helping in Ireland; whenever I visited I was amazed at the wonderful hospitality. No matter what time I arrived at the Barrett household, the table would instantly be laid with the most wonderful spread. I found the Irish generally to be very welcoming and friendly people and my only regret was that I did not like

Soggie in action!

the Guinness which seemed to make up the major part of the evening celebrations! Brian and Paul began to build the sanctuary up under Paddy's skilled knowledge and with the help of his whole family who were all dedicated donkey lovers.

I previously mentioned the Poitou donkeys, which were threatened with extinction. There were now only sixty left in the world. Bob Camac, one of the trustees of the IDPT, had always been extremely interested in the breed and had visited France to see how the Sanctuary could help. We had been working in fairly close co-operation, and had received a visit from one of the world experts on the Poitou, Jacques Moreau. We sent our senior vet, John Fowler, over to France to have a look at the situation for himself, and to offer help in advising on donkey welfare and management to help preserve this species. Following our assistance, June and I were invited to France by SABAUD, an organization set up to save the Poitou, and they took the unusual step of allowing two of their mares out of the country to be cared for by us. Jonquille was 13 years old, and the other donkey was a very elderly mare by French standards – Amande – who at 22 was past breeding, so came as a companion for Jonquille. They also promised that we could later have a suitable stallion who was not related to Jonquille, in the hope that we would be able to breed successfully in England should the project in France fail. They kept their promise and Torrent was purchased later in the year. We then realized that our previous most favourite donkey, Buffalo, must have been part Poitou. The Buffalo Fund is therefore being used to attempt to preserve this breed, and hopefully one day perhaps the offspring can be used for the Slade Centre, for, as you are probably aware, the maximum weight limit that can be carried by ordinary donkeys is eight stone, and many of our children have to stop riding when, perhaps for the first time in their lives, they are just making some progress. To have a 14- or 15-hand donkey that could take a heavier child would make an enormous difference.

Unfortunately the Mayor of Villanueva de la Vera and his wife didn't turn up for Donkey Week. I think he thought discretion was the better part of valour, and he sent the councillor for tourism instead. She was a delightful lady, but turned out to be scared of donkeys, and it was quite amusing when the press tried to photograph her with Blackie, who seemed to enjoy her discomfort and got a little of his own back. Unfortunately, despite converting her, and obtaining her promise to try to persuade the villagers to accept our model life-sized donkey, we received a negative response. However, we intended going to Villanueva de la Vera again, with the hope that if we presented the donkey to the villagers on the day before the fiesta, they would accept it and a live donkey would be spared the terrible ordeal.

We knew a visit to Mexico was badly needed, but as it was extremely busy at the Sanctuary, June offered to go with Fiona Taylor, our vet, in my place, and when she came back she brought the most horrific report of a market they had found in San Bernabe, some fifty miles from Mexico City. This was the most barbaric market I'd ever heard of; animals with compound fractures being forced to jump on and off lorries, and no one being allowed to put an animal down, even though it was in extreme distress. I made up my mind that I would go to Mexico later in the year with June, to see the situation for myself and see what we could do.

This we did, taking Dr Aline de Aluja to San Bernabe market with us and our new vet, Guillermo Rodriguez, who was actually threatened with a gun whilst we were trying to treat some horrific injuries to a donkey which had been thrown off the back of a lorry. It was heartbreaking to see the donkeys so ill and being forced on and off the lorries, and I felt helpless in the face of such massive cruelty and indifference to the animals' plight. I was able to sit on the ground with a dying baby donkey's head in my lap, to give it what comfort I could in its last few moments; it had been crushed under a load of donkeys and horses during its journey from the farm to the market and, running my hands across its chest I could feel many of the ribs had been crushed and broken. There was nothing I could do for this poor little mite but just sit and comfort it as best I could. We made a direct appeal to the Governor of the Veterinary University hoping it would result in the Ministry of Agriculture inspecting and improving the horrific situation.

I was extremely busy. The well known publishers, David & Charles, had asked me to compile and write the first really big book on donkeys, and this had taken quite a bit of time. *A Passion for Donkeys* was about to be published and it included contributions from such famous people as Leslie Crowther, Charlie Chester, Thora Hird, Angela Rippon, Catherine Cookson, Sir John Harvey-Jones and just plain lovers of donkeys. Although the price would be nearly £15 I knew that if we could sell enough these would bring in an enormous contribution to the Sanctuary. Mal spent literally hours ploughing through press cuttings and articles, selecting those she felt could be considered for inclusion in the book, and landed up doing most of the research work. We were both absolutely astounded at the number of orders we received for the book before publication.

I was also deeply involved in thoughts of a new charity I wanted to form. I'd long wanted to expand the work of the Slade Centre to other parts of the country. The Queensway Trust in Birmingham had suddenly had to stop using donkeys, due to a change in government policy: previously people on work-experience had been funded to run the project. The children who had been enjoying donkey rides on a weekly basis suddenly found the donkeys were no longer arriving, and I knew from our own experiences what a disappointment it was going to be for them. I decided that, as the Slade Centre was restricted to working within an area of 25 miles of Exeter, a new charity would have to be started, and we decided to call it 'The Elisabeth Svendsen Trust for Children and Donkeys'. Stuart Way, the Charity Commissioner who had helped me so much in the earlier days, and had now retired due to ill health, helped me in setting up this new charity, along with John Lovell, our Slade Centre Trustee and patient solicitor. John has been such a great help to us over the years and both Brian and I highly respect him and his advice, and are deeply grateful to him.

With the help of these experts the charity was set up, with Birmingham in mind as the first venue. Sue Brennan, a qualified A.I. (British Horse Society Advanced Instructor), who previously worked for the Queensway Trust, was ready and willing to join us and we knew our Inspector, Bert Duncan, would supervise the project. Pat Feather was also keen to be involved. The application was duly made to the Charity Commission and we awaited confirmation that The Elisabeth Svendsen Trust (EST for short) was accepted and registered as a charity.

I have always been interested in children as well as donkeys, and the necessity for training future generations on the needs of donkeys is never far from my mind. The Donkey Breed Society run Junior Camps using the Slade Centre facilities during the holidays and I am only too happy to oblige. Wonderfully organized by Rosemary Clarke and Margaret Taylor, the children spend a happy week practically living with the donkeys. I was amused whilst watching the 'handy donkey' classes to see the child doing the jump and the donkey walking placidly round it.

We had been approached by the RSPCA to hold similar camps for their junior members, and Julie took it in hand to organize a wonderful day for them, starting early in the morning and covering as much of donkey care as was possible in one day. We always send the children away with a donkey book as a happy memento, and I sincerely hope that all these children will remain donkey lovers as they grow up.

The question of research had always been a thorny problem to me. Whilst we needed to know all we could about the donkeys and their welfare I was determined that no donkey should suffer during any trials that we carried out. To make quite sure that not only ourselves but other charities did the same, I decided to set up a committee comprising some of the top people in the country so that we could draw up some guidelines for future use: these were for use in the Sanctuary, but it was thought they could be used throughout the country. Brian Singleton, a retired Director of the Animal Health Trust, agreed to take the chair and on the team were Professor Murray of Glasgow University, Professor Anderson of Liverpool University, Bill Jordan, John Fowler, Roy Harrington, Derek Taverner of the Home Office and myself. We had two meetings in London and were able to define quite clearly what we all accepted as 'normal practice' and what we considered would be 'intrusive research'. I feel this official guideline will now be very helpful to all those wishing to further animal welfare without any suffering to the animals.

We get many interesting visitors to the Sanctuary and when I was away in Mexico John Stirling, the film producer, had visited. He wished to make a film of my life and the lives of six donkeys. I just felt it wasn't right at this time, and had to turn the offer down. I think I'd rather any film about my life, if such a thing were ever to be made, should be much later on. At that time we were so busy and working hard for the future, and I felt our job was far from ended.

By this time we had over 3,800 donkeys in our care. Our second vet, Fiona Taylor, left to travel around the world and John Fowler needed to find a replacement. Looking after animals is certainly not a 9 a.m. to 5 p.m. job and for two vets to provide veterinary cover twenty-four hours a day, seven days a week, at all our farms, was proving quite a task. Brian and I had a long talk with John and decided we would write to veterinary practices in the area to ask if they would like to associate with the charity, by putting either one or two vets on our list so that we had their expertise to call on when the work became too much. Eventually, after a lot of discussion, we selected Peter Ikin's practice in Sidmouth. Apart from being nearby, we got on very well with Peter and he had seven fully qualified veterinary people in his practice. He immediately agreed to take on a new person who would be allocated full-time to the Sanctuary, and it was arranged that we could call on any of the other vets we needed in times of crisis. We accepted his offer with alacrity and I felt much more comfortable that we had so much expertise to call upon.

In fact it was not just the Veterinary Department that was being over-stretched. Some of the terrible cruelty cases and donkey problems having to be dealt with by the Welfare Department were taking their toll. One morning Roy Harrington came down to my office, and I was appalled at how ill he looked, and how he suddenly seemed to lose the thread of the conversation. He kept harping back to a very difficult case that we'd had some years ago, and seemed completely disorientated and worried. I wasn't surprised when his wife, Sandra, came in the next morning and said that Roy wasn't very well and was going to see the doctor. In fact it proved much worse than that, and Roy had a complete nervous breakdown which meant he had to leave his job. Fortunately we had a pension plan in hand for senior staff who became ill or had to take early retirement, and this did at least mean that Roy could retire in some comfort. His wife, Sandra, who had been with me for many years, would of course be able to stay on at the Sanctuary and provide some extra income for the family.

Paul, who was already involved in the rehabilitation side of the donkeys, agreed to take over the running of the Welfare Department completely, and found his time more than fully occupied in view of this extra large commitment. He had to start travelling all round the country following up direct complaints of cruelty, arranging courses and lectures, not only for our own staff but also for staff of the RSPCA, who were keen and interested in our expertise and with whom we were now liaising closely, and with his chief welfare officers, to make sure all the voluntary inspectors were kept up to date.

The year ended with the most delightful donation. A telephone call was received from a Mrs Bourne saying that she and her family were very fond of donkeys and she would like to donate a bracelet to the Donkey Sanctuary and asked if we would accept this. Obviously we are pleased to receive any donation, of any sort, and agreed happily, suggesting that she sent it and every effort would be made to sell it for a good price. However, Mrs Bourne thought it better that the bracelet went through one of the London auction houses and suggested Bonhams, as her son knew somebody there. She wished specifically to confirm that we were a registered charity and that if she gave us this gift in total then it could be put to a special use. At that time a new intensive care unit for the isolation facilities was just being built and any money towards the project would be a great help.

We heard no more for many weeks and then received a phone call to say the auction was the following Friday at Bonhams and could a brief description, around one hundred words, of the Donkey Sanctuary be

(ABOVE) *Donkey Breed Society Juniors enjoying their training.*

(BELOW) (from left to right) *The grandchildren: Kate, Dawn, Mark and Simon.*

written to include the story of Islander, Blackie in Spain and Timothy, the poor donkey whose ears had been vandalized. This was so that the auctioneer could specifically mention that the money raised from the sale of the bracelet was going to the Donkey Sanctuary. A hundred words seemed rather a tall order to give so much information so, being in London during that week, I decided to call in. Bonhams were very pleasant and after I had explained the work of the Sanctuary to them, they offered a catalogue so I could see a picture of the bracelet. To my amazement this turned out to be a Cartier diamond bracelet and was featured on the front cover with a suggested price of £14,000 to £18,000!

Having recovered from the shock I decided to attend the auction personally to see what the bracelet made. After an extremely nail-biting two and half hours, lot 243 was announced and was eventually purchased at £19,000 by a very quiet gentleman seated in front of me who only joined the bidding at the very last moment. Overcome at the price and the knowledge that this amount would pay for the complete unit, I bent forward to thank the gentleman on behalf of all the donkeys. He immediately asked if I was Mrs Svendsen and he said, 'I am Mr Bourne.' It transpired that this was Mrs Bourne's son who had always loved and admired his mother's bracelet, which had been a present to her from his father, and he felt sad that it was going out of the family although he fully appreciated his mother's desire to put the proceeds towards the funds of the Sanctuary. Rather than try to strike a deal with his mother to buy the bracelet, which he felt could never have been very satisfactory because whatever price they reached would not have been an independent one, he decided to let it go through the auction and purchase it, the purpose being to give it to his wife on her birthday. This delightful story shows how much kindness there is in the world and has an almost fairy-tale ending for all concerned.

Chapter · 10

A PERFORMING DONKEY
1989

I COULD HARDLY believe that Sarah was twenty-one this year. We arranged a birthday party for her with a dinner at a Honiton restaurant, and all her friends turned up. Sarah had left the hotel and since the previous November had been helping at the Slade Centre. It was lovely having her home but I knew that she wanted to get away and was looking for a suitable yacht charter job. Niels was keeping his ears open while he was in the Mediterranean and offered that Sarah could stay with him so that she might be on the spot to take up any jobs that came along. Eventually Sarah took up Niels's offer.

Sailing must run not only in the family, but also among the executives. Brian Bagwell was a member of Sidmouth Sailing Club from the age of ten and sailed regularly competitively. Paul also had been brought up in our sailing environment, and he decided he would enjoy regular racing locally as a relaxation from work. Having spent a year suffering from crewing problems, he decided to go in for a Laser – a single-handed racing machine. By chance Brian had a brand new Laser tucked away in his garage. His wife, Eunice, had bought it for his fiftieth birthday present but, for some reason, Brian had never sailed it; he joked it was not fast enough for him. After a friendly negotiation, Paul bought it and, to commemorate the fact that Brian never sailed it, he named it 'Bagger's Folly'!

Paul really loved that yacht, and, wet or fine, windy or calm, he sailed every free minute, progressing to the National Championship at Poole Harbour where the photograph was taken.

We all need relaxation sometimes and we had some wonderful family holidays on the Broads. I bought a lovely old cruiser hoping to spend time on it as I grew older but, once again, time was the problem and I never had time to use it fully.

June, apart from doing an immense amount for IDPT, was helping voluntarily in the Donkey Sanctuary. As we were living together at Little Slade we had to be careful that we didn't talk donkeys morning, noon and night! My days were already very long and we both found it hard to turn off the subject of donkeys in the evening.

I was dreading going to Villanueva de la Vera again, but all too soon it was Shrove Tuesday. This time we were taking the model donkey and so Neil Harvey and June set off two days earlier for the long drive with it to the village. I flew out with Trini Hanson, our interpreter, and we met them at Madrid airport to drive the final leg together. They had already had quite a 'run-in' with the Spanish authorities before I met them. On arriving at the airport parking lot Neil and June had put the money in the slot, the barrier had lifted, but before they had time to get the trailer through, the barrier had dropped again between the Land Rover and the trailer. The impact completely smashed the arm of the barrier. The conversation that ensued must have been quite amusing because, although June has some knowledge of Spanish, I don't think she was able to cope with the torrent of Spanish words that poured forth from the car park attendant's lips! By the time I had joined them, however, all was very peaceful and I noticed that, not only was the barrier lifted as we went (this was the exit barrier and still intact), but the attendant stood at attention firmly holding it up until the whole of the vehicle was through.

We picked up Derek Baker, our contact vet who lives in Spain, and drove down to the village. We took the model donkey in the box to show the Mayor and after two hours of persuasion he finally came out and had a look at it. We rolled it out of the horse box and he gazed at it with great admiration. It certainly was very beautiful, and we'd had it built to take the weight of a 20-stone man. However, he shook his head in dismay and said he didn't think the villagers would be pleased to have it, but that he would mention it to them. Unfortunately some of the local people who had already been enjoying the previous two days of the Fiesta happened to see the donkey. Later in the day we returned to the village to try and get a place for June and Trini to stand on the balcony the following day, from which June could take photographs. We went down to the village, leaving Neil to look after the trailer where it was parked. We had been trying to negotiate for a balcony in the local bar, when Neil arrived, red in the face, saying, 'Please come back straight away. There's an enormous gang of youths around the trailer, and I'm afraid they're going to smash it.' He was very right. When we got back, to our horror, we found men with axes already attacking the back of the trailer in order to get at the model donkey. They turned on us as we

(ABOVE) *Somebody loved our model donkey.*
(BELOW) *Paul leading in his Laser.*

tried to get into the vehicle and we were lucky to get in safely; Neil put his foot down on the accelerator and we managed to get out of the village. As we left they shouted at us, 'If you bring the donkey back tomorrow, the donkey will be axed and so will you.'

During the evening at our hotel, the Mayor rang and spoke to Trini; she came back with a very long face to say that we had been advised by the Mayor not to come at all, because feelings were so high in the village that we had offered a model donkey instead of a real live one. The next morning we were up early, and standing in the village square, where we had to suffer taunts and shouts and jostling, until that poor donkey, already deafened by the sound of guns exploding in its ears, was pulled out of the town hall to start its terrible journey through the streets. This time the mood was extremely hostile and at one stage a group of five men rushed at Neil, June (she had refused to stay on the balcony and had joined us to follow the donkey round the village) and myself, literally knocking me to the ground. Neil and June quickly picked me up and we managed to keep up with the, by then, almost desperate animal. At this stage one of the men with a 12-bore shotgun, supposedly loaded with paper instead of shot, fired almost directly at us, and a terracotta pot full of plants smashed to smithereens and showered down on our heads. We still carried on and at the end, despite threats and shouts, we managed to get the donkey away and off down a side street again, where it could recover. We never saw the Mayor during all this time; he was hiding out of sight, and it wasn't only the donkey that had tears running down its face by the end of that terrible day.

On our return home, I made an appointment to see the Spanish Ambassador in London, and the *Daily Mail*, who had accompanied us on this trip and had been as horrified as we were at the treatment meted out, not only to the donkey but to our team, asked if they could come with me. I refused, as I knew I had to see him on my own and I didn't want the press interfering and making it sound as if we were after publicity, rather than stopping the donkey being used, which was our only aim. Senor Bellacasa, the Ambassador, was extremely kind and quite upset when he heard of the events of that day. I think he had felt everybody had been exaggerating before, but I'd taken photographs and I know that he believed me when I told him the true story. The *Daily Mail* were waiting outside, and to my horror, having heard how he'd promised to help me all he could, they rang him from a local phone box and said, 'If Mrs Svendsen comes back could we take a picture of you both together?' To my surprise he agreed, and so I went back into the Embassy into one of the beautiful big reception rooms, and there I had my photograph taken with Senor Bellacasa, and for the first time began to be hopeful that perhaps next year's terrible events could be stopped.

I'd hoped that all the tragedies were over for the time being, but as I arrived back from London June met me, looking pale and upset. I couldn't believe what she told me: my darling Eeyore had died in the night, and I hadn't been there. Nobody had realized he was ill, but he suddenly collapsed, and before I got home, he had died. We found out later that it was due, of course, to the terrible start in life he'd had. When I'd rescued Smartie I really didn't think she would live – she was so thin and emaciated, and the fact that she was heavily in foal made her recovery almost more miraculous. Eeyore had been born very small but apparently healthy, but the autopsy showed that part of his heart was totally deformed and he would never have been able to live any longer, no matter what treatment he'd received. Poor Eeyore – he'd been such a naughty little donkey, but he'd given such pleasure to so many thousands of children, and especially to me, and I really couldn't believe he'd gone. There were, however, many more donkeys to be looked after. I already had around 3,500 in care, and there just wasn't time to mourn for long.

I wrote and told Sarah, as she had loved Eeyore. Sarah had been accepted on board a yacht called *Edgewater* and her main problem seemed to be the fact that the colleague with whom she shared a cabin had a parrot to which she was very attached. Sarah wrote to me asking that I get a book on parrots sent out in the hope that she could communicate better with her. Sarah was at that time on route for Antigua, and was thrilled to be crossing the Atlantic.

It was really exciting to go up to Birmingham in April for the Elisabeth Svendsen Trust official launch. We had now appointed the trustees – Pat, Paul, Brian, myself and Steve Springford, who had made a wonderful video for us entitled *Down Among the Donkeys*. Steve was a director of a video production company and a great supporter of our charities. The first mobile unit was started in Birmingham under Sue Brennan, and Pat took on the task of making sure that everything ran smoothly. The donkeys were in stables at Sue Brennan's house; at first only four donkeys were taken out to the schools, but because so many children were involved, the number had to be increased to eight. About two hundred children a week participate – their ages ranging between 2½ and 19 (those too big to ride are taught to drive) – from 16 schools. During the winter mainstream schools are visited, usually with one donkey, to teach donkey welfare. The response from the schools has been overwhelming. Bert Duncan was always at hand, living in that area, and I was absolutely delighted to see the joy on the children's faces when our very first visit was made to a school. Hopefully we were going to start a similar unit in Glasgow before too long, which would bring pleasure to another group of city children, equally in need of help.

We get many calls from the public reporting donkeys in poor condition. One such call was received by our Voluntary Inspector, Jimmy Gough, who spoke to a very upset and anguished lady regarding a donkey owned by a friend of hers. She explained that the donkey had a terribly large abscess on its neck but the owner totally refused to have a vet and the lady was deeply concerned that the donkey was suffering and in great pain. It is never easy for our inspectors to go into a household and ask to see their donkey about which we have had a complaint, but Jimmy is one of our most experienced officers and he was well received with his tactful comments and immediately taken to see the 'suffering' donkey. The donkey had been so well fed that a large roll of fat had appeared on its neck, and not an abscess, and Jimmy was very pleased to be able to give the advice that slightly fewer daily treats be given so it could slim down a little.

The second call we received in the same period was of a different nature altogether. We were told that the donkey was in a terrible condition, looked really ill, never brayed and took no interest in people. Again a concerned inspector had the job of visiting and once again the situation was rapidly solved – the donkey was in fact a llama!

I managed to get away for a long weekend to visit Clive and Grainne in Cambridge. They had spent the last year in Japan as Clive had been working with an American company in Boston who manufactured a machine that analysed blood and urine samples to detect and identify abnormalities. These varied from impending cancer to neurological disorders. There were some problems to be sorted out in Japan, and so Clive had taken on the job. Now they had returned – for two reasons. The main one perhaps was that they were expecting their first baby, and the second that Clive wanted to obtain his Doctorate and had been offered the opportunity to take his PhD in Cambridge. It was lovely to see them again, and with a new grandchild on the way, for me things could not have been better.

Little Katrina was born on June 5th. Clive sounded just a little subdued when he rang me two days later. It seemed Katrina had a heart defect of some sort, but modern medicine being so advanced we all assumed it could be sorted out, and happily celebrated the newest little Svendsen's

Eeyore in his prime.

arrival. Paul, Uschi, Sarah, Dawn, Simon and I descended on Cambridge for a lovely christening party.

Brian and I were looking at a farm which had been offered – Woods Farm – near Ottery St Mary, within easy reach of our current properties. It was a delightful farm, with many outbuildings, two houses on the property and 132 acres of land. Once again Brian found himself deeply involved in the negotiations, not only for this farm but also the farm over the hill that was coming up for sale. Unfortunately the second farm proved too expensive and Brian was unable to work out a deal, but we were able to purchase Woods Farm, and, with the authority of the trustees for the purchase, and after a careful valuation, a figure was agreed. It is a glorious place for donkeys, with plenty of barns so that the winter is no problem. Once again we had an aspiring young manager who'd been through our selection programme, and Rob Nichols was appointed as manager for the new farm. His wife, Christine, had also been working with us for many years, but had taken maternity leave for the birth of her first child. They loved Woods Farm and settled down immediately. The house alongside was earmarked for Julie and Charles Courtney, who were living at Brookfield Farm, where Charles was manager; it was becoming apparent that we needed more help in the office and Charles seemed an excellent person to bring into the management team. We again had a good manager, Malcolm Salter, waiting to move into Brookfield Farm.

At this time a most delightful little donkey with a very special talent came in. Mrs Cooper had written to us five years previously, asking if we could possibly take her donkey, who was called Concorde, when the time came that she could no longer care for him; she was getting on in years and suffering from arthritis. We knew we might have problems, as very well loved donkeys take much longer to settle in than donkeys that have come from uncaring backgrounds. However, Concorde arrived and settled in very well after his isolation period, and was transferred to Town Barton Farm under the care of John Pile. As many past owners do, Mrs Cooper asked if she could come and visit Concorde, and of course John was delighted to agree. It was amazing how Concorde immediately recognized his past owner, and she only had to go to the fence at the side of the field and call his name, and over he came. Aged between 17 and 18, he was a delightful grey donkey. As John and Mrs Cooper stood talking, and she was admiringly loving and stroking Concorde, she turned to John and asked, 'Has he shown you his special trick, then?' John looked suitably puzzled, as he had no idea that

Concorde had any particular talents. Turning back to Concorde, Mrs Cooper said firmly, 'Do your party trick then,' and to John's surprise Concorde immediately lay on the ground, rolled right over and stood up, looking really proud of himself. Mrs Cooper fished in her large bag and pulled out a packet of polo mints for Concorde, who was obviously expecting to be rewarded for his performance. John was suitably amazed, and after Mrs Cooper had left, quietly went back to the field and walked up to Concorde. 'Do your party trick, then,' he said, very firmly, and to his complete joy and amazement, Concorde responded. Very quickly and quietly, so that the donkeys wouldn't see (as giving titbits is strictly prohibited) Concorde received a large juicy carrot.

When I regaled two of our overseas inspectors, Sharon and Bob Drakeley with this story, they told me of a similar one; a friend of theirs who is a horse dealer, John Hancock, fell in love with a beautiful little Appaloosan pony, and bought it at Market Drayton market. After training the pony for some time to pull a cart, he set off proudly to Market Drayton on their Monday market day. Arriving in the main square, he tapped the pony on the neck a few times with his long whip to turn it to the right, and to his absolute horror the pony dropped between the shafts, almost tipping the cart over, and lay apparently unconscious on the road. As you can imagine, a crowd quickly gathered and a very embarrassed John had to admit he had no idea what was wrong with the pony – he certainly hadn't hit him hard. However, suddenly and with no warning, the pony stood up, and the journey was resumed. Exactly the same thing happened on the following market day, and John then realized that it was something to do with tapping the pony on the side of his neck, but he was still extremely puzzled. Fortunately an elderly gentleman who lived nearby had seen the pony in the past and explained that he came from a circus, and had been taught that if he was tapped on the left side of his neck he should fall down and play 'dead'!

Paul accompanied June and I on another trip to Mexico. Conditions were still bad at San Bernabe market. In another of the little villages, Capulhuac, we spent a very busy day. Capulhuac has a wood market, which is purely used for barter; no money changes hands. People from as far as 15 miles away travel there carrying wood which they have taken from the local forest, and exchange this for goods. The donkeys and horses are very tired on arrival, and we felt that if there was a specific enclosed area, they could rest and be given any medical treatment necessary. With Aline I went to see the Mayor of the village to try and arrange for some of the donkeys to be able to stay in a 'set aside' area for the day. The Mayor agreed, and showed us a beautiful yard which he said we could have for our exclusive use. We'd had a strange request from our veterinary surgeon that, instead of using gentian violet antiseptic (purple) spray to treat the wounds of the donkeys in the village, we should use a clear spray. Apparently, taking the wood from the forest was illegal, and up to now the police had been unable to trace any of the culprits. However they were now aware that if a donkey's wounds had been treated with purple spray, it had been at the clinic at Capulhuac and so they were now fining the owners. With the help of one of the drug companies we managed to get a clear liquid.

We continued to use purple spray in other areas and I was quite amused to watch one elderly Mexican. He'd obviously come into the village very early and tied his donkey to a post, which was near where our clinic was set up. At the end of the day the poor donkey was still standing waiting for his owner, and he had the most appalling long distorted feet. Unable to drive away and leave the donkey there, I told Guillermo (the new IDPT vet in Mexico) to clip his feet and treat the wounds, which he did. The donkey looked completely different; apart from having neat little purple hooves, he also had his various cuts and wounds treated. Just before we drove away the owner came rolling along the street – it was quite obvious where he'd been for almost the whole day – and he stopped by the donkey, looking at it in amazement. He then decided it couldn't possibly be his donkey and lurched up past the next few posts. Realizing there was no other donkey tied up, he came back and stood looking at it, scratching his head, and eventually he untied the donkey, slumped over the saddle, and the donkey, knowing its way home, set off with a very bemused owner.

Paul was interested in the overseas work. Since we were so busy abroad, it was decided that Paul should take over the running of the Mexican project. We approached the International League for the Protection of Horses to see if they would agree to share the cost of two mobile clinics, as the conditions were equally terrible for horses and ponies in Mexico. After looking into the matter, George Stephen of the ILPH willingly agreed. Arrangements were then put in hand by Paul for two mobile clinics which would treat horses, ponies, mules and donkeys. We all feel that this close liaison between charities is absolutely essential in Third World countries where the maximum aid is needed with the minimum cost.

In Ireland, Paddy Barrett's mother had died. Brian had visited, advising on administration and arranging housing for the donkeys. Paul moved

(ABOVE) *Working equines in Mexico.*
(BELOW) *The joint IDPT and ILPH teams in San Bernabe market.*

there for two months helping with sorting out problems and in the setting up of the rehabilitation scheme. Uschi, Simon and Dawn moved over there with him and all got involved, as they lived in a mobile home in Paddy's garden and the children attended the local school.

I had long known Pam Jermyn, a member of the Donkey Breed Society, who'd taken a great interest in the Restfields Home for many years. Her son was now a solicitor in Cork, and we made contact and used his professional services for the legal matters relating to the Restfields.

A team from BBC television accompanied us on our next trip to Kenya, as they were making a film to be called *Mama Punda* which is Swahili for 'mother of the donkeys'. The film was broadcast on BBC2. We held our donkey competition in Lamu, and over 160 donkeys attended. As promised, we gave good prizes – the winning owners received Walkman sets and rosettes for their donkeys, plus 500 Kenyan shillings (more than a week's wages). Abdalla told us afterwards what an enormous difference it had made to the villagers, and how they were now determined to keep their donkeys in tip-top condition in order to win the prizes next year.

We did our usual trip round all the islands, exhausting though it is, and were delighted to see that on Chundwa and Faza, two of the far distant islands, the donkeys were beginning to show definite signs of improvement. On our visit to Matondoni, we were surprised to see practically the whole village waiting for us as our boat anchored in the soft mud as near to the village as we could get. Struggling with all our equipment through the thick mud, I was surprised to see one of the people in the crowd rush forward, stumbling through the mud, regard-less of his long robes which dragged behind him, and alarmed to find that he fell on his knees at my feet, crying, 'Bahati – m'toto, m'toto.' He had tears pouring down his face and I realized that it was Bahati's owner. For a heart-stopping moment I was sure Bahati had died, and turned to Abdalla and asked, 'Abdalla, what's happened, has Bahati died?' Abdalla grinned cheerfully and pointed up to the crowd of villagers standing with a rather plump-looking donkey and next to her, the sweetest little foal I had ever seen. This was Bahati's 'm'toto', the African name for a baby foal. To everybody's joy and surprise, Bahati had recovered magnificently, enough to present her poor owner with the gift of a little foal. The welcome we received that day in Matondoni was out of this world. Coconut matting had been laid for us to work on and instead of the usual eight donkeys arriving for treatment, over a hundred appeared, the leader of the village having been so impressed with

Bahati's progress that he had insisted on every person bringing their donkey to be dosed. The villagers had even gone to the extent of getting Coca Cola for us to drink: an absolute luxury, and greatly appreciated.

We were making two trips a year to Kenya to treat the donkeys, and it was certainly rewarding to see the results. On one of the islands lived what I considered was a very old lady, until Abdalla told me she was only in her late forties. She'd lost all her family and lived only on scraps given to her by the people in the village. It gave me great pleasure on each trip to give her a little bag with various gifts in, and I always slipped in a few hundred shillings, which I knew made all the difference to her life.

After my first gift, Abdalla drew me on one side and said, 'Do you know what she's done with the money?'

I said, 'No, tell me, Abdalla.'

He said, 'She's been round giving some money to all the villagers who've been helping to feed her over the last few years since her husband died. She now feels she can hold her head up with pride again.'

It made me feel really humble.

We take toys out for the Lamu children, and vitamins, and it's wonderful to see the expression on these children's faces when they receive a little toy car which has cost us perhaps 10p in England, and which our children here would not even bother to look at. To them it becomes the pride of their life, and they will still be playing with it when we return six months later.

On one of the Kenyan trips, Bill Jordan and I were the only passengers in the tiny Pioneer aircraft and the captain had met us off our dhow and walked with us to the plane, chatting about our work. 'Seat belt fastened?' he asked me, looking back, as we taxied along the tiny airstrip. Bill, as was normal practice for the front seat passenger in the intense heat on the ground, was leaning out holding the door open for air. As I nodded, Bill shut the door, fastened his belt and with the engine revving we set off down the runway. Suddenly, I was pressing against the belt as the pilot applied full brakes and we shuddered to a stop, slightly askew.

'What's the matter?' I yelled.

'Elephant dung,' the pilot replied calmly.

'Can't we run through it?' I asked naively.

'Problem is,' he replied, 'when one elephant crosses the runway, there are usually more, so we have to wait,' and wait we did, for ten minutes, before he risked taking off. Not the sort of problem encountered at Heathrow!

On another trip June and I had to go up to Isiolo, which is in northern Kenya, as we had been asked to visit by Chris Dunston, a Peace Corps Volunteer, who was working with a Danish Welfare Community project there. Not having travelled to this part of Kenya before, I was very careful to arrange that we would be met at the airstrip to be taken the hour's drive to Isiolo. The actual airstrip itself is situated in the bush near the Samburu Game Reserve and we were the only passengers on the tiny plane when it dropped down to an apparently deserted area. We climbed out into the blazing sun hoping to see a vehicle waiting for us, but to our horror there was nobody there. We were met by a rather laconic guard who was leaning on what can only be described as an antique rifle and who didn't seem particularly interested in our reasons for waiting at his small airport. The heat was intense and we struggled across to a small bench nearby which thankfully had a small makuti (palm leaf) roof cover. We gazed hopefully around for a sign of the arrival of the vehicle and it was most depressing to see no dust stirring anywhere on the horizon. As the sound of the departing plane faded away, we began to have serious doubts that we were in the right place and I spent some time looking through my notes to ensure that we had in fact got the right airstrip, the right time and the right day.

I had noticed a very small hut situated a short walk away and eventually, the call of nature making its presence felt, I wandered across to find a toilet situated inside the hut. There was a front door which I opened and looking in I was shocked to see that there was no back to the hut and the toilet seat was just supported on two wooden boards! Still, looking out through the back I could see there was nobody in sight so I nervously sat down on the seat. To my horror I realized there was absolutely nothing under the seat and within seconds a small trickle appeared between my feet and ran down through the closed door in front. I wasn't enamoured with the plumbing in Samburu!

We waited on the bench under the makuti roof for nearly three hours before, in desperation, we returned to the guard with the antique gun. Using his walkie-talkie he called someone to explain our predicament. It took three-quarters of an hour for a jeep to arrive from the Samburu Game Reserve and they advised us that for a fee they would run us back to the game reserve for the night. By this time we had given up all hope of seeing anybody from Isiolo. We were just climbing into the jeep when a cloud of dust appeared and a truck drew up. A very flustered Chris Dunston explained that they'd had two breakdowns on the journey from Isiolo and were deeply upset for being late. We all travelled to the Samburu Game Reserve and had a brief meal there, which was very·

(ABOVE) *Lining up to be judged.*

(BELOW) *Bahati and foal, two years later.*

welcome after our parching time in the scrub, and we arranged that we would go on to Isiolo the following morning.

In Isiolo we found a most unusual project taking place. They were trying to use donkeys to plough, and had taught the local women how to make the harness necessary for this project. In many countries oxen are used for this purpose but they are extremely expensive animals both to purchase and to keep, and gradually countries in the Third World are becoming more and more aware of the agricultural value of the donkey. We were able to offer a great deal of help and advice and also to dose all the donkeys used in the scheme, which we could see was going to be a tremendous help to the local people.

We'd also been called to Tanzania, where the Germans were working on a similar project. It was a long drive from Mombasa, and at one stage we thought our vehicle wouldn't make it. However eventually we arrived at the small community where the ploughing project was in operation. Here, both local people and those from as far as a hundred miles away were being brought in and taught how to use donkeys for cultivation. The funding came from Germany and Switzerland in the form of bicycles, and the administrator had to exchange these for donkeys in the village. He wasn't amused when I pointed out that all the donkeys he'd exchanged for bicycles were elderly. Until donkeys are regularly dosed with anthelmintic they can die between the ages of 11 and 12 in that part of the world, and most of the donkeys he had purchased were over 10 years old. However, he learnt very quickly, and I gave a lecture to his team of trainees and agricultural officers, and they spent a great deal of time taking us round the country showing us their work, which was most impressive. Many oxen in that part of the world have died from diseases carried by the tsetse fly, and donkeys (which have more resistance to certain strains) are being brought into use more and more throughout the whole of the Third World.

At the Sanctuary the number of donkeys had increased substantially, mainly because of the work being done by Paddy Barrett in Ireland. He rang us one day to say that, at the request of the local Gardai in County Mayo, he had been present at an auction sale, where a group of twenty-three mares, many in foal, who had been turned away by their owners and left to roam free, had been rounded up by the Gardai and put in their pound. An auction was held to try to sell these animals which had become an embarrassment to the authorities, but very few had been sold. The fate awaiting those unsold was horrendous. As Paddy told us on the telephone, in the next field he could see there was a large bulldozer

(ABOVE) *Kambi Odha Women's Group harnessing their donkeys in Isiolo, northern Kenya.*
(BELOW) *Training of local farmer to use donkeys for ploughing.*

already busy digging a hole, and he'd been told that the donkeys which had not been sold were to be shot and buried immediately. Many of them were in foal, and Paddy was almost in tears. We told him to do what he could to get them, and send them back to us if he hadn't room in his Sanctuary, and in response to his desperate appeal for the lives of the donkeys, the Gardai allowed him to take them away with no charge. Many of these donkeys were then brought over to our Sanctuary here. It's not really our policy to bring donkeys back to the UK, but we couldn't let those donkeys meet such a horrific end, and so near home, without attempting to take all of them.

This year 420 people took part in Donkey Week, but it still felt very personal and individual, and the donkeys and staff enjoyed the week as we hope our supporters did. Moving so many people around could have presented many difficulties, but our coach operators dealt with all emergencies, and each farm visit went with a swing. I think the letter from Cindy summed it up:

Dear Mrs Svendsen,

Once again I am writing to say an enormous 'thank you' for organising another Donkey Week this year. Prior to my first Donkey Week in 1984, I had spent almost thirty-five years searching for friends with similar interests to myself. I never gave up hope, but most of the friends I made were just acquaintances who could not understand my love of animals and the countryside. I shall there-fore be eternally grateful to you because since attending Donkey Weeks I have made so many good friends all over Britain.

Many, many thanks.
Cindy Sinclair

A trip to East Berlin for the 13th WAAVP Conference in August proved very successful, and I was able to meet the 'savage' Poitou donkeys in East Berlin Zoo. I just couldn't believe they were kept behind such thick bars, and the horror on the face of the Zoo Director when I insisted on going in and cuddling the donkeys was a sight to behold. He was quite sure that they were fierce and wild, and would attack. I think he was confusing them with the Kiang donkeys or the Somali wild asses which can indeed be very difficult.

Fiesta was the main event during the summer; after months of sun we had a cool day – a miracle, for everyone came to visit the donkeys instead of lying on the beach! Virginia McKenna, actress and star of *Born Free*, who with her husband and son is involved in Zoo Check, had agreed to be a patron of the Slade Centre and she did us the great honour of opening the Fiesta and presenting some of the prizes to the Slade Centre children. Thanks to Pat and Julie's hard work of organization, hundreds of supporters rallied round to provide goodies to sell, ran stalls, organized games and helped to make a record net profit of over £7,000!

During the year Julie was appointed Vice-Principal of the Slade Centre so that she could stand in and the high standards would be maintained, whilst Pat was busy working in Birmingham with EST.

I sometimes could not believe the way things worked out for the charities. The team running the mobile unit for EST in Birmingham was marvellous, and was most enthusiastically welcomed at the schools for the handicapped. The joy of these children in petting and riding the donkeys was touching. I had been dreading the winter, when the children would lose their riding lessons due to the cold and rain. Funding for an indoor centre seemed a dream, but miracles do happen! A letter from a trust fund in London, which had already donated £1,000, intimated they might help put up further funding, and, as an indication of their seriousness, sent me another cheque for £10,000! I rang to thank them personally, but I'm afraid I was so overwhelmed I broke down on the phone and was unable to finish the conversation. Until now, it had seemed such an uphill battle even to get enough to pay the teams' wages. The gentleman on the other end of the line, who wished to remain anonymous, was extremely understanding and suggested I had a cup of coffee and rang him back later. This I did, and was invited to his office in London. You can imagine how I felt when, having seated me carefully and ensured a coffee was to hand, he offered to fund the building of a new centre. I walked the streets of London in a happy daze, but had one problem – land. We needed an area near our handicapped schools, and land in Birmingham would be expensive but, without it, we could not put up the building I had been promised. So – a second miracle. Some time before one of our most dedicated donkey supporters had offered some land to use for donkeys in transit, but because of administration difficulties we had been unable to take up her wonderful offer. With my heart in my mouth, I rang her to see if she would still consider the offer of land and, bless her, she did better, and offered twelve acres as a free gift on which to build an EST centre, plus the use of some of her grazing land. (We spent a considerable amount of time after this having the land surveyed, plans drawn up, etc, but unfortunately due to access problems, planning permission was not granted. The day we were advised that permission had been refused was a sad one.)

Donkeys need miracles too, and when a factory in Oxford was forced to close and all the staff were made redundant, two donkeys got the help they needed. Despite their own problems the staff were really concerned over the fate of two donkeys who had been in a field next to their factory and whom they had cared for during the last eight years. The donkeys were Mrs Brown, who was over forty years old, and her son, Charlie, who was blind in one eye. It was quite heartbreaking to hear of how close the staff and the donkeys had become and how desperately worried the staff were about their future. We promised we would do our best to give the donkeys the same loving care and attention they had been receiving. The donkeys were in due course collected. Unfortunately for Mrs Brown the move proved too much and she died having been with us for only a short while. Once donkeys exceed the age of forty it seems all too easy for a change in their lifestyle to bring about problems and although Mrs Brown had four happy months with us, her will to live must have gone and she quietly slipped away, or perhaps she realized that Charlie was now safely in a home for life.

The year really ended with a bang; a freak bolt of lightning struck the main cable of the computer system, causing over £50,000-worth of damage! The storm hit at 7 p.m., on December 20th. Luckily no one was using the computers at the time, as they could have suffered an electric shock, and of course we were fully insured. Unfortunately our computer held all 85,000 records of our supporters and this, of course, played havoc with our Christmas posting. We were just working at our very busiest time and to have to stop for several days whilst the engineers desperately tried to put us back on-line was most frustrating. Fortunately it is practice to make a back-up copy of the computer data each day, and so nothing was actually lost except the most valuable thing we had at that moment – time. Our computer list has always been guarded most secretly. I think there's nothing more annoying than to send off a donation or a request for an item from a newspaper, and a short time later to find oneself flooded with unwanted mail. The names on charities' lists are particularly sought after by businesses and in fact by other charities, and some are willing to pay a fee of up to £10 for each individual name. Obviously a list the size of ours would immediately bring in a huge income, but we have never even considered it; we feel every subscriber has the right to privacy and we guard the names most jealously. We ended the year getting all the old typewriters out, trying to answer as many letters as we could.

Chapter · 11

I BECOME A SENIOR CITIZEN
1990

THE BAD weather continued in 1990. We were awakened one morning by tremendous gales, and the storm-force winds battered the Sanctuary again and again. We all rushed out, and at one stage there were seven of us in Buffalo Barn as 100-mile-an-hour gusts periodically lifted the roof. We frantically blocked up the Yorkshire boarding on the windward side to try and stop the through-gusts. The donkeys appeared to enjoy it all, and, from the safety of the outside yard, watched our desperate activities with great interest. In the end, we lost the roof on the old barn in the main yard, hundreds of slates, and some of our favourite trees, but no donkeys were hurt, and Buffalo Barn was still intact.

I had hoped that the staff would not realize that my birthday, which fell on January 23rd, would be my 60th, but of course I was wrong, and I don't remember ever having had such a birthday. Apart from the zimmer frame and wheelchair which were waiting to meet me at the door, balloons were placed on every stairway, and when I came into my office I couldn't believe the piles of gifts that rose high from my desk. Paul lurked around with a video camera, gleefully filming everything that happened, and especially my tearful comments when I was called down-stairs to find all the staff lined up with yet another set of gifts. I was then ushered outside, where I found Sam and Dobby, two of my favourite Slade Centre donkeys, with a cart all decorated, for me to be driven up to the Slade Centre. When I got there, what a surprise – an enormous party with the staff, teachers from the various schools and lots of children to help enjoy my cake and the celebrations. That's a birthday I certainly won't forget in a hurry, but I was very pleased to pass back the zimmer frame at the end of the day, having as yet no use for it – thankfully.

One of the nicest visits to the Sanctuary by television celebrities was that of Thora Hird, who wanted to include the Sanctuary on her programme,

Praise Be. She came with a small but dedicated team, and it was a real pleasure to show her round the Sanctuary. It had always been one of Thora's ambitions to drive a pony and cart, but she very happily settled for a donkey cart. Wilma had the great honour of pulling Thora Hird round our little lanes and down our drive, where the crew filmed her as part of the programme. Earlier that morning we had had a very happy event. A foal had been born to a donkey called Harriet, who had only been at the Sanctuary for two months. She had been rescued by a member of the Donkey Breed Society but, as the lady already had nine donkeys in her care and was short of room and shelter, she sent Harriet on to us. Although Harriet had only been with us for a short time she had settled down happily, obviously pleased to receive all the love, food and attention she needed, and it had been a very easy birth. I rather hoped, as I helped the little foal struggle to its feet, that it could be a filly, so that we could call it 'Thora'. However, a close inspection proved that we were not so lucky, but it was a delighted Thora Hird who was introduced to the little foal we named after her, even though he had to be called 'Thor'.

When the programme was televised on the BBC it evoked an enormous amount of interest in the Sanctuary and we had many letters from people who hadn't written before, particularly wanting to know more about Thor and whether they could have any photographs of him. We had to get a whole lot printed specially, and these were sent to many people in hospitals and nursing homes; the replies we received back were most rewarding. We look forward to another visit from Thora to see her 'nearly namesake'. She is an amazing lady; deeply devoted to animals and with a charming sense of humour and humility which one would not expect to find in somebody quite so famous.

On one of my frequent walks across to the Isolation Unit I arrived just in time to see a group of donkeys arriving from the North. As they came off the lorry the staff were carefully helping one very lame donkey to the ground when I looked at the top of the ramp and saw to my surprise the most beautiful donkey head I had seen for years. The donkey carefully picked its way down the ramp and as I took its halter and looked at it, I knew I was looking at one of the best donkeys I had seen in many years. He was called Holly and the more I looked at him, the more delighted I became: his conformation was excellent. It made a pleasant change to see a donkey in such excellent condition and with a lovely temperament. He nuzzled against me and put his head on my shoulder, not at all concerned about his recent long drive or that I was a total stranger.

I visited him regularly during his six weeks in isolation and decided

(ABOVE) *An emotional moment: my first rail card.*
(BELOW) *With Thora Hird: a break in the filming.*

that here was a donkey that could really represent his species at any show in the country. It is rather nice to feel that some of our donkeys from the Donkey Sanctuary can compete with the beautifully bred donkeys of the Donkey Breed Society and it was at this moment that I decided that we would enter one or two donkeys in some local shows to see how they got on. Of course Holly was to be my number one exhibit. We carefully selected another two donkeys which had been rescued earlier and had come into the Sanctuary in a bad condition but were now looking extremely well. Joanne and Tracey, two of my staff, were given the job of training the donkeys to see how well we could do in the show ring. I have not been disappointed, Holly has won almost every prize going and has been a constant pleasure and delight to us all.

I was appalled by the reports from one of the meetings of the Intergroup for Animal Welfare that many thousands of small birds were being shipped illegally into the country, many dead on arrival. During a discussion with Bill Jordan he explained that there were many problems at Heathrow, not so much for those birds which came by cargo transport, but for those which had been carried illegally in suitcases and which were then confiscated by HM Customs and Excise. Bill explained that, because of financial restrictions, various organizations had had to withdraw the facilities they'd made available previously to take these birds in after their isolation period with the Ministry was completed. There seemed little problem with the large birds which had a high market value. What was causing more concern were the very small birds with little market value and which were often in a very poor state, having travelled under such terrible conditions. Bill asked if there was any way I could help, knowing my interest in all types of animal life. I looked at our garden, decided that if I did without my garage I could turn this into three indoor units, and by erecting an enormous aviary, eighteen feet high, covering almost the whole of my back garden, to include trees, bushes and a lawn, this would make the most happy home for the poor birds caught up in this terrible trade. On my behalf Bill contacted the Chief Veterinary Officer in London, and I had a very nice letter from Mr Wiggins, part of which said, 'I have spoken to my staff at Heathrow and there would appear to be few difficulties in carrying out the procedure you outline, so when such birds turn up I have instructed staff to let me know, and I will get in touch with your goodself to make the necessary arrangements. Obviously it's impossible to make any predictions but, from time to time, the odd bird is abandoned which should fit the bill, and when this happens I will get in touch.'

I had great fun designing the aviary and making three large indoor compartments of different temperatures, to suit the different climates which the birds were used to. Obviously this was nothing to do with the Sanctuary and everything was provided by me personally, for my own satisfaction in giving these birds a good home.

I couldn't believe my first arrivals. They were described to me as 'oven ready', and turned out to be three small canaries with not a feather between them! They were the only ones to survive a large consignment, and I gained much pleasure from seeing these little birds gradually begin to grow feathers again, to learn to trust me and, indeed, to learn to fly from the special trees I'd put in the aviary. These had branches starting from one foot up from the ground; I could place the birds on the branches and they learned to flutter down.

It is wonderful to sit in the aviary in the quiet of an evening, watching these little birds recover, and I must say the beautiful Poitou donkeys, who can come up to the fence at the edge of the aviary, seem to enjoy their antics as much as I do!

Most donkeys, although they enjoy their initial isolation, are delighted to get out to one of the other farms, where they have unlimited access to galloping and pasture, but occasionally donkeys literally fall in love with the Isolation Unit, and this was the case with one little donkey who came in called Nuala.

Nuala was a delightful little donkey, aged 25, who had lived for 20 years with her companion, Neddy, but when Neddy died their owner found Nuala became lonely and depressed, and asked if we could take her in. Nuala had made friends with another donkey called Clarence and together they decided that Isolation was their permanent home. As was normal, at the end of the six-week period they were moved, and they went across to our geriatric group in the main yard of the Sanctuary. This is a delightful group of elderly donkeys who receive extra feed and attention every day, but for Nuala and Clarence this certainly wasn't the answer. They stubbornly refused to eat for three days and, in desperation, they were taken back to the Isolation Unit to see if their appetites could be revived. The second they got back they settled in, and ate and ate and ate! After a three-week period we, once again, tried to move them, but met with exactly the same resistance. On their return to Isolation for the third time it was decided at a managers' meeting that a great exception would be made, and the two little donkeys would stay permanently in that part of the Sanctuary.

Horse & Pony magazine, which had helped us so much in the past by bringing children's attention to our work, and had raised an amazing amount of money for us, asked if Sally Warburton, one of their reporters, could come with us to Lamu. She absolutely loved her visit; in the article she told of the panic that a particular donkey caused when he came in as an emergency case. He was covered with blood around his mouth, and I rushed to check it with the vets, but could find no trace of cuts or abscesses. I asked Abdalla to talk to the owner to find out what had happened, and luckily there was no need to panic. The donkey had been eating tomatoes from one of the stalls in the market. So we could all breathe again.

While Sally got the plane back to London, we went on to Ethiopia where we were beginning to get an even better reception from the Veterinary University. We had offered to build them a small clinic if we could find a suitable site, and to my great delight they took us down and showed us part of the Veterinary University's grounds which would be absolutely ideal for us. We discussed it at length with the Dean and other dignitaries, and it was agreed that as soon as possible we would start the project to build a clinic which could be manned by vets from the University on a full-time basis, with little Meron Tsegaye being the secretary. It was so exciting to think that at last we could help the Ethiopians in a more substantial way, as they were in such desperate need. When a donkey died, the family was put under a strain to save in order to buy another donkey. The saving usually involved cutting down on food, and starvation was a threat to the weakest – the elderly, frail or young. In this country we say we can tighten our belts, but in the areas where we are working there is no way they can tighten their belts any further without disastrous consequences.

I had previously written to the British Ambassador in Ethiopia to see if there was any way that the embassy could help to finance a clinic and, to my surprise, I had been asked to visit them whilst in Addis Ababa. June and I duly went to the beautiful building in the delightful grounds and were given the warmest reception possible from the Ambassador. To my great delight and amazement he gave us a cheque for £20,000 towards our proposed clinic, saying he was delighted to be able to help in donating money for a project such as this, which he knew would really help the poor people in his area.

Little Katrina, Clive and Grainne's baby, was a darling little baby, and we all loved her very, very dearly, but sadly as time went on her heart defect caused more and more problems. Clive and Grainne spent much time with her visiting hospitals and specialists, and eventually Katrina was

(ABOVE) *Holly being shown at the Bath and West Show by Jacqui.*
(BELOW) *'Where did you get that hat?' See page 198!*

admitted to the Great Ormond Street Hospital in February.

We were already planning our next trip to Villanueva de la Vera. Determined to make other animal welfare charities aware of the terrible situation, I'd invited all of them to join a British Animal Welfare Task Force, and had been extremely impressed by the number of charities, including the RSPCA, the International League for the Protection of Horses, the International Fund for Animal Welfare, the World Society for the Protection of Animals, the National Equine Welfare Council and the Donkey Breed Society, that had agreed to take part. We also asked Margaret Langrish, a devoted campaigner, to join us as our guest, in view of her bravery and persistence in trying to stop the Fiesta. I drew up plans of the village, with points where each of us would stand as observers. In the past we'd always been behind the procession, and I felt that with so many professional people watching, we should get an accurate and unbiased survey of the whole situation, which could be sent to the authorities when the event was over, to back up our claims of the stress suffered by the donkey during the Fiesta.

However, little Katrina went into hospital a few days before the fateful Shrove Tuesday. I went up to London and spent as much time as I could with Clive, Grainne and Katrina, but it was obvious that she was desperately ill, and on February 17th she underwent major surgery to try to repair her heart. Clive and Grainne stayed with her in the intensive care unit, and although at first she seemed to be making some progress, on February 21st I received a desperate phone call from Clive telling me that little Katrina had died. You can imagine my feelings. Neil Harvey drove June and me up to London, as Clive and Grainne were waiting at Great Ormond Street for me to come, and we then had four of the most terrible days I can ever remember, until the actual funeral. Niels came for the funeral, and although we all stayed in the same hotel, I was too shattered by Katrina's death to even worry that he was there. The sight of that little coffin in the church is a memory I can never forget.

On the day of the funeral the terrible fiesta in Villanueva de la Vera took place and the team rang me to let me know what had happened. The donkey had been named Misty. He was dragged for two terrifying hours around the streets, the ring of men around him for protection having been cast aside. The donkey was petrified with fright and kept falling to the ground. Each time he was lifted to his feet by the mob who seized handfuls of skin along his flanks while the rider was still mounted. Forty-five minutes after the fiesta the donkey was still sweating and appeared to have lost nearly 20 kilos in weight. Two hours afterwards his heart rate was still double normal resting rate. His flanks were a series of bruises and his knees and fetlocks had been skinned hairless.

I had little time to recover when I got home, as a French television crew had visited and wanted to make a documentary. There were also three crews from Germany and one from Belgium. People were asking for articles on the Villanueva de la Vera affair from all over Europe, and in fact as far afield as India, but perhaps it was a good thing that I was kept so busy; it kept me from thinking of little Katrina too much.

Sarah's best friend, Kate, had now moved to London and was sharing a flat with some friends. Kate telephoned and suggested that Sarah went to London to try to get a secretarial job there. So Sarah went up to the big city. She loved it, but despite many interviews she could not get a job, so it was back to studying again as she took a business course and remained in London.

So many things seemed to be happening at the Sanctuary; not only were the donkeys pouring in and the constant work and daily rounds still to be kept up – the joy and tears of the donkeys' recoveries, the tragedies when we lost one – but things were happening all round the world. To cope, everybody had to give a hand. Pat and June went to Crete to visit the Friends of the Animals Group there, who rescue donkeys – amongst other animals – and to see if we could help fund their project. Brian went to Tenerife, where we had been having tremendous troubles with the donkey safaris. The Code of Practice which had been set up meant that safari owners had to care for their donkeys much better, and very often this meant that they couldn't afford to run the projects. In addition, the number of tourists visiting the island had dropped dramatically, and one particular person, George Brand, desperately needed help. He'd tried to rescue many of the donkeys on the island that were in trouble, and Brian went over to see how we could assist. He found the buildings in a bad state of repair and the only advice Brian could give to George Brand was that he try to re-home as many of the donkeys as he could, so that he could afford to keep the few that needed extra care. Brian arranged for him to have a small amount of funding to ensure that the donkeys were fed.

We had been approached by a Dr Onoviran of Nigeria to see if we could help there, as he was sure that anthelmintics were the answer to the problems for his donkeys. He was Registrar of the Nigerian Veterinary Council. June and I visited for ten days; little did we realize that half of the time would be spent being introduced to VIPs in each little village we passed as we travelled from Lagos to the north. For the first eight days we grew more and more frustrated, as we saw hardly any donkeys and couldn't get down to any work. There were some funny incidents, however. Each area in Nigeria has its own Emir (the equivalent of royalty for the area) and we were invited to visit the Emir of Keffi. We hadn't understood how important these people were until we were ushered into the large house which was used as the Royal Headquarters. Dr Onoviran had warned us that we should be prepared to curtsy and to call the Emir 'Your Highness' but we weren't prepared for the scribes sitting along the side of the room, the presence of the important elders of the village and the bodyguards dressed in brilliant red, green and yellow long-flowing robes. June and I were accompanied by Dr Onoviran, his veterinary surgeon colleagues, the Keffi Chief Veterinary Officer and the Agricultural Officers. We were seated on large chairs which were placed down the left-hand side of the room from the Emir. Each of our party made a speech in turn and then I was asked to speak. I was able to point out how we hoped to be able to help the Nigerians by improving the health of their donkeys and extending their lifespan, thereby increasing the working capacity of their donkeys. The Emir then asked me to step forward as he wished to make a presentation and, completely unsuspecting, I stood in front of him wondering what was coming next. A large leather and straw hat was passed to the Emir who, with great ceremony, placed it on my head. I realized that this was a moment of great seriousness and importance, and I was, indeed, very honoured; unfortunately the honour had not been bestowed on women before and, in particular, not on English women! The fact of the matter was that men have larger heads than women, and in Nigeria the head to be crowned would normally be wearing a turban, so you can imagine what happened; one moment I was looking at the Emir and the next, my vision was completely obliterated and I could feel the hat resting firmly on my nose! There was a moment of embarrassed silence until I thought of what a spectacle I must be making of myself. I gave a desperate look at June from under the hat – she was convulsed with laughter – and then at the veterinary surgeons who were equally amused and, finally, lifting my head back so that I could see the Emir from under the brim of the hat, I burst out laughing myself. To my great joy his face broke into a big smile and he had to sit down as he was laughing so much.

In the end we found all the donkeys were north of Kano – in fact over one million in a very small area between there and the country's border with Niger – and, having dosed all that we possibly could with anthelmintic, we set off for Lamu with the promise that we would try to help further in the future. Travelling to Lamu from Nairobi always causes problems; the planes from Wilson Airport to the islands are tiny and the luggage allowance ranges from 10 to 15 kilos. Apart from our own personal luggage, which is obviously extremely small, we often carry two or three times this weight in medical supplies and equipment needed for our clinic in Lamu. I don't think we have ever gone through Wilson Airport without arguments, discussions, pleadings, etc., to be allowed to take our vital luggage on the plane.

This time, after a particularly difficult episode when we had to personally ask the captain if he was prepared to take our extra luggage, we found ourselves rather hustled when boarding the plane. I had to climb in from the back and clamber across to sit in the only vacant seat next to the pilot. While clambering through I was just about to put my hand on the seat to steady myself when I realized that the pilot had left his headset right where my hand was going! I was already off-balance and had to reach out to try and grab the door handle to steady myself. To my horror I caught my finger in the door with the full weight of my body behind it. I settled in my seat trying to make no fuss but, having looked at my finger, I realized that at worst, I had broken it, or at best, dislocated it. My finger was beginning to swell so much it was difficult to tell. Fortunately, I was so concerned that the plane wouldn't be able to take off due to our heavy excess luggage that the pain didn't seem to sink in for some time. I was so grateful when we actually took off and were able to gain the necessary altitude. On landing in Lamu and showing my hand to June, we both realized that there could be problems. Indeed there were. Within five days my whole hand had swollen tremendously, probably due to the tropical climate and trying to work under an obvious handicap. In the end we had to cut short our visit and come home three days early. I'm glad to say that after hospital treatment in the UK, although it took some time, my finger healed and was once more back to its original shape.

Because of the constant need to attend to donkeys' feet in the UK and Ireland, we had employed Robin Somers, a practising farrier for over eighteen years. Robin was working out in the field, attending to problem cases where there was difficulty in engaging the services of a good farrier, and his professional skill was already showing good results amongst our large family.

We'd always had good relationships with our local Young Farmers, and when they decided they'd like to do a special event in aid of the Slade Centre, we helped all we could. They wanted to pull a big model of

Dick Whittington's cat up to meet the Lord Mayor of London, and they asked if I would help organize this and get the Lord Mayor to see them. I'm delighted to say it all went absolutely beautifully, and we were allowed right into the Guildhall in London, along with a group of handicapped children from the Honiton Partial Hearing Unit. Bridget Roberts, their teacher, came with them. Of all the teachers I've ever met, Bridget gets more of my admiration than any other. The time and effort she gives these children is amazing; she makes their quiet lives happy and cheerful, and every little sound they make is encouraged by her into more normal speech. The children themselves are a great credit to her efforts. Our lorry went up as well, loaded with donkeys, and the children had a marvellous time, riding around the grounds of the Guildhall, and having tea with Sheriff Derek Edwards and his wife. A really wonderful day was enjoyed by all.

It was just as well that we were on such friendly terms with our farming neighbours. Once Brian had had an extremely trying day and was feeling very uptight. He was accosted just outside the office by an equally agitated John Rabjohns.

John said, 'Quick, Mr Bagwell. There's been an accident up on the corner and the trailer is stuck alongside a big posh car.'

Brian raced out with him and within a few minutes was at the scene. Three or four of our staff were desperately trying to rock the car in order to lever it away from the side of the trailer which was completely jammed against a smart, sleek, shining Alfa Romeo. As Deputy Administrator, Brian immediately took command of the situation.

'Stop rocking that vehicle,' he said, after weighing everything up. 'What we are going to do', he continued, as the men gathered round, 'is to cut away that part of the trailer, as the metal ring is jammed right inside the door handle recess of the car.'

John immediately stepped forward, saying, 'You can't do that, Mr Bagwell . . .'

Before he had time to continue, Brian said, 'Don't tell me what I can and can't do. That is what we are going to do and I'm going to get someone to saw this part of the trailer away.'

Without further ado Brian stormed off to find one of the carpenters working at the Sanctuary and returned a short while later. It took about ten minutes to saw away part of the trailer and to Brian's great relief his plan worked and the Alfa Romeo was free.

'There,' said Brian, looking triumphantly at John, 'don't tell me we can't do that. There's your answer.'

'Mr Bagwell,' said John quietly, 'I didn't mean you couldn't do that, but it isn't our trailer, I've just borrowed it from our neighbour. You've just sawn up our neighbour's trailer.'

As you can imagine our staff enjoyed this joke for some time, but I'm not so sure about the neighbour!

Many years ago through the Donkey Breed Society I had met Jim and Phyllis Roberts and at that time their daughter had a very good donkey racing team. I was surprised, however, one afternoon when Julie came to my office to tell me she had been in contact with them and they were interested in meeting me with a view to holding a Variety Club Sunshine Day at the Sanctuary. We all met up and discussed this special day for the children. This was, as we would say up north, 'just up Julie's street'. She loved that sort of organizing and if handicapped children were involved that was an additional bonus. I knew I could rely on Julie to make the day a real success and she did not prove me wrong. Sunday June 10th duly arrived and the staff turned up to help – I knew that they would be pleased to help without payment once again. On Slade Centre fiesta days and the weekends of Donkey Week the staff always work without pay and there have been numerous other occasions; they are very loyal. Julie had thought of everything; there was a bouncy castle for all the children, clowns to entertain, free ice cream, etc., etc., and of course, donkey rides. Numerous coaches arrived from all over the south and south-west and it really was an enjoyable day. Mr and Mrs Roberts were delighted and we all agreed we should hold another Sunshine Day in the future. Thanks to Jim Roberts I joined the Variety Club of Great Britain in the hope that a south-western committee could be set up to do more for the handicapped in this area. (I must admit I also had in mind that this could possibly lead to getting a coach for the Slade Centre. However, I was wrong!)

Donkeys have to endure many cruel acts: Timothy, whose ears were slashed by young boys, and Matthew, who was castrated by boys with broken jam-jars, must rank as some of the worst cases but Nobby Adams certainly had a very tough life. His owner tied him to a fence by the side of a main road; tied in fact by a car seat belt. Groups of youths on passing motorbikes would frequently stop and torment him, throwing stones and teasing him. Occasionally he managed to escape and he was arrested at least once by police as he wandered amongst the traffic in the local town. A local lady, seeing his plight, befriended him and used to go and feed him regularly. Eventually when she saw how ill he was becoming she paid for her vet to go and see him. On hearing the vet's report of the terrible state that the donkey was in she decided to advise us of the situation. Our inspectors, after a great deal of time, managed to persuade the owner to sign the donkey over to us and the lady who had been so kind looked after Nobby until he was fit to travel to the Sanctuary, nursing him day and night. We are quite sure that her actions saved his life. It was such a relief when Nobby came in and we were able to ensure that his future was going to be a great deal happier than his past. It was very sad indeed to find that he was little more than a baby himself, being just over two years old and already having been through such a terrible time.

A donkey who arrived at this time caused us a lot of problems. Jon Joseph Harrison was rescued by the RSPCA who had been told that his owner had died and they thought 'that a donkey had been left alone in a paddock'. The RSPCA lost no time in finding him and phoning us and we were delighted to take him in to do what we could for him. His feet were quite appalling and were described to us by the RSPCA as 'chronically neglected'. Although we were able to cope with his feet, despite all efforts by the staff, he just refused to eat. Day after day he turned his nose up at everything we offered him. We realized that the situation was becoming really serious. Our local inspector went back to Jon Joseph's original home and from conversations with the local people found that for the last few years he had been fed on saffron cake and Jaffa cakes! It was quite amazing that after we had rushed down to our local bakers and returned with a packet of Jaffa cakes, Jon Joseph regained his appetite and from that moment began to improve. We gradually weaned him on to a more suitable feed and he started to look much better. He soon made friends with another gelding in his group and now seems settled.

We were fortunate with a legacy for the donkeys, however. It all started with a telephone call from a Major John Millet-Smith. He asked, in the most educated voice, that I meet him as soon as possible at the Savoy Hotel in London to discuss a large legacy which he wished to leave to the Donkey Sanctuary, adding that he only had a very short time to live. We had a long conversation, as he took pains to tell me of the many happy hours he and his wife had spent petting the donkeys at the Sanctuary in Devon.

I arranged to meet Major Millet-Smith at the Savoy Hotel on Wednesday, July 11th, at 11 a.m. I duly arrived at the Savoy and waited for his arrival in the large lounge below the foyer. I ignored two messages for 'The Lady Elizabeth to contact reception' and it was only when I went to enquire if there had been any message from a Major Millet-Smith that I

(ABOVE) *Jon Joseph Harrison. He'd been 'chronically neglected'.*
(BELOW) *A new tractor: part of our legacy with Bull i'th Thorn farm.*

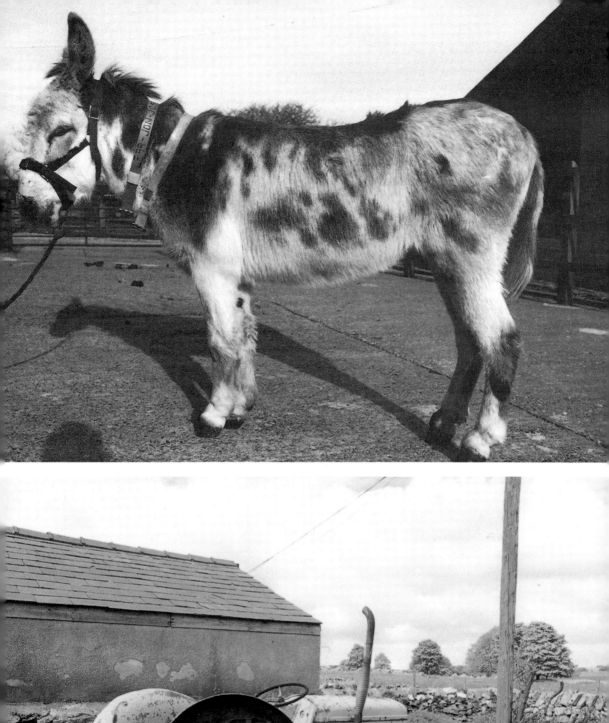

realized 'The Lady Elizabeth' referred to me. I put them right, and received the message that the Major had been delayed but would be with me by 12 noon. Once again I settled down to wait, but my attention was drawn to a commotion in the main foyer. I wandered up, to be greeted by the strangest sight. It consisted of two immaculate managers trying to restrain an irate Major, with a dog larger than any of them, intent on entering the sacred dog-free premises of the Savoy Hotel.

The Major eyed me above the mêlée, shouting, 'The Lady Elisabeth will allow the dog in. She is an animal lover, and my friend Elizabeth Taylor came in here with her five dogs, and you allowed that!' It was my first meeting with the eccentric Major, and certainly not one to be forgotten. 'Lady Elisabeth,' said the desperate manager, 'we cannot allow the dog in. Please ask the Major to leave quietly with his dog.' 'I'm not a Lady,' I said, as I looked hopefully at the Major and beckoned him towards the door. But my pleas were also ignored, and within moments we were all being propelled ignominiously out of the foyer.

It was the first time I had ever been thrown out of anywhere, but I suppose it was an exceptionally high-class place to be thrown out of!

Major Millet-Smith told me he had joined the Irish Guards at 16, by lying about his age, and re-joined when he was old enough. Apart from his Sandhurst training and army life, he had also featured in films with Errol Flynn. His life story was laced with humorous anecdotes but it was obvious he still grieved terribly for his wife, and was fully prepared for his death. His big worry was Wicklow, and I found myself promising to look after him, as I couldn't bear to let that beautiful dog be cremated and buried with him.

The Major told me he wanted the donkeys to have the residue of his estate, and particularly asked that I attend his special funeral, and that I take Wicklow as soon as he died. He gave me the name of his solicitors, and very sadly I saw him into a taxi with the feeling I would not see him alive again.

I rang the Major's telephone number constantly the following day to ensure his safe return home, but there was no reply. On our ansaphone that night was the message that he'd had a serious accident and was in a military hospital, and would I come up to see him. I spoke to him the following morning, and to my surprise, he said he had discharged himself and would be returning home. I rang his solicitors, who were really nice. They too were very concerned about him, and gave me the number of the Social Services with the name of the person looking after his area. The Social Services promised to visit the Major and had obviously been closely concerned with his welfare.

The Major phoned me on numerous occasions over the next two months, and indeed, on our last phone call, he said he'd decided to come and live with me in Sidmouth; he was by then very ill, and my heart ached for him and Wicklow. I'm not sure of the feelings of the other residents of the block of flats in which he lived, as he used to let Wicklow out for a run at all hours of the day and night, recalling him with his bugle!

The Major died during the night of Monday, September 17th. His cousin Victor was with him. He left the fullest instructions for his funeral. Wicklow was taken into immediate care by his good friend, Andrew Turner, but he was soon desperately ringing for help, as an untrained Wicklow and a small daughter were not compatible. Wicklow arrived under escort at Honiton Station on the 3.10 p.m. train from Waterloo. It was lovely to see him again, and he went straight to John and Monica Fry, who run Three Gates Farm. They had two spaniels and a collie, and Wicklow, running free with his new friends over the two hundred acres, decided he was in heaven!

As for the Major, all I can say is that his funeral was a triumph. From Mary Walker, his solicitor, who made sure every wish was carried out, Canon David Jackson, who conducted the service in the most outstanding and personal way, the undertaker, Frederick Paine, who dressed him as instructed in his officer's uniform plus medals and photographs and placed his sword with a faded red rose (which obviously had immense personal memories) through the handle, to the Royal Military School of Music who provided a drummer/bugler, all did their bit extremely well.

It was a wonderful end to an incredible man, but Major John Millet-Smith's name will live on – his name has been placed on our memory wall here at the Sanctuary in grateful thanks for the help he gave to our charity.

On September 24th I received a letter from a legal firm in Buxton, Derbyshire. The letter was headed:

TO BE GIVEN AWAY

(to a charity caring for animals)

BULL I'TH THORN FARM, HURDLOW, NEAR FLAGG, BUXTON, DERBYSHIRE

There was then a full description of this farm, together with a letter with regard to William Arthur Newton deceased. The letter started:

'Charities wishing to be considered as the beneficiary of Bull i'th

Thorn Farm should complete this form with as much detail as possible, and return it to us before the end of October.'

It then went on to explain that Mr Newton had died, and during his lifetime he had been very interested in caring for sick and abandoned animals or animals who were at risk of being destroyed. Apparently he'd left instructions that he would like the farm used as a sanctuary for animals, and in particular, 'horses and donkeys which are sick, abandoned or being at risk of being destroyed'. So the executors of the will had the job of finding a charity which they felt would fulfil all Mr Newton's requirements. For us, the thought of a base in Buxton was extremely interesting. We bring a lot of donkeys down from the north to the south, and a place where they could stop and be cared for by our own staff would be of tremendous advantage. Very hopefully, we completed the forms as fully as possible, and I spoke to Mr Horne, the solicitor, on the telephone. Paul went to view the property, as we wanted to know what we were being offered. He said the bungalow on the property was in a reasonable condition, except that there was a flat roof which was leaking, but the farm buildings were very rough. There were approximately 12½ acres of land, with typical Yorkshire stone walling, again in need of some repair, surrounding the property. We were absolutely delighted to be informed on October 29th that our application had been accepted.

They requested that we re-name the farm to something including the name 'Newton', and so Newton Farm it became, despite the fact that I rather liked the name 'Bull i'th Thorn'. Two of our senior staff were selected to run it. Ray Mutter had been with us for many years driving the bus at the Slade Centre and working with the donkeys. He had attended one of our internal interview sessions and proven his potential as a manager; when his name was put forward to manage Newton Farm I felt this would be an ideal appointment. However, after discussing the matter further Brian and I felt it would be better if a married couple ran the farm. I was aware that Ray had been courting Julie Hussen who worked as a secretary and research assistant in our Veterinary Department; Julie was superb in her job and a well respected member of staff. I had a chat with Ray and I think I probably hurried their marriage along a little! After Ray and Julie were married they moved straight into Newton Farm and we were delighted to know that the farm would be in such excellent hands.

Neil Harvey was a most enthusiastic member of staff. He had gradually worked his way up through the ranks of the Donkey Sanctuary from gardener to driver to accompanying us on trips abroad, and eventually to the position of Welfare Officer. He loved the donkeys so much it was a pleasure to watch him handle and talk to them. Whatever Neil Harvey wanted the donkeys to do they always seemed to do it willingly. I was not over-concerned when he came into my office one day and said he had been having stomach pains and that he had better see the doctor. None of us, least of all Neil, were prepared for the terrible events of the next four weeks culminating in a trip to the specialist where, with no prior warning, he was told he had cancer of the stomach and a maximum of six months to live. I do not think I could have been more upset over the next few months as I watched Neil succumb to the cancer than if it had been one of my own family. I spent as much time as I could visiting him but it was just so terrible knowing that there was no hope and it seemed so cruel that it should happen when life was just becoming so good for him. Everybody else was equally concerned. Brian drove him back and forth from the hospital and Julie took him to the Bristol Cancer Centre.

The offer from the New Zealand Donkey Breed Society made to me previously had come to fruition and they were paying my fare over so that I could do a lecture tour from the north to the south. This meant being away for a long time and June and I went to see Neil in Sidmouth Hospital the night before we left. I think we both knew we would never see him again, and it was an extremely sad departure. It was heartbreaking to be telephoned in the middle of the night by Brian, who had managed to trace me at one of the lecture venues, telling me that Neil had died, and this cast gloom over our tour. Following our visit to New Zealand, we went over to Australia, where I managed to meet members of the New South Wales Donkey Breed Society.

I always try and visit Lise, Jan and the grandchildren twice a year. I had fixed to go out for a weekend during November. Normally it is just a quiet short flight to Tirstrup, which is an airport directly between Arhus and Randers where the children live, but on this particular night things did not seem to be going too well. We were due to land at 9 p.m. but by the time we flew in over Jutland there was a full-scale gale blowing and on its first approach to the runway the plane got within fifty feet of the ground and then we suddenly saw the runway lights swerving away to the left and were forced back in our seats as the plane revved up to full throttle and aborted the landing. We tried to land three times and each seemed worse than the last and then the pilot advised us that he was going to have to take us to Copenhagen. This caused almost an uproar amongst the passengers as it would mean one night in Copenhagen and another flight back the following day. Eventually the pilot was persuaded to try and land at another airport called Karup. Once again we had a hairy approach but this time managed to land at this small, almost unused airport in the middle of Jutland. We had to take our own luggage off as there were not, of course, any facilities and we were not expected.

Various announcements were made in Danish, which left me totally confused. A very nice lady who had been sitting beside me explained that they were providing coaches; one to go directly to Randers and one to Arhus. She very kindly helped me telephone Lise's house to enquire what they were expecting me to do. The au pair answered the phone and said quite firmly, 'Lise and Jan are on their way out to pick you up. You are to wait there,' and so I let the buses go. It was almost deserted apart from one other young man who was waiting for his family who had also said they would drive over and pick him up. By this time it was 10.30 p.m. and blowing a gale outside and pouring with rain. We sat in the deserted airport, occasionally seeing an elderly man who was riding up and down on his bicycle through the long corridor where we were waiting. Eventually at 12.15 a.m. my companion's family arrived. They were extremely kind to me and very concerned and said perhaps Lise should be phoned again as they had driven from even further than Randers. They helped me phone and to my absolute horror she answered the phone saying, 'Where were you, Mother? We drove all the way to Randers and you did not take the bus.' I explained what had happened and she said, 'Well, we will have to come out and get you now but it will take at least two hours to drive there.' The young man's family were extremely kind and concerned when the attendant cycled up and said he now had to close up the building, turn off the lights and lock the doors as it was well past closing time. Fortunately they were able to persuade him to leave one light on and to let me wait in the building until Lise came but once they had gone it felt very creepy, all on my own with just this strange man cycling up and down now and then. In the end he made me a cup of tea and came and sat next to me waiting. It was absolutely pouring down outside and it was not until almost 2 a.m. that poor Lise and Jan arrived, nearly as exhausted as I was, having had to find their way to an airport they had not heard of before either. It was 3.30 a.m. before we got to bed and it seemed the weekend was over before it had started and they were running me back, thankfully this time to Tirstrup Airport.

Later that month I had the honour of being invited by Her Majesty's Government to Lancaster House to a reception in honour of organizations representing disabled people. I was over-awed on entering a beautiful room at Lancaster House, full of people, many of whom obviously knew each other well. Whilst wandering around on my own looking at the paintings, I met another lady also on her own, who began to talk to me. She asked what I did and I explained our projects for children and donkeys. I also mentioned that I was having terrible planning problems for our new EST Centre in Birmingham, and she said, 'You must talk to my boss – I'm sure he can help you. Stay here and I'll fetch him.' I waited and to my great surprise she went straight to The Right Honourable Nicholas Scott (Minister of State for Social Security and Disabled People) and, tapping him on the shoulder, drew him away from the VIPs he was speaking to, and brought him over to me. We moved to a quiet corner where I was able to explain our problems. He was so kind, promising to help all he could, and in fact asked The Right Honourable Denis Howell to give help and advice, which he certainly did. My goodness, that chance meeting was to prove immensely helpful to the handicapped children in Birmingham.

Paul was working very hard on advertising and publicity. One of his projects had been the production of a calendar which was sent round to all the solicitors in the country. This meant that when somebody wanting to make a bequest to a donkey charity in their will went to their solicitor, he could just refer to the calendar and he had all the details he required without going to any extra trouble. On my return from London Paul was happy to show me the *Professional Fundraiser* magazine which had arrived. They'd carried out an anonymous survey on forty charities. The Donkey Sanctuary came out as the fifth best for replying promptly to donations, supplying lots of information, explaining where the money went, and how much their support was appreciated. I have always felt that prompt replies and the fullest possible information should be sent to everybody, no matter how small a donation they send, but we'd had no idea that we were involved in a survey of this sort.

Many of the donkeys at Slade House Farm are permanent residents and each needs a great deal of individual attention. Obviously the majority of the staff have set routine tasks which have to be adhered to for the benefit of all the donkeys, but it was decided it would be an advantage if we had a couple of staff to give the extra special care needed by some of the donkeys. June and Natalie ensure that these donkeys' dietary needs are attended to and that additional feeds are given to those losing weight. They also dish out the medicated sandwiches. The Veterinary Department have developed a wonderful way of dosing the donkeys; donkeys love brown bread and so each day three different shapes of sandwiches are made up. The triangles and rectangles contain medication for two types of breathing problems and the small squares contain pain killers. June and Natalie also spend hours grooming and just talking to and observing the donkeys, and are able to note even the smallest change in condition. One Saturday morning June left her tray with six sandwiches balanced on a post, well away from the donkeys, whilst taking other sandwiches to another group of donkeys. When she returned, to her horror there were only five left! Not without some irritation she set off back to the hospital to replace the sandwich when she came across a large pheasant tucking into the missing quarter!

One of the problems donkeys face is that of dust getting into their lungs from feed or bedding. Donkeys can be allergic to dust and it can cause severe problems. In the past we've always kept these donkeys, which we call 'bad breathers', on peat bedding, but with today's scarcity of peat and our feelings on the conservation of natural resources, we decided that we would try to look into a way round the problem. Unfortunately by this time John Fowler had moved on to new pastures, but Peter Ikin, our new Senior Veterinary Surgeon, was extremely interested in this idea, and spent a lot of time going into various types of dust extracting machines: the idea was that we should remove the dust from hay and straw ourselves. He selected the one that appeared best for our needs, and at last we found a good use for the buildings at Weston. Weston is a very small, closely knit community, and as our farm buildings are almost in the centre we had not put donkeys there because of the possible noise factor. We were using the barns for storage, but even storage of hay seemed to cause problems, as the large contractors' lorries arriving with loads were not always welcome in the narrow lanes. We decided it would be a good idea to put the dust extractor in the Weston complex, and so, under Peter and Brian's supervision, this was set up. The results for the donkeys were quite amazing – the bedding totally dry and dust-free, and the hay was thoroughly enjoyed by the donkeys. The piles of extracted dust included many seed heads, and these were spread on some of the fields. John Rabjohns came in chuckling one morning to say that a local pheasant shoot was in operation, and he was absolutely delighted to find 26 pheasants sitting safely on our land, where shooting is not permitted, enjoying the seeds they were picking up from the dust!

I was highly honoured to be invited to the Woman of the Year luncheon. The question of what to wear was of course a concern as I remembered seeing previous television programmes showing the most elaborately dressed women. After a great deal of thought I decided there was no way I could compete and I would wear uniform. I had thought that as so many women were going I would be unnoticed but for some reason, probably because I was the only one wearing uniform, they put me on the top table next to Esther Rantzen and only a few places along from HRH The Princess Margaret.

It really had been a very, very busy year. I had given lectures at the British Veterinary Association Congress in London, and at the Edinburgh Colloquium, a meeting held on donkeys, mules and horses in tropical agricultural development. We'd invited vets from Third World countries to join us, and we knew that the work we were doing was making a tremendous impact worldwide on academics and veterinaries.

We'd managed to buy a small strip of land between the Donkey Sanctuary and Paccombe Farm, which had extended our boundaries and could mean in the future that the donkeys could walk up the track in the woods through to the new land, which we named Hurford's, and up the hill, just having to cross one road and back to the main Sanctuary again. For sick donkeys this would save the problem of being transported in a lorry, which for many of them could be a very stressful experience, bringing back memories of earlier terrors.

Even with the addition of Newton Farm, however, we knew we were running out of space again, and the year ended with Brian and I seriously contemplating the purchase of yet another farm. We decided to buy one somewhere near to John Fry, our excellent manager in Dorset. This would mean that when the vets drove out to Three Gates Farm they could visit another en route and spread the time and cost of the journey. I drove off on my own one day and visited three farms; the first two were beautiful, but the farmhouses were far too elaborate and at least a third of the cost of the farm was in the residential side. Donkeys have always come first, second and third with me, and I was far more interested in finding property where the facilities for the donkeys were as ideal as possible. The third, East Axnoller, was absolutely beautiful, with lovely sloping fields, and what finally made up my mind was the fact that the source of the River Axe rose in the lower meadow. As I sat in the car halfway down the lane, looking around, I knew that if we could get sufficient funds to purchase this farm, another donkey heaven was about to start.

As it turned out East Axnoller Farm was purchased on December 3rd, 1990. Steve Stone had worked at Slade House Farm for several years and had been made Relief Manager, covering holiday periods for the other farm managers. When the purchase of a new farm was discussed it was agreed that Steve should be appointed as Manager.

Chapter · 12

JENNY IS OUR 5,000th DONKEY
1991

DESPITE ITS distance, the Gulf War had quite an impact on our work. It was almost a disaster to us, as Lamu is a Muslim community and many of their sympathies were with the Iraqis, as were those of the Nigerians. For this reason, during the period of the war, we had to curtail all trips in these directions. Fortunately the staff on Lamu are so good that the work kept going, and we looked forward to the hostilities ceasing, so that we could get back.

The year started with a very quick trip to Zurich. I had been invited to lecture at the International Veterinary Students Association Congress, and they agreed to pay my flight and hotel for two nights, so that I could speak to this large group of students. It turned out to be very interesting; I was able to be more informal with the students and I ignored the podium and sat on the table at the front of the arena-style lecture theatre. I was amazed at their excellent grasp of English and they roared with laughter at the funny stories of the Donkey Sanctuary, and showed genuine concern when I had to relate some of the terrible experiences the donkeys had suffered.

The students were tremendously interested, and as they came from many countries, they unanimously agreed to spread the donkey word throughout their universities. After my lecture, which I was told should be for one-and-a-half hours, I was invited to stay for the student presentation, and was delighted to hear their criticism of using laboratory animals bought in for surgery practice. Today's veterinary students are far more animal-welfare-minded. A development from this lecture was that one of the attending students came to see practice at the Sanctuary later in the year, and has professed his interest in pursuing a career in equine veterinary medicine.

When I arrived back in the UK, I went straight to London to meet the new Spanish Ambassador. Unfortunately, Senor Bellacasa, who'd been so kind to me, had left, and I needed to meet his successor, Senor Morena, so that I had a contact in the embassy before the next Fiesta in Villanueva de la Vera. He proved as polite and delightful as Senor Bellacasa, but once again I had the feeling that his ability to help in preventing the use of a donkey in the Fiesta was almost negligible.

I have previously mentioned the setting up of guidelines for non-intrusive research. We had funded projects with Glasgow Veterinary University and other veterinary universities in the country. Sarcoids, the nasty growths which appear on donkeys and are a form of cancer, were becoming a big problem to us, not only in England but throughout the world. Every time we'd had to surgically remove a sarcoid at the Sanctuary we had sent it up to Glasgow, and Stuart Reid, who was doing the work for us, rang me with some quite amazing and terrific news. From these skin scrapings they had found that the tumour was being caused by a virus, and Stuart said they had definitely produced evidence that this was the same virus which caused cervical cancer in women. The Cancer Research Council in Glasgow was also excited at this new discovery, and I was asked to go straight up to Glasgow University, where they were able to demonstrate the findings to me. I also visited the Cancer Research Council, and we all felt it was so rewarding that donkeys, as well as helping with agriculture in the Third World, were now helping human beings; at last I felt the donkey's value was being appreciated.

Later in the year I received a very important-looking invitation in one morning's post. It was an invitation from Sir William Fraser, the Principal of Glasgow University, to attend a dinner, so that I could be introduced to the Senate. On my previous visit to Glasgow, Max Murray had talked quietly to me, and suggested that it might help my work if I were to have some veterinary qualifications. I told him that I regretted many times not having pursued a veterinary degree when I was younger, and he said that it might be possible that I could be given an Honorary Degree in Veterinary Medicine, which we both knew would be of immense value when working abroad. Apparently the invitation to meet the Senate was to be the first step in seeing if I was going to be a suitable recipient for this great honour.

Our work with EST was now well underway; the Birmingham project was working well, and Sue Brennan was continuing to take our team of donkeys round to as many schools for handicapped children as we were able to fit into the week. Julie Courtney had been up to Glasgow and had managed to set up a small unit there, run by Margaret Leith, one of our welfare officers for many years, who was a great donkey lover and a member of the Donkey Breed Society. One of the hospital schools we were visiting in Glasgow had built a new wing, and the Princess Royal had agreed to open it. We were delighted to be asked to put on a donkey display for the day, and once again, I had the great honour of being introduced to Her Royal Highness. She immediately recognized the work being done as connected with her previous visit to the Sanctuary, and was really kind and interested in the expansion of our work.

The chance meeting I'd had in London, when I'd been invited to the government reception at Lancaster House, was now paying dividends, and EST had been offered some land in Sutton Park, Birmingham, which would be an absolutely ideal site for the centre to be built. I went with Brian and Bert Duncan and we met many of the councillors of Birmingham City Council to discuss the forthcoming project. On the way back we called in at the TSB in Birmingham, who kindly presented a cheque for £5,000 towards the funding of equipment for the proposed unit. It was encouraging to have local people helping.

The problems in Ireland did not seem to be improving. The harder Paddy and his team worked in Ireland, the more problems were found. We discovered that many unwanted donkeys were being shipped by dealers over to England. They travelled in cramped and poor conditions in lorries and were often sold in markets for slaughter. It has been known for the lorries to travel 48 hours, during which time the donkeys are not let out and scarcely have room to move inside. Paul became involved in trying to rescue 16 donkeys waiting to be shipped to the UK. They were in the most dreadful condition. Eventually, with the help of the Ulster Society for the Prevention of Cruelty to Animals he managed to get 11 of the donkeys away; very sadly the other 5 had died. Our driver carefully transported the 11 donkeys, stopping regularly to feed and water them and to check on their condition. When they arrived I found it difficult not to break down on seeing the toll of years of neglect and cruelty on these pathetic new arrivals. They were put into the Isolation Unit for the night with, of course, deep bedding, food and water. Paul and I went over to the Isolation Unit in the morning to find the staff staring in concern and horror at the sight that met their eyes. There was no doubt it would take a long time to get these donkeys back to being fit and able to enjoy life but we hoped they would be able to spend 'donkeys' years' with us. They are doing fine.

I had to take my walks to check on the donkeys earlier in the morning then. We estimated that during the year we had approximately 90,000 visitors, and it could take up a great deal of time just going through the

(ABOVE) *Some of the Irish donkeys fully recovered after their horrific experience.*
(BELOW) *Jonquille, proud mother of five-minute-old Danielle.*

yard, with so many concerned and interested people stopping to talk and ask questions. The staff in our Information Room had been increased and Ron, Syd, Brian and Fred could be found there at various times ready to show visitors around or just answer questions and advise on our work here and abroad. I am sure that, like me, they all enjoy their work.

I seem to be able to get through a mountain of paperwork fairly easily. However, I can honestly say it does not seem like work to do something you enjoy. I love every minute of the day and the job never seems too hard. The concern and compassion shown by the many visitors and supporters of the Sanctuary keep me cheerful and just knowing that we have so many supporters and that the staff are now so skilled and experienced, gives me a glow of pleasure when I realize that all the donkeys in care can indeed look forward to a safe and happy future.

One of the most exciting events to take place at the Sanctuary happened on March 2nd. One of the staff ran across to tell June and I that they thought Jonquille, our Poitou mare, was about to produce her foal, and we were just in time to see Danielle being born. She really was the most unusual foal anybody had ever seen in England, already larger at birth than most of our foals are at three or four months old. She was extremely responsive to human beings, and Jonquille made the most charming and gentle mother. We had great plans for little Danielle, and looked forward to her growing up and being introduced to the donkey world in general.

When the Gulf War was over, I set off for our regular visit to Lamu, where the annual donkey competition was being held and we were, of course, worming on all the islands. On this occasion we weren't taking any staff, as we were going on to Tanzania afterwards to check the situation with the donkeys there. The trip was successful and we had no need of our team of staff from Devon, as we were fully supported by the veterinary services and had as many helpers as we could cope with. Once again we treated hundreds of donkeys around the islands, but we did have rather a near miss on our way back to Lamu. The staff in the primitive hotel where we had spent the previous night had not prepared any food for us, and we had a 6 a.m. start in the morning to catch the tide in our small motor boat. I spent a good time in the hotel kitchen preparing a picnic for the day. We left Kiwayu and went through the 'narrows', which become high and dry when the tide has dropped with only just enough water to scrape through, and landed at our first destination to treat a group of donkeys. After we had finished treating the donkeys and climbed back in the boat, Abdalla said, 'Mrs Svendsen, we have a problem.'

'What is it, Abdalla?' I asked, and he explained that they had just tried to refill the almost empty petrol tank with the second drum of fuel, only to find, to their horror, that it had been filled with water instead of fuel. We didn't have enough fuel to get back to Lamu. We worked out that the tide would have dropped too far for us to get back to Kiwayu to refuel and the nearest other source of fuel was about sixty miles away. As the discussion deepened it became obvious that there was no way we were going to be able to get back along the protected sides of the islands, where the sea is relatively flat and calm, and our only hope would be to go out to sea through the bar and try and get round the shorter but rougher route before the fuel ran out. However, it was impossible to do that at the moment because of the heavy tide running and so it was decided to make our way to a sand atoll where we could wait until the tide turned. We would then have the advantage of a returning tide to try and make it back to Lamu. To get out to the atoll we had to go through a narrow cut with a heavy sea running but, fortunately, still with the tide. We decided that this was the only way out and with our small boat, slightly overloaded, set off through the channel to try to make the atoll where we could spend the day until the tide went down.

The boat almost turned over two or three times and I had just jokingly said to June, 'Well at least we're all good swimmers,' when a shark surfaced within three feet of the boat, so close that its tail actually touched the boat as it went down again. All thoughts of swimming rapidly faded from our minds. We were fortunate to make the atoll safely and there we spent six hours in the blazing sun waiting for the tide to turn so that we could attempt to get back to Lamu on the incoming tide. We were hot, burnt and very short of liquid by this time.

We eventually left at about 4 p.m. and nursed the engine with every ounce of fuel we could get through the tanks. It was 6.15 p.m. before the engine put-putted to a stop. We were in one of the most dangerous mosquito areas in the world, in a boat with no fuel, night fast approaching and little chance of any boat other than a sailing dhow coming within reach. For twenty minutes we drifted, and then a miracle happened. We heard the sound of a speedboat engine and coming across the sea towards us were three Dory type motor boats, on which, incongruously, were seated wealthy Italians in deck chairs enjoying an evening boat trip to see the sunset off Pate Island! They immediately came to our aid and we learnt that it was the first time this particular excursion had been organized by a group of Italians who had opened a small safari camp on the mainland. Our luck was certainly in, and they were able to give us just enough fuel to get back to Lamu.

We travelled to Mombasa to meet up with Dr Fischer, who was heading the project in Tanzania. We did not take the fact that June was feeling ill too seriously at first; it started one evening after dinner, and we decided that she must have eaten something that disagreed with her. During the night she had to make frequent visits to the bathroom, and by morning she was quite pale and feeling far from well. We decided to abandon the trip to Tanzania and to get a flight back to Nairobi. I had arranged to meet the Chief Veterinary Officer there; the veterinary premises right next door to our Sanctuary in Lamu had burnt down, and we were going to discuss funding its re-building. It was very useful to have qualified vets within touching distance of our donkeys there.

June gamely carried on, and we managed to make it to Nairobi, where she immediately went to bed in the hotel. We were due to arrive home just before Easter and I'd arranged the first big family 'get together' that I'd been able to organize for some time, due to my hectic schedule. Lise, Jan and the children were coming over from Denmark, Clive and Grainne from Cambridge, and of course Paul and Uschi would be joining in, plus Sarah. In Nairobi, having settled June into bed in the hotel, I set off to start my work – visiting our accountants there, following which I was going to do some shopping for our family party. However, I had a sudden very strong twinge of stomach pain, and, deciding that discretion was the better part of valour, I returned to the hotel. Within an hour I was in the same condition as June. I don't think I can remember a worse night in my life. Fortunately by now June had stopped vomiting, and it was my turn to be closeted in the bathroom. The fact that all running water is turned off in the hotel from 11 p.m. until 6 a.m. did nothing to help my desperate situation. We had to be at the airport by 7 a.m. and it was indeed a very sorry pair who arrived there. Fortunately we were flying British Airways and the staff on the aircraft were absolutely marvellous. One toilet was reserved entirely for me, and as we disembarked at Heathrow the steward said, 'I don't know why you bothered to pay for the ticket, as you've spent the whole flight in the loo!' We'd arranged to be met by one of the staff rather than drive ourselves home, and on arrival I don't think I've ever been so pleased to see Devon in my life! I did feel a little better that night, but had become aware of a gnawing pain down my left side which seemed to get worse every time I vomited. The following morning I managed to go down to Sidmouth to buy much needed food for the big party we were holding that night.

All the family turned up at around three or four o'clock in the afternoon and I was busy preparing a beautiful dinner. For quite a while I

(ABOVE) *My eldest daughter, Lise, with husband Jan, Mark and Kate.*
(BELOW) *Eldest son Paul with wife Uschi, Dawn and Simon.*

managed to conceal how very ill I felt and it wasn't until we were halfway through dinner that I realized I couldn't go on any more, as the pain in my side had become totally unbearable. I had to go to bed and by 11 o'clock that night I was in agony. June became increasingly concerned and eventually the doctor arrived. He confessed himself completely puzzled by the symptoms, as I now had a high temperature, but gave me some sleeping tablets and said he would call in the morning. Nothing seemed to work; I spent the most terrible night in extreme pain, and by the morning, when the doctor arrived, he decided I must have amoebic dysentery. For three days I took the treatment for that, getting steadily worse, and in the end June was so concerned that she rang Glasgow Veterinary University to see if they had any influence with the School of Tropical Medicine, and if they could suggest what the problem might be. Unfortunately my doctor had gone away on holiday, and was not aware of the deterioration I was undergoing, but another doctor called, and with the help of Glasgow University and the School of Tropical Medicine, and many more samples, found that I was suffering from a tropical disease known as shigella.

The family had all left by then, and I'm afraid I was so ill I hardly saw any of them. It was so disappointing I really could have cried. June fed me on porridge and junket, the only foods I could manage to keep down, and the next two weeks were a complete nightmare. By the time I began to feel a little better I'd lost one and a half stone, and could remember little of the time I'd had to spend in bed. Slowly, however, I began to recover, and my bedroom became an office with Mal almost a permanent resident, until I was able to stand on my feet again for more than a few moments.

Our trustees' meetings were due in April, and I did manage to get to the Donkey Sanctuary trustees' meeting, but the strain of that was such that I was totally unable to be present for either the IDPT or the Slade Centre meetings the following day. June had to give the reports for me, which she did extremely adequately.

Just before Donkey Week Paul had arranged for an Equine Welfare Weekend to be held, to draw people's attention to the proposed EEC abolition of minimum values for animals in transit. In the UK the Minimum Values Clause of the Animal Health Act puts a controlling financial limit on most equines that are destined to leave the country. The purpose of this legislation is to try and safeguard the cheaper animals, most likely to travel from country to country in cramped lorries only to end up on the butcher's slab. Although the main impact was on horses, we were well aware of the suffering caused to donkeys on these very long trips, usually ending in a slaughterhouse. Spearheaded by the ILPH and the RSPCA, a national campaign was under way, and the Donkey Sanctuary decided to join in with a special weekend to make the public aware of the problems. The high spot of the weekend was the Donkey Walks: visitors for the day could pay to take a donkey for a walk which consisted of almost a mile of grassland track round the perimeter of the Sanctuary. This may sound quite easy, but it didn't always go as well as the walkers intended. Some donkeys decided they'd rather stop and eat grass at the side of the track; others decided the best way to get back to their field was to go at 90 miles an hour, and we had much need of our staff who were placed strategically round the walk! However, everybody enjoyed it – not least the donkeys – and it certainly drew attention to the problems we were all facing on the transport of live equines. After the campaign, at a meeting of agricultural ministers in Luxembourg, special dispensation was given to temporarily retain Britain's system of minimum values for equines intended for export. This is not a permanent solution and EC regulations on equines will have to be agreed at some future date.

Donkey Week arrived, and for the first time I couldn't participate in all the events. I was still finding it hard to stand for any length of time and I even wondered at one stage whether I would manage to give my talk at the 'Sob Sunday luncheon' as it's now become known! This year we'd arranged for it to be held in the Great Hall at Exeter University, as we'd really outgrown our large barns, despite Sheila Rabjohns's brilliant catering. It turned out to be an ideal venue; the catering was excellent, and we'd put at each person's place a gas-filled blue balloon with 'I love donkeys' written on it, so the hall had a most festive air. My speech ended with the following poem which everybody seemed to enjoy:

> It's really a pleasure to stand here today
> I've been praying that I would be able
> I can feel the support, the help and the love
> Which is coming from every table.

> Since I last spoke, almost twelve months ago
> At this lunch, which so many attended
> Over 200 donkeys have entered our gates
> Broken down, and with wounds to be mended.

> Not one turned away, but all given care
> Each one has individual attention
> They get love and care all the day and the night
> From the staff – too many to mention.

And think of the children, the blind and the lame
To whom donkeys give so much pleasure
What a quiet gentle creature this animal is
Who can ever appreciate his measure.

And think of the work that he does, far abroad
As he toils through the heat and the dust
For the Third World nations, hungry and tired
His efforts for them are a must.

On a lighter note, as we worked far abroad
I was thanked by this Third World fella
For saving his donkey – he kissed me with thanks
And I think that he gave me *shigella*!!

At least this brought forth a laugh!

We'd thought it would be nice if Abdalla could visit for the week so that he could be introduced to all our interested visitors and talk to them about the Sanctuary in Lamu. Unfortunately, as so often happens when trying to arrange visas and transport from Africa, he arrived on the day they were all leaving, but a grinning and cheerful Abdalla was able to wave goodbye to everybody after another very successful Donkey Week.

We take donkeys and mules in from all sorts of circumstances, but I think two of the funniest to come in were Timmy and Jenny from McDonald's Circus. The circus contacted us to say they had two mules which they no longer required. They didn't want to sell them; they wanted them to have a happy retirement, so they decided the Sanctuary was the best place for them. They seemed to have settled very well and their past owners visited, and were delighted to see them so happy. However there was one thing they'd forgotten to tell us. We knew the mules had been trained to work with the clowns, but it wasn't until one of the isolation staff bent down to pick up a brush and found herself flying through the air, that we learnt that this was their act. Any bending clown got a firm tup up the rear! Needless to say, the staff learnt their lesson very quickly and no one turns their back on Timmy and Jenny unless they want a quick rise.

We had a delightful visit from our French friends from SABAUD, who were interested in the birth of Danielle, and were impressed by the condition of Danielle, Jonquille and Torrent, the stallion. Amande had by this time sadly died, after being carefully nursed for many months. For a Poitou donkey she had exceeded her expected lifespan and had enjoyed her time here with Jonquille. They asked if I would come to France later in

(ABOVE) *Sarah, my youngest daughter.*

(BELOW) (from left to right) *Julie Courtney, who has been with me for 18 years, Paul, and Sandra Harrington, office manageress, with me for 13 years.*

the year to present the trophies at their annual Poitou Show, which of course I had the greatest pleasure in doing.

June and I decided to take a short holiday, and we took the Danish grandchildren with us to Butlins Holiday Camp at Bognor Regis. Having been on every pleasure ride in the amusement park numerous times, we decided a good way to keep the children happy was to buy each of them a skateboard. This would have been fine had we not found that we were the ones who were expected to pull them everywhere, and one evening, quite exhausted, we landed up in the amusement arcade. Both the children ran off to play with something else, leaving me with Mark Charlie's skateboard. I decided to have a go on a one-arm bandit machine, and was playing happily with the skateboard at the side of the machine, when a middle-aged man stopped and said, 'Excuse me, but is that your skateboard?'

'Yes,' I replied, not thinking.

'My goodness,' he said, 'Do you use it often?'

I couldn't resist saying, 'Yes, I always come down on my skateboard.'

The only problem was that he stood watching until I'd finished, and I then had to nonchalantly put one foot on the board and do my best to get out of the arcade in a dignified manner! We did love having the children with us, and it was such a break to have a complete change of activity, that I'm quite sure it must have done us good.

It seemed impossible to believe that on Monday September 23rd we greeted the 5,000th donkey into care! It was a long time since Naughty Face, my very first donkey, joined me – in fact it is over twenty years – and I never thought then that she would be joined by 4,999 others! I wonder what would have happened had I been able to look into the future and see the immense problems that would have to be faced – the personal sacrifices, the sadness in seeing such cruelty inflicted, the constant battle to maintain each and every donkey individually with all the tender loving care it needed, and the daily battle to find funds!

The 5,000th donkey was called Jenny. Her history included two years when she was locked in a garage, eventually being moved to a small back garden and finally into a field with seven large horses. Although donkeys generally get on well with horses, it was obvious Jenny was taken advantage of, and she received several nasty kicks. Being afraid to use the main grazing of the field she had retreated to a muddy corner and was eventually found standing up to her stomach in mud. The lady who found and rescued Jenny had no land but a friend kindly loaned her the temporary use of a field. Several charities were asked to take Jenny, but no home was apparently available for her. Eventually Redwings Horse

Sanctuary, who send bad donkey cases to us, gave the lady our telephone number and we collected dear Jenny.

I had been asked to provide a book which would be interesting to both adults and children and so *The Bumper Book of Donkeys* came to be published. Once again Mal had to spend hours getting details of patterns, etc., together and Sue Harland, who had joined the secretarial team, was kept busy at the word processor. Between us one of the most popular books was produced. Although the books helped the funding we still depended on donations sent in by our supporters when they received our newsletters, and by advertising. I wrote the newsletter for the UK twice a year but Paul had now taken over the writing of the newsletter for Ireland. Much to my relief Paul had also taken over the advertising. He seemed to have a natural flair for this which is a great asset to the Sanctuary. We'd managed to cut advertising costs down as new equipment had been purchased which allowed Paul and Sarah, his assistant, to actually set up the advertisements in a format which was accepted by the press. This saved an enormous amount of money in preparing the advertisements for publication, and also meant that Paul could check and know that exactly what he wanted was going to appear. It was getting more and more difficult for him to calculate where our donations were coming from; although a key number is put on each advertisement in the hopes that those sending a donation or letter would include this key number on the envelope, many people now know us so well that the advertisement just jogs their memory and they send a donation to us, addressed only to the Donkey Sanctuary at Sidmouth, Devon. However, there is no doubt that his campaigns were working and the desperately needed money came in to enable us to keep our work continuing satisfactorily.

With so many mouths to feed and so many donkeys needing extra care we have to have sufficient staff to do the job properly, and sufficient land so that the donkeys can have the best conditions possible. Paul had suggested to the trustees that perhaps we should try a television commercial now that the regulations had been lifted with regard to charity advertising. We'd recently had a marvellous new video called *Devoted to Donkeys* made by Steve Springford, and this described the current work that the Sanctuary was doing. The cost of making a commercial advert almost ruled out the feasibility of trying this type of advertising. However Paul decided that if he could make it himself he could cut the cost down very substantially, and so he designed his own film and brought me the script to look at. Quite frankly, I thought it was excellent and Paul set about making the film. Of course, once again, we needed what every film producer here needs – myself surrounded by a large group of donkeys, and we chose Woods Farm for the venue on this occasion. Somehow Paul managed to get the footage he wanted, with over 400 donkeys milling around me, and eventually the soundtrack was added. Steve Springford agreed to go to London over the weekend to do the editing when we could get an editing studio at a cheap rate. We succeeded in making the commercial, which was shown in the London area and created a great deal of interest.

One morning I was called across to the Isolation Unit to look at a donkey which had arrived; I found circumstances very different from what I'd expected! Usually when I am called across it is to see some poor tiny terrified donkey with appalling feet or with terrible sores or covered in lice, but on this occasion it was the exact opposite! Lucy Costello must have been one of the most well cared-for and pampered donkeys I think we've ever had in. We always ask owners who have had their donkeys as pets for many years to let us know their usual feed and also what titbits they receive, so that we can try to make the transition from a home environment to the Sanctuary environment as easy as possible. Usually people give us one or two lines as to what their donkey has been given; on this occasion we were told: 'Morning – small hay net, two Denes nature log biscuits, two hours in the paddock eating grass, and the hay net late morning, plus one polo mint. In the evening she has a small hay net, one large carrot chopped into smallish cubes, two to four Denes biscuits (see sample), a small amount of wholemeal toast, two polo mints and plenty of clean bedding as she sometimes eats her straw.' We were also told, 'Lucy has always been stabled in a light airy stable and *has never been wet.'* I could tell Lucy had been well looked after; she was immaculately groomed and, running my hands along her back, a small puff of perfumed talcum powder wafted up. Her owners had obviously really loved and cared for her, but now, elderly and ill, they were having to move from their home and losing Lucy must have been a most heartbreaking time for them. We immediately rang them to let them know how Lucy had travelled, and I'm pleased to say that Lucy settled in well and her owners, despite their own adversity, insisted on sending money towards her keep.

Since Misty's ordeal in Villanueva de la Vera, we had been collecting signatures for a petition which we decided would have the most impact if we presented it to the European Parliament in Strasbourg. We collected 1,300,000 signatures, but, in view of the many boxes taking up half the space in my secretary's office, we had a problem as to how to physically get them to Strasbourg. The answer, of course, was the model donkey! I took a full team there; David and Marie (our Irish French interpreter) drove to France with the horse box laden not only with Blackie II, the model donkey, complete with soggies, but also with the 1,300,000 signatures. June, Mal and I travelled by plane, and we all met up in the small hotel we'd booked in Strasbourg. I had advised various members of the European Parliament that we would be arriving, and Lord O'Hagan had promised to help us get Blackie II into the actual Parliament building. He had not, however, at this stage been able to convince the security guards, and when we arrived with the horse box, we found ourselves surrounded by them as we tried to get through the barrier system with Blackie II. At first they were amazed, then incredulous and then quite definite that there was no way that Blackie II would be allowed into the building. Leaving David to find a parking space for the horse box, we went in and, with the help of Members of the European Parliament – Lord O'Hagan, who claimed the donkey was one of his constituents, Ken Collins, Chairman of the European Parliament's Committee on the Environment, Public Health and Consumer Protection, who I was presenting the petition to that day, and Ken Coates, who obviously had influence with the security department – Blackie II was finally allowed in. He stood in magnificent splendour in the main hall, and, during the two days he was there, 500 or more signatures were collected, many from MEPs. We had written to all Members of the European Parliament in the UK prior to our visit and they were very interested and supportive. Literally hundreds of visitors being escorted through the building stopped to read our display board and give their support.

We were extremely fortunate in receiving permission to present the petition to the President of the European Parliament, but as he was called to an urgent meeting with the Yugoslavian delegation at the last moment, it was accepted by the Vice-President, David Martin, on his behalf. World television recorded my appeal to him to try to prevent the unnecessary torture of a donkey annually at Villanueva de la Vera, and heard his promise for the European Parliament to do their best to prevent it.

Helped by a team of maintenance men Blackie II was then escorted upstairs to the large council chamber where the Intergroup for Animal Welfare meeting was to take place. By this time a further 500,000 signatures had been added to the petition being brought by animal charities in France. The final presentation of the petition was made to the President of the Intergroup for Animal Welfare, Mary Banotti, MEP, and further photographs were taken by the press. The petition was then forwarded to the Petitions Committee in Luxembourg, and apparently is the third largest animal welfare petition to be submitted since the European Parliament opened.

We had planned to go to Nigeria to do another dosing project in the Kano area, and I had a full team lined up ready and waiting. We had already sent the anthelmintic over to Nigeria three months previously, and were absolutely horrified, two days before our trip commenced, to be told by the Nigerian vets that it just hadn't arrived. We couldn't believe it – the shipping agents for our suppliers of Eqvalan – Merck, Sharp & Dohme – advised us that it had definitely been sent but the Nigerian Veterinary Council were adamant that it was not there. Very regretfully we had to cancel the trip, as it was pointless going without our veterinary supplies, and of course, as so often happens on these trips abroad, the anthelmintic was located in Nigeria a week after the trip had been cancelled. It was decided to leave Nigeria for the time being, as there were so many other countries in trouble where we seemed to be getting more support.

Another place we'd been asked to visit was the Turks and Caicos Islands. We were asked to go at the request of the government and local people. They were having real problems with feral horses and donkeys. When the dry season came many donkeys died as the waterholes dried up, and others wandered into the town looking for water and food. Of course the clever donkeys soon worked out a few things, which made government action imperative. Each house by law had to collect any rainfall during the year, and they have plastic drainpipes from their roofs leading into water storage tanks. The donkeys worked out that if they kicked hard enough at the pipe leading into the tank, a miracle occurred, and there was water for all. They got so clever at it that the islanders became desperate, and the government decided to ship the donkeys to Haiti for meat. At this the islanders rose up in revolt and we were called in.

It would have been quite easy to get to the Turks and Caicos Islands had Pan Am Airlines, on whom we were booked, not gone into liquidation the day we were due to fly out. It took nine hours of negotiations to get transferred to an emergency flight put on by Cayman Airways, and we were completely exhausted when we arrived on the island of Grand Turk. The small island hotel was very adequate, but we woke in the middle of the night to find we were not the only inhabitants of the bedroom. This time it was cockroaches. I realized they were there when, in the early hours, one dropped on my face from the ceiling, and as I leapt out of bed with a yell June turned the light on to reveal others, which we could hear scurrying away across the floor. On visiting the bathroom and sitting on the loo, I felt something wriggling; on lifting the seat, to my dismay I saw five large cockroaches sitting on the rim waving their antennae and doing what appeared to be 'knees-bend' exercises. I have a horror of these insects, and I'm afraid I knocked as many as I could into the bowl of the toilet where, despite frequent flushing, they remained until the following night, during which time they were joined by more insect bodies!

We were fortunate to meet the minister responsible for the donkey project, and in the short time we were there were taken to meet the governor of the island and a small committee which had been set up to deal with the problem. We managed to design a suitable Sanctuary, which we were willing to help fund, and we also offered to send a veterinary team to castrate all the stallions. An approach has been made to the ILPH, as there are many horses in trouble on the island as well, and they have agreed to join us in this project. We're hoping that this will be as successful as the joint project in Mexico, and that the feral horses and donkeys will have an assured future.

Leaving the island proved even more disastrous than our arrival. The absence of Pan Am meant that the Cayman Airways flight on the Friday was grossly overbooked and, although we arrived at the airport at 8 a.m. for the flight at 3 p.m. they refused to issue seat allocations, saying that the first on the plane got the seats. Unfortunately they gave the same message to the 500 or so other prospective passengers waiting for the flight, which could seat approximately 280. After waiting four hours in the appallingly hot departure lounge, when the flight was announced there was such pandemonium that the one policeman on duty was totally unable to cope. Fortunately we were sitting near the front of the lounge, and, despite being crushed almost to the point of unconsciousness by many very large American ladies, I burst onto the tarmac reasonably intact. A few moments later, June, who was wearing a dress which fastened down the front, emerged from the throng, and to my horror I saw that all her buttons had been torn off, leaving her dress wide open. It was at this stage we realized that the governor and Mr Hall, the Minister of Health, had just been seeing a VIP on board – they recognized us, but appreciated our embarrassment! A brief 'goodbye' was all we could manage as we sprinted for the plane.

We then visited Antigua, where a similar problem of donkeys had been reported, but found the situation much less critical there, and were able to make an arrangement with the Humane Society to deal with any donkeys which got in trouble, and for which we would help with funding.

It had been a very hard year; physically for the first time I'd had a real struggle. Normally I'm absolutely full of energy, but the shigella still seemed to drag on and cause me problems. It appeared to have slowed down my overseas work, although this gave me much more opportunity to be working at home, and there was so much work everywhere that I was never without anything to do. There seemed to be a never-ending stream of people wanting to write articles, television producers wanting to make programmes, but everything had to be kept in perspective, and even though we now had over 5,000 donkeys in our care, the rules of the Sanctuary never change. Each donkey coming in must be given individual attention, tender loving care and the best conditions we can possibly give it for the remainder of its life.

Chapter 13

HONOUR FROM THE NORTH
1992

A S MY last attempt at a family get together had been so disastrous, it was with some trepidation that I decided to try and invite everybody for a week's holiday, and we chose to go skiing in Switzerland. I was quite sure my grandchildren would prove to be experts at this, and felt they should have the opportunity while so young to have a try. Unfortunately, but for the very best reason in the world, Clive and Grainne were unable to come with us – Grainne was expecting a baby in March. For the rest of the family it proved a marvellous holiday. The family had a chalet, with a chalet girl to run it, and June and I retreated to a hotel at the top of the village of Wengen, which had a swimming pool, so that we could entertain the children after their day's skiing was over. It was a splendid week's break and a really lovely 'get together' for us all.

Back home and into work again we found the Lockwood Donkey Sanctuary causing concern, and once again I visited. Mrs Lockwood was determined not to let anybody else look after the donkeys. It was sad to see them looking miserable and over-crowded on the relatively small acreage of ground, but of course, as it was not a registered charity, but Mrs Lockwood's own personal project, unless direct cruelty could be proved there was no way anybody could intervene. Despite the difficult conditions, there was certainly no direct cruelty, and so we had to leave the donkeys in the hopes that, at a later stage, we may be asked to help.

Merck, Sharp & Dohme rang me one day. I imagine we must be one of their biggest customers for Eqvalan, our favourite worm paste. They explained that they had 2,500 tubes, the expiry date of which was the following September, and they said that if I would like them, they could let me have them all at half price, shipped free, anywhere in the world. This was a real bonus for us and the donkeys. To be able to treat six donkeys for the price of three had to be a good buy, but I knew that we needed to have teams already in the field to use the doses up before they expired. I had recently had much more contact with SPANA (The Society for the Protection of Animals in North Africa) and, not only had their Mr Dorman visited us, but some of the dressers from overseas had been on a training course with us, and a short while previously, Andrew Prentis, a new Veterinary Surgeon appointed by SPANA in Morocco, had visited the Sanctuary, and been most impressed. We had talked about the worming and I had told Andrew that if it was possible to get him any anthelmintic over to Morocco, I would do so. He was the first person I sent a fax to, and he was more than delighted to receive 1,000 syringes, and guaranteed that these would all be used on 3,000 donkeys before the expiry date. We then approached our teams in Mexico, and they took a further 1,000 syringes, and the balance went out to Kenya to provide the dosing for the team going over in September. The whole exercise had been beneficial, not only from a financial point of view, but obviously to many, many donkeys.

Although not yet officially open, Newton Farm was ready to take in a few donkeys, and Billy Boy Green was one of their first inmates. We had taken on a new chief welfare officer for the north, Bill Tetlow. I had known Bill for some time; he had been a Donkey Breed Society member for many years and at one time we had been on the DBS Council together. Bill made an ideal chief welfare officer and it was he who had eventually to collect Billy Boy. Billy Boy was a stallion, and every day he had watched a large mare trotting past his field with a rider on her back. In the end it proved just too much for him. He broke through two fences in time to see his love vanishing on a road near the Thirsk by-pass! Undaunted, he pursued at a gallop, and, with his goal in sight, attempted to mount the mare! Obviously chaos ensued, the rider fell off, and the horse, pursued by Billy Boy, set off down the path. The horse veered at the entrance to the main road but Billy galloped onto the by-pass, thundering down the wrong side, causing motorists to face a crisis of amazing proportions. He was caught by a local policeman and held in a lay-by and, according to newspaper reports, an unusual arrest was made!

Slade House Farm had grown larger and larger as we'd managed to purchase land surrounding our original premises, and we were having up to 90,000 visitors a year. Visitors in those sort of numbers can cause various diversions, and John Rabjohns, our Farm Manager, was finding the job becoming almost untenable, as he had to cope, not only with donkey welfare and donkey care, but the movement of donkeys; the agricultural policy for all the land, some of which had to be carefully

Bill Tetlow and Billy Boy Green.

rested, some of which had to have a rotation of crops; as well as the management of the sheep which play an important part in parasite control. In addition to all this, he had to cope with demands from the Veterinary Department and Slade Centre, not forgetting frequent comments and suggestions from myself. It was agreed that John Pile, who was running Town Barton Farm, would come and assist John, and we would have joint managers – one manager mainly responsible for the agricultural side, maintenance of fences, water, etc., and the other dealing with the day-to-day donkey problems, movement of donkeys and stabling requirements. Jim Pinn, who was now trained to management standard, moved down to replace John at Town Barton Farm, and Neil Coles, who was selected following another successful interview session, became trainee Farm Manager at Slade House Farm.

John found to his cost that one of our sheep for some strange reason is always full of static. As long as the wool is on her there is no problem, but at shearing time, whoever is unlucky enough to be handling her as the wool is stripped from her body, certainly feels the effect. Poor John Rabjohns was the first to learn of this peculiarity. As he said, 'I had my arm round her body to support her, and as the fleece came off I changed my grip to the sheared area. A shock ran up my arm and my hair stood on end!' Now named Mrs Sparky, all the staff try hard to identify her (not easy with such a large flock of sheep), and usually it's poor John who lands up with a shocking experience. There seems no logical explanation – just the one sheep in almost two hundred.

Paul was getting on extremely well running the Mexican project with the support of Dr Aline de Aluja. At San Bernabe market, rather than being threatened, our vets were now being welcomed and were able to treat the donkeys. Our charity and ILPH now had two vets, one farrier and three dressers working freely in the market with the equines. Water troughs had been installed at the market and Paul's suggestion of tying rails was being taken up. An agreement had been drawn up between our charity, ILPH and the University of Mexico and Brian had visited with Paul to sign necessary documentation. It was Brian's first trip to a Third World country and he was really impressed by the very practical help we were giving to such poor people. The units daily visited villages around Mexico City and the locals often queued, waiting for the free treatment to their equines when our van arrived, and many for the first time ever were starting to take a real pride in the condition of their animals.

As Villanueva came nearer we held a conference to discuss the best way we could tackle this year's event. The same donkey Misty was to be used again and this caused us great concern. In the end Paul volunteered to go, as he was not known in the village and, with his small video camera, felt that he could take good pictures which we could then send to the Spanish Ambassador and other interested parties. A film was to be made featuring Julian Pettifer as part of a *Nature* series on BBC television, and this was going to discuss cruelty to animals and whether or not we should interfere in other countries' customs. The television crew decided to accompany Paul to Villanueva de la Vera, and spent two days filming at the Sanctuary before the event took place. Poor Paul – it proved a terrible experience for him. Like me, he felt so helpless, and unable to come to the aid of an animal in such obvious distress and under such terrible conditions. Despite being harassed and threatened, he managed to film the harrowing event, and we know the video will have an enormous impact on anybody who sees it. When they managed to get the donkey away at the end, the press and animal welfare people received the most hostile reception, and Paul was extremely concerned by the whole episode. My heart went out to him during that terrible Tuesday. I knew exactly what he must be going through, but it's absolutely impossible to prepare somebody going out to that sort of event for the emotions that they're going to feel.

The *Nature* programme was due to be televised a few weeks later, and the BBC rang and asked if they could come back and do another interview with me, as they needed some more comments on the event. They came down, and I was interviewed by Julian Pettifer, and I must say I was concerned at the whole tone of the interview. They tried their hardest to make me admit that it was wrong to interfere in the ancestral culture of Spain, and that Britain should keep out of things like that, but I'm afraid there was no way I could accept the programme's reasoning. The solution to the whole problem is so simple; they could either use the model donkey which we have produced for them, as once the procession starts, very few people can actually see the donkey at all since it's completely surrounded by crowds, or they could lead the donkey at the front, protected from the mob of drunken youths, and still achieve the same effect. There really is no way that the use of an animal under these circumstances can be acceptable. The suggestion that it was a tradition and why should we stop it reminded me of the ancient ducking of witches, bear baiting, cock fighting and the many other cruel practices which were carried on in the past in the name of either religion or nationalism. Spain is part of the European Community and as such really should try its hardest to prevent these ancient festivals and sports using live animals from taking place.

Paul has since come up with the good idea of writing to the residents of Villanueva de la Vera explaining why we dislike the use of a donkey so much, and suggesting the alternative method of leading the donkey in front of the crowd. I have also just written a children's book called *Blackie and Beauty*; not with the usual happy ending, but ending in fact with the request for children to write to the schoolchildren in Villanueva de la Vera to add their voices to our genuine horror at Misty's continuing ordeal.

I was very interested to meet Dr Charissis through the Greek Animal Welfare Fund. Dr Charissis, a Greek Ministry of Agriculture vet, came for training at the Sanctuary, as the first animal welfare department within the ministry was to be set up, and Dr Charissis was to head this. He was most impressed by what he saw here, and we decided to send Robin Somers, our farrier, over to Greece for a month, to help them with their donkey foot problems. It's nice to feel that in the last six months we have been able to help teams from SPANA (Society for the Protection of Animals in North Africa), from GAWF (Greek Animal Welfare Fund) and from the Brooke Hospital in Egypt in their search for more donkey knowledge, and that we are able to work happily with so many other charities towards a common end.

We also had a visit from Betsy Hutchins who runs the American Donkey & Mule Society. Her husband visited last year, but this was the first time Betsy had been able to visit. She edits the most marvellous donkey magazine, *The Brayer*, in the USA; each issue is almost a book – I don't know how she manages it. She is a real lover of donkeys, and we get along amazingly well. It was lovely to be able to take her round some of our farms and to see her delighted face as she was surrounded by almost 600 donkeys on one farm – to her a dream come true.

I had arranged to go over to Lamu again, taking the team which was so disappointingly unable to work in Nigeria at the end of last year, but, two days before we were due to leave, a crisis developed once again with the Lockwood Sanctuary and a visit was arranged with Peter Davies, the new Director General of the RSPCA. I also arranged to meet the Charity Commissioners in London to see what could be done to help the donkeys. By now June had gained great experience working with the donkeys at the Sanctuary in England, and also by accompanying me on nearly all my trips abroad. I was extremely grateful when she stepped in at the last moment and agreed to lead the team to Lamu; for the first time we were taking the farrier, and this provided even more impetus for the

(ABOVE) *Clive, Grainne and baby Sam.*
(BELOW) *Clive receiving his doctorate.*

local people to bring their donkeys. They were fascinated by Robin's skill, and the way the lame donkeys they took in came out practically walking on air, ready and willing to help in their daily workload. The team comprised Malcolm Salter, our manager from Brookfield Farm, Robin Somers, the farrier, and Andrew Hartnell, a young man from Sidbury Young Farmers, whom we had promised to take out to see agricultural conditions in another part of the world.

It seemed I had not been meant to go to Lamu, as on March 24th I had the exciting news that Clive and Grainne had a son who was to be named Sam. Grainne had an extremely hard labour as she refused any drugs in case they had any effect on the baby, but fortunately the hospital was very keen on natural childbirth and offered her the opportunity of an underwater birth. I am sure they will never forget this and the joy of having a healthy baby. It really was an exciting time for Clive as during that week he finalized his PhD. With Paul, Uschi and family I rushed up to Cambridge for the weekend to see the new baby. I think the news of Sam's arrival was one of the happiest of my life.

On Monday April 13th we were horrified to receive a desperate phone call from Brian McConnell, our number one driver, as he told us in a shocked voice that the donkey lorry he was driving had caught fire on the M6 motorway, at a junction on the outskirts of Birmingham. Poor Brian – he'd been driving along and noticed a light flashing on his dashboard, and the smell of smoke. He pulled over to the hard shoulder of the motorway, got out, tried to open the side door, but the handle was so very hot that he had to wrap his handkerchief around his hand to open it. The minute he opened it a great belch of smoke and flames came out and he shut the door quickly. The whole vehicle exploded into flames. Thank goodness there were no donkeys on board – Brian was on his way to North Wales to collect some. It was the most terrible shock for him. The fire brigade, who were there within five minutes, as the motorway police had reported the lorry was on fire after catching this on camera, told him there had been an electrical fault in the sleeping quarters. Our two main lorries are fitted with simple accommodation for the drivers who have to do long journeys, as we don't like them to leave the animals alone during the night. On this occasion an electrical fault in the cooker had been the cause of the fire, and the picture sent to us by the *Birmingham Post* (see p. 240) gives some idea of the scale of the disaster. Fortunately the Sanctuary's insurance covered the cost, but until the lorry was rebuilt, it didn't solve the problem of how to pick up donkeys in desperate need.

At our managers' meeting we were all highly delighted by the general condition of the donkeys at the Sanctuary. Before last Christmas a special appeal had gone to our subscribers to donate, if they possibly could, enough money to buy a wintering rug for some of our elderly donkeys. In the past, the elderly donkeys had felt the cold more than the younger ones, and they had tended to stay in the warm barns all the year round, and not take advantage of a brief walk or trot round the outer yards to which they all have permanent access. Wearing these warm rugs, they had all been venturing out and getting much more exercise, and were consequently very much fitter. We all agreed that this was a marvellous project, and we hoped that even more rugs would be given for the coming year. As a measure of appreciation to those who had contributed, we had arranged a book in the Visitors' Room in which the name of everybody who had donated a rug was inscribed. We had asked people to send donations for these rugs in our Christmas 1991 newsletter, which also included details of perhaps the most beautiful Christmas card we have ever produced. June had gone across to the Sanctuary on one of the very few snowy mornings that we'd had the year before, and had managed to take the most exquisite shot of Blackie and Lola standing together at their gate, apparently looking for the arrival of anybody bearing carrots! We spent a lot of time this year trying to find a suitable subject for our 1992 Christmas card, finally deciding on an artificial Christmas tree with presents underneath surrounded by a small group of donkeys. Two or three parcels were totally destroyed before June finally got the picture she wanted. The donkeys thoroughly enjoyed themselves.

We'd just received a large number of donkeys from the most unusual source. As you know, most dealers are fairly hard-hearted. They have to be, I suppose, to do their job, and so we were most surprised to receive a telephone call from one. The dealer had been persuaded to take donkeys, having previously handled only horses destined for the meat trade. On the arrival of the consignment, however, the dealer must have spent too long in their stable and, instead of proceeding with their shipment, he decided to keep them 'just for a couple of days'. He then found that two of the mares were pregnant, and every time he went in the stable, one particular donkey always came up and nuzzled him. Each day for two months, he tried to persuade himself that it was only business, but finally we received a very restrained quiet call – could we pick the donkeys up at night when other dealers wouldn't see what was happening, and bring them back to the Sanctuary? Within twelve hours the lorry was on its way, and the driver swears the dealer had tears in his eyes as they drove away. So thirteen more donkeys were rescued from a dreadful end.

Some time ago I had been asked if I would give a paper at a Conference in Cairo, Egypt, organized by Transport of Animal Welfare Studies (TAWS) on the subject of working animals, and we'd also agreed to fund three overseas vets to give papers on our donkey work abroad. We arrived in Cairo the day before the meeting, and met up with Dr Feseha Gebreab from Ethiopia and Dr Ragheb, who had been helping us with our anthelmintic trials in Egypt. Dr Ragwa, who was attending from Kenya, had still not arrived when we all met the next morning in Cairo University buildings. We sat as the President of the Veterinary Association, Dr M.R. Shalash, gave his address, and he then said he was giving presentations for merit. I was absolutely amazed when my name was called out, and as I approached the platform I vaguely heard him saying, 'For her work on donkey welfare throughout the world,' and I had the most enormous medal placed round my neck, with a picture of a large buffalo and the inscription 'Egyptian Veterinary Association for Buffalo Development – Science Pioneer Prize'.

That evening at the President's dinner party for all the delegates, I sat with my little team at the end of one of the long spurs jutting out from the main table. Before we had even started to eat, I was tapped on the shoulder and told I was sitting in the wrong place. All the team started to move, and then it was pointed out that it was just me, and I was supposed to be sitting at the top table. I was very loath to leave our group, as Dr Ragwa had only arrived just minutes before and it was so good to have the opportunity to speak to our foreign vets. However, as instructed, I went to the top table, which meant of course having to eat all the food put in front of me. I had rather hoped to avoid this, in view of my past experiences. Even worse was to follow. The President stood up to make his speech, and I was absolutely appalled to hear him say that although he normally made the opening speech, he had somebody there who he felt everybody would like to hear from, and therefore he was asking Mrs Svendsen to make the speech! I did my best at no notice whatsoever, but I think the maximum enjoyment was gained by the mosquitoes, who were having a great time with my legs under the table. The dinner was being held in one of the Ministry of Agriculture's buildings, with all the windows wide open, and quite obviously the mosquitoes were enjoying a pair of white legs for a change.

On the day that the delegates to the conference were to make visits to the various places of interest in the Cairo area we were invited to go to the Ministry of Agriculture and Veterinary Services to meet Professor Moussa, who was Dr Ragheb's immediate superior. Asked if I would perhaps have a little discussion with them about the work we wanted to

(ABOVE) *The indispensable Brian Bagwell, my Number Two.*

(BELOW) *Disaster on the motorway.*

do in Egypt, I readily agreed. I had been hoping for some time that we could perhaps set up a mobile unit in Egypt, but hesitated to trespass on Brooke Hospital's projects which I knew were based in Cairo, Alexandria and Luxor. However, I took the opportunity to visit the Brooke Hospital with Dr Ragheb, and to speak to their new manager before we went on to the government offices. I mentioned to him that perhaps we might set something up down in the Nile valley, to see if this would conflict with any work they were doing, but he was immediately enthusiastic and very grateful for any work we could do to help the donkeys in that area.

On arriving at the veterinary offices I was surprised to be asked to speak to an audience which was larger than that at the conference. However I gave a talk, which was extremely well received, and we then went to the principal's office. I explained what I wanted to do with the mobile unit, and was quite overjoyed at their reaction. They not only offered me full support and said that they would supervise the whole project for us, but they offered me the free use of their surgeries in that area so that, should any donkeys need operations or longer treatment, we could use all their facilities. We suggested that Dr Ragheb came over to the UK to have a further course of training at the Sanctuary, and that perhaps he might like to join us at the end of June when we were planning another trip to Mexico so that he could see for himself how the mobile units worked. We would then go back to Egypt in September to try and set up the project with the assistance of the government. We returned to London extremely pleased with the results of the trip.

Donkey Week this year was a very special one – our tenth! Twelve of our supporters have managed to attend every year, and so we decided to give them a special treat. In addition to a certificate which I presented at the Sunday luncheon, we decided to break our age-old rule and name a donkey foal after each of the ten-yearers. It made Donkey Week a very special occasion, as two foals were born during the time our visitors were here and so two of the Donkey Weekers, Robert and Blanche, were able to meet their own very special namesakes. We shall hold a special ceremony with the foals at Donkey Week next year.

We've had some wonderful letters and poems from our supporters; here is a poem from Lilian Shaw, about Donkey Week May 1992:

> I'm going to Sidmouth on the train
> Donkey Week is here again
> Can't wait to meet up with my friends
> The welcome there never ends.

They are there in the field below
I can almost hear them braying 'Hello'
I love to whisper into those long ears
The cuddles, petting and grooming 'Three Cheers'

The next few days will be like heaven
Even though there are only seven
Thanks, Mrs S., and all her crew
Where would the donkeys be without you

And part of a letter from Sylvia Horne about the same event:

Dear Mrs. S.,

This is my 5th Donkey Week. When I came to my first, it was partly out of curiosity to see the place in which our 2 'rehab' donkeys had spent part of their life; partly to discover more about donkeys in general. As we had no-one to care for our animals while we were away, my husband stayed at home to look after them.

It was clear from the newsletter that many people enjoyed D.W. but I rather wondered . . . however, it was only a week and I remember saying that even if it was really dreadful I could surely stand it for so short a time!

Of course I loved every minute and at the end of the week, I joined the Torbay Hotel 'regulars' and booked my room for the following year. Like so many people, I've had a lot of sadness and stress since then and really wonder how I would manage without D.W. to look forward to.

In addition to enjoying the happiness at the Sanctuary, meeting the lovely donkeys and chatting to the staff, I have made many friends among 'us visitors' and I am lucky that some live near enough to visit us – although I suspect that they mainly come to feed carrots to 'Bill & Arthur'.

Normally the luncheon ends after the various speeches, but this year our visitors had a surprise for us. They had decided to have a special ten-year celebration and, to the Sanctuary staff's amazement, two little figures appeared in beautiful donkey costumes and presented a most amusing and clever stage show to the music of *The Stripper*. The two little donkeys then came to the top table and led me onto the stage, and to the rapturous applause of everybody I was able to take off their 'heads' to reveal Mo Flenley and Sylvia Horne!

On the last day of the week we were able to take nearly everybody on trailer rides to the land at Hurford's, as we call it, to see the beautiful new facilities down there, where over 200 donkeys lead an idyllic and delightful life.

The support and donations of the 'Donkey Weekers' are really essential to the continued running of the Sanctuary. We are going through one of the hardest times I've known since I started – just the daily feed bill has reached enormous proportions – add staff wages and it can be a nightmare. The recession has not only made people tighten their own belts, but put many out of work and their donations to charities have just had to be reduced – a situation we understand completely. To add to our problems, the fact that houses are not selling means that solicitors are unable to wind up estates, and money willed to us is tied up in unmarketable property. If it is sold it is at a very much reduced price, then all charities join the suffering.

Fortunately we have such a good team that we can weather most of the storms. Our trustees are excellent and a constant source of information and support, and our senior staff are now totally professional in their own areas. Brian's expertise on legal, building and planning matters deflect many problems which could arise and, combined with Paul's love of the donkeys, backed now by many years of experience, and his advertising and literary skills, their ability to represent the Sanctuary at the highest levels gives the Sanctuary a secure future should I meet a sudden unforeseeable end!

When everyone had left after Donkey Week, I had my first quiet Saturday morning. A foal had just been born to Hatty during the previous day and he had been carried from the expectant mares group to one of the beach box units with mum trotting alongside. After taking the post upstairs, I walked up to see him. Bobbie, our vet, was just coming out of the unit, and there was this beautiful little brown colt foal with the longest legs I'd seen for ages. I don't know who the father was, as the mare had been pregnant on arrival at the Sanctuary, but he would have been proud. So far the foal had not been allowed in the paddock as Hatty needed veterinary attention, but Bobbie agreed now was a good time. It was so peaceful – the grass, newly seeded, was lush and green, and baby rabbits scuttled away as Hatty came into the tree-lined paddock. Little Walter did about three skips and a jump, and a series of short gallops which ended in his legs folding as he realized he wasn't going to stop in time to prevent a collision with Hatty. I couldn't stop laughing as he picked himself up, looking forlorn – then suddenly off he went again around the paddock scattering birds and rabbits. I heard a strange

(ABOVE) *Hatty and Walter exploring the paddock.*

(BELOW) *Danielle, still only a yearling, at the Bath and West Show.*

whinny from the next stable and went to comfort Scar (well named, as he was covered in them!) recovering from an operation. Before castration Scar had been a really aggressive mule. He would have loved to be able to play with Walter, but it was not to be his day. I was interested to see he had dunged in exactly the same place during the night, and remembered that Jubilee, our mule, had the same habit. It made it much easier to keep the stable area clear and I'm sure the grooms would love it if they could give the donkeys some lessons – especially at the Slade Centre!

After fourteen years running the Slade Centre, Pat very regretfully decided that the time had come to retire, and we were all heartbroken to lose her. However, Julie Courtney, who for so many years had been such an integral part of the Donkey Sanctuary, asked if she could possibly take her place as Principal. She had been Vice Principal for over two years, and the trustees of the Slade Centre were highly delighted by her offer. Although of course she'd be sadly missed in the office, which she ran at the Sanctuary for so many years, she would be only just round the corner and I had no doubt at all that Sandra Harrington, who took her place as Office Manageress, would be calling on her frequently, as Julie's advice and expertise are quite invaluable to the running of the Sanctuary. Uschi, who had been working at the Sanctuary for the last few years, would be Sandra's deputy.

The donkeys were still coming in at a never-ending rate, each with their own tale of sadness and woe, but thankfully we were here to help them all. Now there were to be two doctors in the family, as I had heard that I was definitely to be honoured by receiving an Honorary Doctorate of Veterinary Medicine and Surgery, and would be going to Glasgow on June 17th to receive this great honour.

I have already mentioned Holly and his success in the show ring; we now had a small group of donkeys that we took to local shows. Joanne Parsons took charge of this little team and at first she was helped by Tracey Warren. When Tracey left to run a riding stable, Jacqui Welsman stood in. They had much success with the donkeys, training them to drive, jump and even had them pulling a plough, which aroused great interest in the farming community.

Our Poitou foal, Danielle, had been growing steadily and, under the careful supervision of Joanne Parsons, was enjoying her basic training. She was already almost 12 hands high, although only a yearling. To give her some experience and to give the public an opportunity to see her, we decided to enter her in two shows, the Devon County Show at Exeter and the Bath and West Show. Joanne spent absolutely ages getting every tangled knot out of Danielle's coat – incidentally using all my hair conditioner in the attempt! However we both managed to arrive at the Devon County Show looking reasonable, and Danielle caused the most amazing interest. She moved beautifully in the ring and was twice the size of her nearest yearling competitor. I felt really sorry for the judge, as obviously Danielle should have been in a completely separate class, but I was delighted when she won a second prize. The following week we all went to the Bath and West Show where there was a 'Large Donkey' class. If she had created an impression at Exeter, this was nothing to what she achieved at this show; other breeders were there, and stewards from many of the other rings came to see when they heard of her arrival. I couldn't have been more proud than when the first prize rosette was pinned to her bridle, although I must be absolutely honest and add that she was the only one in the class!

Paul had been over to Ireland on a special rescue bid, and one morning soon after his return he came into my office and invited me to see the result of the video he had taken. He has become really skilled at filming, and it was a lovely story. Paul, Paddy and the local Welfare Officer, John Daley, had gone over to one of the smaller of the Aran Islands off the west coast of Ireland at the request of the local Gardai. Apparently there were about fifteen feral donkeys there and they were ruining the picnics of tourists who no sooner had their goodies laid out ready to eat than they were overrun by the hungry herd who had apparently been lurking nearby waiting for the right moment! It meant hiring a small cargo ship and renting large open containers so that the donkeys when walked onto the container could be lifted comfortably onto the ship.

The night before the team arrived, the Gardai managed to round up twelve of the donkeys, but the last three proved impossible to catch and Paddy, Paul and John herded them onto the docks. How easy it appeared on the video. Despite other avenues of escape they trotted happily to the boat and onto the container. Perhaps they sensed the lovely life they were about to partake in once they got back to our Sanctuary in Liscarroll!

Despite having taken in so many donkeys, each one has its own personality, and many recognize me as I walk amongst them despite the thousands of visitors who come to see them. Woe betide me if, on my way to the Slade Centre, I pass Blackie and Lola without stopping for a quick cuddle. I'll think they haven't seen me, being in a great hurry and surrounded by visitors, but before I've turned the corner I hear them both – it's not a bray, more like a loud sobbing, 'eee . . . eee . . . eee' which gets louder and louder and turns into a desperate bray if I don't come back. Visiting the farms and walking through the fields with the managers means taking twice as long as ever intended; every donkey wants to be noticed and touched – and I want to touch them too.

It's not only the donkeys. This affection and trust spreads through the staff as well – not that we rush to touch each other, but Brian and I like to feel they can come to us with their troubles and we can give them the time they need. The very first person I ever employed, Herb Fry, despite having retired twelve years ago, still comes in voluntarily every week to gently rub the eyes of all the old donkeys with oil, and to talk to his favourite donkey, Timothy. Time is our biggest enemy; the days are just not long enough, and having 160 full-time staff in the UK alone we decided the time had come to take on a personnel manager who could take over some of the staff problems and ensure that the training programmes we had set up could continue, and to cope with everyone's individual needs as we expand. After a full day's interviewing, Richard Barnes joined us – a super, jolly chap with enormous experience in his job, and he is really settling in well. I had never thought that there would be so many donkeys in need but, of course, every one coming in needs tender loving care and to do this we have to have enough staff, so I can't see Richard's work reducing. Many of the visitors who come – and anyone can visit freely without appointment from dawn until dusk – comment on the quiet and happy atmosphere, due entirely to the attitude of those employed, who love the donkeys and enjoy their work so much.

The date of my graduation grew nearer, and I became more and more nervous as the importance of the ceremony gradually sank in. June was to be my special companion and when we received the itinerary we both decided we'd better go shopping to find some suitable clothes. The event was to start with a tea provided by the Principal of Glasgow University, Sir William and Lady Fraser, followed by a formal Senate dinner; the next day was to be the ceremony itself. We had invited some of the trustees and senior staff, as well as Paul, Uschi and Sarah. Unfortunately my other two children were unable to come. June and I arrived in Glasgow on Tuesday at lunchtime, and quickly changed into our afternoon tea dresses, just in time to be picked up by the university car very kindly laid on for us. All the other honorary graduands were there; there were 12 of us, including the Right Honourable George Younger, a Glaswegian poet and author, and a Chinese professor. It was very interesting to meet so many academic and important people and the hour passed extremely quickly. Then it was back to the hotel to change into our evening clothes

(ABOVE) *Herb, my first employee, now retired, but still visiting Timothy.*

(BELOW) *The new waterproof, padded rugs.*

for our dinner with the Senate. This was indeed a formal dinner but, once again, everybody was so kind we both thoroughly enjoyed ourselves.

On the actual day of the ceremony we were picked up at ten minutes past nine, and taken round to the main university building. June was whisked away with the other partners of those to be honoured, whilst I was escorted up to the robing room at Bute Hall where I donned my gown, along with the others, and then in a very solemn procession we proceeded to the University Chapel for the Commemoration of the Benefactors.

It was one of the most moving ceremonies I have ever attended. The graduands were placed each side of the altar in the high choir stalls, and over a hundred professors must have filed into the main chancel of the chapel. The whole of the rest of the chapel was taken up by visitors and the hymns sung with such gusto that it really brought tears to my eyes. Following this, and a very welcome cup of coffee, we were once again assembled, and in a very dignified manner made our way to Bute Hall. I must say I was slightly concerned at the high level of casual conversation as we stood waiting to enter the hall. I stood next to Professor Charles K. Kao, who is Chancellor of the Chinese University of Hong Kong, and he turned to me, casually asking, 'How would you organize the infrastructure needed for a capitalist society?' I was able to point out to him that I was only receiving a Degree of Veterinary Medicine and Surgery, and promptly passed him on to Professor Slaven, who is a professor of business history and, I knew, far more qualified than I to answer such a question.

Fortunately the pealing of the organ ended our wait and once again we walked solemnly into the huge Bute Hall. I was presented for my degree by Professor Norman Wright, Professor of Veterinary Anatomy at Glasgow Veterinary University as, sadly, Max Murray, my original presenter, was unable to do so, due to illness. I had to sit in the beautiful chair raised high on the dais whilst he read some lines, starting with: 'Mr Chancellor, by authority of the Senate, I present to you this person on whom the Senate desires you to confer the Honorary Degree of Doctor of Veterinary Medicine and Surgery.'

It all sounded like a five-minute obituary, and ended with: 'Mr Chancellor, as this is the 130th anniversary of the Foundation of the Veterinary School I would now ask you to confer the Honorary Degree of Doctor of Veterinary Medicine and Surgery on Elisabeth Doreen Svendsen, only the second ever to be awarded by the Faculty of Veterinary Medicine.'

I then knelt on the purple stool below the Chancellor, who sat on what I can only describe as a high throne overlooking the whole proceedings. He then came down from his throne and, placing a round purple hat on my head, intoned several words of Latin, after which my hood was placed over my head, and I became a doctor.

The proceedings ended with a delightful lunch for close family, and then it was back to the hotel, where the university had put on a special lecture for those of our trustees who attended, showing them the precise non-intrusive work they had been carrying out for the donkeys.

Both Paul and Peter Ikin had been called out for phone calls during the proceedings, and immediately the ceremony was over, they told me what had happened. Though things had improved for beach donkeys generally, we had been increasingly concerned over one operator on Blackpool beach, and we had known things were coming to a head for some time. We had become quite desperate to gather enough evidence to get the donkeys away to give them the care and attention they needed. It is heartbreaking to know that animals are suffering but, because of legal complexities to be unable to help. However, Paul and his welfare officers had been pressing hard and, with the assistance of the RSPCA and the police, they had finally managed to get the 35 donkeys away. Paul had been busy on the phone arranging for our lorries to pick them up and take them straight to Newton Farm, Buxton. Thank goodness we had Newton Farm, because now we had a holding base where the donkeys could receive all the care, attention and love they needed, not too far from the Blackpool area, in case things went terribly wrong and they had to be returned. Paul and Peter decided they would set off at the crack of dawn the following morning, as the donkeys would by then be at Buxton, so that they could give them a full medical examination, which would be needed for the prosecution that the RSPCA would bring, as we normally leave this to them, our object being only to get the donkeys away. Paul and Uschi, who were taking my sister, Pat, home, and Peter and his wife, set off early in the morning aiming for Buxton, but June and I had to wait for a press conference which had been called between nine and ten o'clock before we too could set off to Buxton.

By the time June and I were in our car and on our way down south, Paul phoned me to tell me that two more crises had arisen. Just prior to the graduation he and Peter had held a conference for the RSPCA at Buxton, and one of the inspectors from the conference had left inspired by donkey welfare. He rang the Sanctuary to say he had found five donkeys in terrible trouble, and had managed to get them away from the owner. He asked if we would collect them urgently. The five donkeys

were collected; although their body condition was good, their feet were too long. They are now at the Sanctuary.

Paul also told me that two lorryloads of donkeys had been shipped from Ireland to Scotland, en route for the Continent, and we needed to keep a very close eye on these shipments to see where the donkeys were going and what the transport conditions were like. We have a special arrangement – always ready to be put into operation – whereby the lorries are followed and, if necessary, we can get them stopped by the police and the RSPCA to check that the donkeys are being transported legally and properly, and to try to establish their destination. In this case our inspector, John White, was able to follow them as far as Preston, but he needed someone to pick them up from there and follow them down to the south.

After driving the hundred miles south from Glasgow to Buxton, June and I arrived at Newton Farm to see the most pitiful donkeys that I have seen in many years. It was quite clear to see why we had been able to get a certificate to say that the donkeys were suffering, and once again I was surprised, when walking amongst them, to see how gentle and loving they were, and how they appreciated our quiet attention as each one received a full medical, with necessary medication for some of the wounds they had received. At long last they were able to enjoy a really good meal and a roll in the lovely long grass. It was obvious that Ray and Julie were very good managers at Newton Farm, but they were finding it difficult with so many donkeys in such terrible trouble needing individual care, all coming in at once. Following a series of telephone conversations with the Sanctuary Mal was able to organize for Peter Savage, one of our farm workers, to join Ray and Julie the following day for as long as necessary.

After a hectic hour, when all our plans had to be reorganized, we all left in literally different directions: Paul and Uschi back up to Preston to pick up the trail of the donkeys in the lorry; Peter Ikin and wife now taking Pat home to Devon; and June and I setting off to London where I had a meeting the next day!

June has been such a marvellous friend over all the years, but it still seems incredible that on September 4th this year, 1992, we will celebrate our 57th anniversary of friendship. Although we both felt emotionally, and now physically, drained, neither of us could help laughing when June turned to me and said, quite seriously, 'Do you feel different now that you've been doctored?' I could only reply that, if I did, I hadn't had time to notice it – I was quite sure it would never make any difference to the first love of my life – the donkeys.

Me getting doctored.

Afterword

It is hard to believe that within minutes of this book being completed Naughty Face died. So the book starts and ends with one of the most special little donkeys in the world.

Naughty Face on her thirtieth birthday.

INDEX

Page references in bold refer to illustrations